STORIES FROM THE ICE STORM

Edited by Mark Abley

M&S

Canadian Cataloguing in Publication Data

Abley, Mark, 1955–
    Stories from the ice storm

ISBN 0-7710-0653-5

I. Ice storms – Canada, Eastern – Anecdotes.   I. Title.

QC926.45.C2A25 1999   363.34'92   C99-931724-5

Every work in this volume is the property of its individual author.

We acknowledge the financial support of the Government of Canada
through the Book Publishing Industry Development Program for our
publishing activities. Canadä

We further acknowledge the support of the Canada Council for the Arts and
the Ontario Arts Council for our publishing program.

Photo at opening of each chapter by Carolyn Molson

Typeset in Bembo by M&S, Toronto
Printed and bound in Canada

McClelland & Stewart Inc.
The Canadian Publishers
481 University Avenue
Toronto, Ontario
M5G 2E9

I 2 3 4 5   03 02 01 00 99

To my family
and to all the families who endured the storm

CONTENTS

ACKNOWLEDGEMENTS

First I want to extend heartfelt thanks to everybody who volunteered their stories for this book. Not all of the stories could be used, but all of them were appreciated. Among the contributors, I particularly want to thank Steven Heighton for his work in a time of great adversity.

For specific help of one kind or another, I'm indebted to Debbie Astroff, Ann Beer, Jake Belanger, Soeur Lise Berger, Winnifred Bogaards, Charly Bouchara, Marjorie Bousfield, Suzanne Charest, Peter Cooney, John Farrington, Sheila Fischman, Myra Giberovitch, Michael Goldbloom, Peter Harper, Maria Jankovics, Fiona Jordan, Margaret LeBrun, Micheline Le Royer, Sharon Musgrove, Julie Oelmann, Gordon Rosenoff, Anna Rumin and Jane Urquhart. My special thanks go to Natasha Bookalam for her story of the Rigaud shower, to Wendy Sturton for her aid at Laurentian Regional High School and to Hussein Warsame for his translation from Somali.

Douglas Gibson initiated this project; I much appreciate his leap of faith. The advice of my agent, Jan Whitford, was invaluable. Thanks also to Alex Schultz for his calm editing and to Lisan Jutras and many other people at McClelland & Stewart for helping transform a manuscript into a book.

To my family – my wife, Ann Beer; my daughters, Kate and Megan; and my mother, Mary Abley, all of whom I saw too little during the concentrated work on these stories – I give my love and gratitude.

INTRODUCTION

IT WAS, TIME helps us see, not so great a disaster. Compare it to the sufferings the weather inflicted elsewhere in 1998 – Hurricane Mitch and Hurricane Georges, the floods that laid waste to much of China and Bangladesh – and even the word "disaster" hardly seems apt. But we are who we are, we live where we do, and even though our difficulties are small on a global scale, there is nothing to be gained by forgetting the deaths of thirty-five people, the destruction of millions of trees, and the economic damage that stretched into the billions of dollars. For many Canadians, the January ice storm that paralyzed eastern Ontario and southwestern Quebec remains an event of durable fascination. Besides, the ways in which we responded to the crisis tell us much about ourselves.

There are several reasons for this, one of them being that the storm tore a hole in the fabric of daily routine. For some, especially the very young, it was a magic time, a few days or a couple of weeks in which grown-ups behaved surprisingly, unpredictably, while the outside world appeared to imitate the haunting landscapes of a fairy tale – a tale, I mean, from the Brothers Grimm. The busy round of custom and duty came skidding to a halt. Daily life under a weight of ice appeared as risky, as wayward, as the lives in stories. Not until the crisis was over could anyone be sure that his or her story had a happy ending.

This breaking of routine surely helps to explain why so many people recall the time of the storm with tremendous clarity. No sitcom or docudrama could match the intensity of life in the dark. Ask most residents of the affected area what they were doing on January 8, 1999, and you'll be met by a puzzled frown, a blank stare. Ask them what they were up to on that date a year earlier – the last hours of the freezing rain, the moment when power networks were closest to ruin – and the answers will come fast and clear. "It was the afternoon I set out for the shelter with my daughter." "The day the police came and checked up on us." "The morning I said to the neighbours, 'We have a woodstove, come on over and stay with us.'"

Weeks like that one are, mercifully, so rare that they lodge in the mind. But the uniqueness of the ice storm lies not only in the harsh ease with which the weather trampled expectation and ruptured normal life. More significant is the way in which the crisis served as a testing ground for millions of people whose daily routines are designed to avoid challenge and minimize danger. So, how *do* you cook a meal over a fireplace? So, how *do* you occupy a child accustomed to a diet of Nintendo and Pokemon? Faced with a rapidly cooling apartment or a freezing house, a driveway spiked with broken trees or an iced-over set of stairs, those of us who lived through the storm no longer had the luxury of asking questions of life. Life was asking the questions of us.

"Do not bring us to the time of trial," Jesus teaches his friends to say in a contemporary translation of the Lord's Prayer. Still, a large number of people look back on the ice storm as a trial that ended in victory, an ordeal to be remembered with pride, a hard-won success. These stories have a sense of closure, and generally one of fulfilment. Urbanites and country-dwellers were confronted by different challenges, but the tales that both groups tell are often ones of triumph as well as of hardship. Some of the voices in the following pages speak in a manner that recalls, to my mind, the voice of a student who faced a ferocious, unexpected exam – and passed.

The search to find batteries or generators, the battle to keep plants or goldfish alive, can even take on, in the telling, the tone of a quest narrative. There was a task to perform within a limited time; there were lessons to be learned along the way; there would be dire consequences unless the task was accomplished. As I began to read through the stories that arrived for this book, I was struck by the sense of an underlying pattern of quests. Perhaps this is merely a convenient framework that

A festive wreath of bittersweet, encased in ice outside Bill Dodge's home in Vermont.

helps us arrange and organize our memories. But I don't think so. I suspect, on the contrary, that by turning the crisis into a kind of mission, many people were able to fill the random, haphazard days with meaning. By concentrating on practical goals that needed to be met, they could give the freezing days and nights a quality of purpose. They could make the ice storm an event with a shape, an inner design.

The storm provided many people with something else: the chance to help others. Story after story in the following pages describes an experience of giving or receiving care. The recipients of generosity are often keen to show that they, too, kept an eye out for people even less fortunate than themselves. Care became, as it once was, a widespread matter for individual attention, not something that could be easily consigned to governments. Neighbours became, as they used to be, people of some importance. In such ways of the mind, as well in the body's more obvious return to candles, logs and oil lamps, the ice storm marked a brief return to the past.

There was also an incipient democracy about it. In places like St-Hyacinthe and Brockville, no one was exempt from the storm's impact and demands. The rich as well as the poor had to devise strategies of coping. Old people who are, with sad frequency, shunted off to the waiting-rooms of death found they could again be useful, as though, in a time of upheaval, the world still had a need for them. Teenagers whom society often treats with a mixture of fear and disdain had a genuine challenge to confront, a genuine opportunity to prove their worth to the community – and many, though by no means all, did exactly that. As Dag Hammarskjöld once observed, loneliness does not lie in having nobody to share one's burden – it lies in having nobody's burden to share. In the ice storm there were burdens aplenty for young and old alike.

Those who worked in the shelters or helped to set them up; those who laboured to rebuild the networks of light, heat, and communication; those who made sure that other, more vulnerable people would survive the darkness – their stories appear in this volume. But although I have tried to make the book as comprehensive as possible, I confess that certain kinds of stories are absent. The price-gougers, the generator thieves, the foul-brained minority who used the shelters as a place to steal or terrorize or molest: their tales remain unwritten, unspoken except by their own conscience in the dead hours of night.

After the immediate crisis had passed, further opportunities arose to exploit the storm for personal gain. In particular, governments did not always require proof that the money they provided to repair specific losses had in fact been spent in that way. I spoke to a businessman in eastern Ontario who told me – off the record, alas – that the storm's aftermath had changed his view of human nature. He used to believe in the basic honesty of people; now he was convinced that a large percentage of his fellow citizens are happy to defraud the system. It's as though the public and private altruism that the crisis brought out could last only so long. To cheat the government out of hundreds or thousands of dollars seemed, to many people, a downright pleasure. Nature had broken the rules; so could they.

Stories from the Ice Storm took shape in the spring of 1999, more than a year after the events in question. But quite a few of its entries were written earlier, in what I hesitate to call the white heat of experience. Large numbers of people who seldom keep a diary felt compelled to describe day-to-day, blow-by-blow life in January 1998, and several of these candlelit accounts appear in the pages that follow. Other people turned to their computers as soon as the power came back, using words as a tool to keep their memories perpetually fresh. Still others seized the opportunity of a Christmas letter to tell distant friends and family what had befallen them. The eloquence of the professional writers in this book is striking, but no more striking, I think, than the eloquence of others who rarely write for pleasure and never for profit.

The book is a social history of an arduous time. It contains a mixture of written and oral narratives. Far too many of the entries have been carefully authored for the book to be a true "oral history," yet about thirty of the stories do fall into that category: they are the product of personal interviews that I carried out between March and May of 1999. Memories, I found, were still fresh; in a few instances, they still hurt, although probably as many people look back with amusement as with anger. After I had come up with a rough text from each of these interviews, I sent the result back to the speaker, and in most cases the speaker suggested changes, sometimes extensive. Many of the written submissions have also undergone revising and reshaping.

Whether each story originally took the form of a handwritten letter, an e-mail message, a set of printed pages, or an interview transcribed from my tape recorder, I have tried to preserve the sense of a distinct, indeed unique, voice behind each contribution. The spelling and (usually) the grammar are now standard, but I hope that nothing else has been "standardized." Certain entries read more formally than others because certain people write and speak more formally than others. If this book gives an indication of how Canadians lived through a crisis, it also shows something of how, at the end of the twentieth century, we talk about it.

The book is panoramic without (by necessity) being all-inclusive. I was sent far more stories, especially from the Montreal area, than it was possible to use; but I felt obliged to go in search of certain kinds of stories that had not arrived by any sort of mail. (Hence my days on the road with an aging tape recorder.) In particular, it seemed important to include – and, where necessary, translate – the voices of a good number of French-speakers, immigrants, and indigenous people. I am especially

Many of the stories in this book express grief for the fate of the trees.
(Photo: Carolyn Molson)

grateful to those contributors for whom the time and energy devoted to remembering and telling their stories would not result in that story being published in their own language. But I admit to wishing there were more of their voices in the book, particularly from the "triangle of darkness" in Quebec. Residents of cities where the power went out for just a few days would do well to remember the tens of thousands of people living south and east of Montreal who were starved of light and heat for three, four, or even five weeks.

On an institutional level, I found that many speakers in both Ontario and Quebec lavished high praise on the Red Cross and the police. The work of the Armed Forces drew more mixed reviews, while criticisms of the electricity companies proved frequent. Given the personal, totally unscientific nature of this sample, I was intrigued to find that the Red Cross and the Quebec provincial police were quick to offer help for the book. The Armed Forces, too, were generous with their assistance, but two of the officers whom I interviewed insisted that the resulting text had to be checked and cleared by their public affairs department; that department, in turn, insisted on a heap of changes. I agreed – with reluctance. As for the electricity companies, I approached Hydro-Québec twice but was not granted an interview. The only lineman whose story appears in this book works for Detroit Edison, and I tracked him down on my own.

If it was an exhausting task to prepare this book within a few months, it was also an exhilarating one. Some days I was struck by the common images and themes that stretched across age and place and language: most of all, by a recurrent sorrow for the dying trees. In city and countryside alike, no sound or image of the storm had as much impact on people as the crash of snapping branches, the thud of falling trees. It was as though by mourning the trees, people found a way to grieve for many kinds of loss – including, perhaps, the stability which the trees had seemed to embody. Other days I was impressed by the differences of mood and tone, the diversity of individual experience, and the sheer honesty of raw emotion that so many letters displayed. I hope and trust that all those qualities have found their way into the book. When I embarked on the project, I was a little uncertain if a collection of ice storm stories would have enough variety in it. I needn't have worried.

"A STUBBORN SEAM OF LIGHT"

BY STEVEN HEIGHTON

N KINGSTON, by the night of January 7, enough freezing rain had fallen that wires and large boughs started coming down. From time to time one of the century maples beside our house, weighted to capacity, would shake off a load of verglas with a sound like a ton of gravel being dumped on the sloped roof and avalanching off. Trees in neighbouring yards were writhing, flailing as if consciously trying to free themselves of an unbearable weight, then loosing cascades of ice shards onto the roofs of houses, garages and sheds. Their efforts weren't enough. They were dropping limbs fast, and two fences away a thick oak heeled over beyond hope of recovery and snapped. The thunder-cracks of breaking wood and the rumble of falling ice were accompanied by flashes like sheet lightning filling the low skies over the city as transformers blew, their lines ripped out by the ice. I thought of the blue-grey footage of Baghdad under bombardment seven years before. From all directions came the howling of sirens. The night was terrible, unreal and exhilarating; the excitement as much as the noise made it hard to get to sleep, and morning with its scenes of wreckage came quickly.

After the fact, people in Kingston were apt to feel that their city's predicament had been downplayed or passed over in the national media. This feeling – no doubt shared in hundreds of communities outside of Montreal and Ottawa – was less a sign of pettiness or parochialism than a reflection of the way the world contracted during the storm to the point where one's own place seemed to lie at the frozen heart of it, ground zero. Could Montreal really have been harder hit than Kingston?

It was. But for many of us during the storm, Montreal and those many nameless communities hardly seemed to exist – a perception heightened by our initial difficulties in getting as much news as we're used to in a wired environment that had suddenly come unplugged.

Overnight, life in Kingston became focused on a lone, stubborn seam of light running down Princess Street, the main drag, so that to the helicopters I heard passing overhead a few nights after the ice hit, the downtown must have looked like some village straggling along a highway in subarctic wilderness. Evenings, many of us would drift in from the increasingly cold, lightless peripheries to warm up in the coffee shops and pubs, eat hot meals, refill Thermoses, make telephone calls and strive to top the storm stories of friends or new acquaintances. The surest social adhesive is always a common cause, or enemy, and in this case it was the ice and its lingering effects.

During the event and later, the various media were unable to capture what struck many as the essence of the crisis: total darkness in a place where nobody expects it. Out in the woods at night, starlight seems enough, darkness feels natural. In a city, when most sources of artificial light are lost, the darkness is uncanny and troubling and the cold seems that much sharper. Uncannier still is the experience of unlocking a door and entering a house not to the reprieve of synthetic warmth but to a cold co-extensive with the outer cold. So that the walls and door are revealed, from nature's patient perspective, as provisional in the short run and fictitious in the long run, like all artificial barriers.

This was the situation in our neighbourhood five days after power was lost. Two days before, in a car with dented roof and cracked windshield, I'd driven my wife and baby daughter (so bundled up, it seemed a self-inflating life-vest must have puffed open under her sweaters) to the bus depot, where they'd embarked with hordes of others for Toronto. Now I was returning from an overheated pub where I'd spent the evening. Like a curler I shuffled over glazed streets barricaded with branches, criss-crossed by yellow police tape, littered with cars and sinuous downed wires I avoided as if they were sluggish pythons or copperheads. As I came through the door, the cold and the darkness – which till now I'd experienced as a kind of dramatic novelty – struck me for the first time as not just inconvenient but a violation, personally aggressive, seeming to pursue some stealthy vendetta. A house comes to feel like an extension or version of its residents, a solo or group portrait in material possessions; to find it reduced to a dark cold shell is disturbing, like seeing a gravestone with your name on it in the snowy churchyard of a dream.

Essentially the telephone had been dead for days but sometimes, somehow, the lines would revive, a caller would get through and it would jangle shockingly in the dark. On two occasions it was dead again by the time I picked it up – and what silence can match the silence of a dead receiver? Once it cut out in mid-conversation, like a field telephone at a crucial moment in a war film.

In the ice vault of the bedroom I slept under quilts and blankets layered so heavily that it was an effort to roll over. Sheepishly I kept a pitchfork by the door in case of break-ins, a house around the corner having just been vandalized. Around me wafted the festive odours of coconut rum and sweet sherry, as if the house had been reduced to this freezing hulk in the course of some manic frat party; in fact I'd run out of antifreeze, and it was sold out everywhere, so I'd had to iceproof the toilet and the traps of the sink and bathtub with Christmas party leftovers. The toilet was now a ghastly punchbowl effervescing with a toxic melange the colour of Windex – three parts antifreeze, two parts Blue Sapphire gin, one part Henkell Tröcken. The bathroom sink had gargled down half a mickey of Yukon Jack and a little dry red wine. With vermouth (only 16 percent alcohol, a fact that would soon prove a bonanza for Dick Hall Plumbing, and disastrous for Equity Assurance Inc., Kingston), I tried to safeguard the kitchen traps.

Next morning on opening the refrigerator I found it to be the warmest place in the house. Already on the verge of freezing, the milk – as I poured it over cereal of an uncommon crispiness – thickened to a crystalline slush. Time to flee. Wild rumours were abroad, and the most attractive was that insurance companies were going to pay for hotel rooms. I packed a bag and checked into a relatively cheap Victorian hotel on the waterfront, above an ersatz but comfortable "Irish" cigarbar. I hadn't expected to find a room so easily, but by now, it turned out, much of the population had decamped for points west. Each night I would return to check on the house, where I lit candles in the front room and sat at the table in two sweaters and a greatcoat and fingerless gloves, trying to rewrite the poems of Dr. Zhivago. At midnight I would leave, aiming the beam of a flashlight loaded with fresh batteries out an upstairs window – a canny expedient sure to ward off those thieves dim enough to believe that anyone but a frozen corpse could be up there reading in the small hours. As I slid back towards Princess Street I watched for signs of similar precautions in other houses, but most were totally dark – deserted, or tended by less neurotic residents. Above silhouettes of old gabled houses the cold had honed the stars, and the Milky Way was a mist on the sky, a ridge of dark conifers dusted with snow.

Despite the bulk of reports and images stressing the storm's catastrophic elements, the experience could also be a good one. There was that sense of community I mentioned before; the manifold beauty of the storm in all its phases; its spectacular pie in the face of high-tech hubris; its anarchic disruption of rote and routine; impromptu poker parties by neighbourhood fireplaces; and the feeling it gave of radical *usefulness*, whether you were pitching in with strangers to free cars from under fallen branches, draining rads and learning how a heating system actually works, tending a house that seemed under siege, working physically instead of just tapping keys to access flickery precincts of a virtual realm. So that everything was suddenly real and concrete. So that each frustration was more serious, each hope more deeply felt, and the return of light and heat, twelve days later, was a moment of disproportionate joy.

By intensifying moods in both directions, the ice storm granted an inkling of how things must have been not so long ago when life was more basic and less secure – the mortal lows more frequent and thus the joys, set off against them, sharper.

A confession. On the whole, although I knew people were struggling (including neighbours too strapped to send their children to grandparents in other cities), although I knew that most sensible people hated the crisis, although I saw that Kingston's old urban forest would suffer, I loved the storm. Several friends – all poets, come to think of it – felt the same way. Others seemed to find my assertion disquieting, perhaps vaguely treacherous, as if I'd been sleeping with the enemy.

It was a cold bed, but I felt inspired there.

It could be that modern amenities, providing a sort of elemental, existential insulation, have an effect on the psyche comparable to that of lithium on the moods of manic depressives, snipping off the extremes of low and high. I'm as fond of central heating, home videos and word processors as anyone, but the storm proved to me that intensity of feeling and immediacy of experience do decline as convenience and comfort grow. The heart thrives on challenge, yet human nature seeks security. We can have that security now, many of us, much of the time, and the price may be the loss of tragic vision.

A year later – looking through photos and remembering the storm in a warm room in front of a humming laptop – what I want to know is this: Is it possible to feel, to write, to live as intensely as the people of less mediated times while embracing things that sequester us ever further from nature? Every benefit has its price, and the technologies that facilitate postmodern life also sever us from primal sources of inspiration – elemental parts of ourselves. So we live lives ever more removed from the real. Not that I can pose as an expert on the unmediated life, or on ice or fire storms in the soul. I embrace those other things, as you do. And there lies the paradox. I loved the intensity and immediacy of the ice storm, but I do not want it to come again.

Steven Heighton is one of Canada's leading younger writers of poetry and fiction. His novel The Shadow Boxer *will appear in the year 2000. He adapted this essay for this book from its original version, which was published in* Books in Canada *magazine.*

2

SURVIVING IN THE CITIES

ities are bulging with people who choose to be anonymous. For a host of reasons, they move away from home and find themselves an apartment, a job, or a place at a night school — a fresh identity, in short. But if some are anonymous by desire, others are anonymous by fate. Some new immigrants and refugees tread the streets of a city cautiously, not understanding the language or appreciating the rules. The lonely and the unemployed, the homeless and the mentally ill, runaways and castaways — a city has them all, along with wealth and expensive pleasure. Life on a country road may change little from year to year. But life on an inner-city block is always evolving. Under the circumstances, how can a city ever be prepared for an emergency?

I don't know. But I do know one thing: during the ice storm, it's lucky Montreal received merely forty-one centimetres of freezing rain. Vankleek Hill, an hour's drive away in eastern Ontario, had more than twice as much; so did the worst-hit places in Quebec's triangle of darkness. The impact of the rain was not directly proportionate to its amount. Cities are vulnerable places; cities are needy. The stories that follow, more than in any other chapter, admit to vulnerability.

One day, when the rain was over but the crisis was still near its peak, I spent the afternoon inside the bright headquarters of Hydro-Québec in downtown Montreal. A press conference had been promised for 2:00 P.M. Reporters, broadcasters and camera crews spent the afternoon milling around, talking in low voices, gazing glumly at each other, occasionally phoning their offices and hoping vainly for scoops. There were no scoops. It was incredibly frustrating, especially as we had no proof that a press conference would ever occur. Not until 5:45 or so did the utility's chairman finally appear, along with Premier Bouchard. When they'd *said what they had to say – which wasn't much – I came out into the early evening. The early night, I mean: the darkness visible.*

The Hydro-Québec building is not far from my office. Rather than wait for a taxi, I walked with a colleague back along the frozen streets. Sidewalks were impassable, but the traffic was so sparse we could easily walk in the roadway. A siren wailed in the black distance. High above Chinatown, the stars lit up the sky. Bouchard's words of reassurance seemed as forlorn as the cry of a lost child.

I wasn't scared. But I wasn't alone, and I had a job to do and a destination in mind. How would I have felt on the same night in the same street if I'd been cold, lonely, and without a place to go?

DANIEL YELLE

Allô, Normand! I hope everything's fine in Guadeloupe. I have news to tell you. In the middle of winter, it rained here for five consecutive days. The accumulated weight of ice destroyed much of Hydro-Québec's distribution network. My home in Montreal was without power for eleven days. Here's my story.

The problems began on Tuesday. Coming home from work, I found that my apartment had no electricity, so I slept at my parents' place in the country. Next day I still had no power, and the rain kept on falling. I went back to my parents'. The TV news carried more and more reports of fallen wires and power outages, and at 10:30 P.M. my parents' home lost power. I stayed the night anyway.

On Thursday I went to work – the company has a big generator – and lots of people there seemed very tense. The news was going from bad to worse: the freezing rain had toppled not only the lines, but also some huge pylons. I found out during the day that my parents were without running water as well as electricity. When I left work at five, I wasn't sure what to do. But I still had water at my place, so I decided to head back.

It was a terrible night. My boss called to say that the office would be closed the next day. I put on all the clothes I could find – ski pants, sweaters, a parka, tuque and Ski-doo boots – and went to bed under a sleeping bag in total darkness. I slept poorly. At one point I woke up feeling panicky, unable to breathe. I jumped out of bed and leaned against the wall, trying to get my breath back. I don't know what happened exactly, but I thought I was going to die. Finally, finally, morning came and I could leave to get something to eat.

Feeling weak and worn out, I took the Metro to Atwater. Most of the stores in the shopping centre were still open, probably thanks to generators. I withdrew some cash and had breakfast at McDonald's. The newspaper said that shelters were being set up, one of them on the top floor of the Eaton Centre on Ste. Catherine Street, and I decided to go see what it was like. It was nine o'clock in the morning, and two big rooms were full of army cots. One of the rooms was beside the movie theatre, the other just across from it. I was told I'd have to sign up to reserve a bed, and I did so – I wasn't taking any chances. Staying there for a day wouldn't be very comfortable, but still, better than home. Anyway, I thought, the power will probably come back soon.

I stretched out and rested a little. But I was very uncomfortable because of all the clothes I was wearing, and my ski pants were too tight. I decided to go and buy a pair of jogging pants. Before I left, the organizers of the shelter asked me to locate a pharmacy in the Eaton Centre. I came back an hour later with my purchase and the information they wanted. I'd also been able to get a pill for my thyroid condition – I'd forgotten to bring my medication with me. They wouldn't give me more than one pill, because my own pharmacy wasn't answering calls. I'd have to go and get my pills tomorrow.

By 1 P.M. I was feeling stronger and, having nothing to lose, I decided to go see a movie. The only one I hadn't seen was *Flubber*, so I bought a ticket and started to watch. An hour into the movie, the cinema lost power and everyone had to find their way out by the emergency lights. All the businesses in the Eaton Centre were now without electricity. But the people in charge of our shelter, who came from a district health centre, tried to reassure everyone. They served free muffins and juice. During my absence, a lot of newcomers had arrived, including some old people in pretty bad shape.

After a while, we began to hear noises from overhead. As the evening wore on, the noises got louder. I'd better explain: the Eaton Centre has a huge glass roof. Unfortunately, it's right next to a thirty-two-storey skyscraper and the deafening booms we were hearing came from huge chunks of ice that were falling onto our roof. The room we were in had a concrete ceiling, but the situation right outside our door was worrying. The organizers had worked so hard setting up this shelter that they were reluctant to move, but it was no longer safe. More and more people kept arriving. We found out that the Metro was now closed and that you had to wait three hours for a taxi.

At around 9 P.M. we were told that we'd be transferred to the thirty-eighth floor of Place Ville-Marie, a couple of blocks away. Two hours later, I found myself sitting on the windowsill of an empty office – no telephone, no furniture, only a colour TV. That's where I saw, for the first time, the magnitude of the whole catastrophe, and where I understood that it wasn't a question of just making a few repairs so that everything would soon be back to normal. As we watched the news, our hair stood up on end. Hundreds of pylons had fallen like dominoes; four out of the five electricity lines that feed Montreal were out of service; it could be weeks before the power came back.

Fatigue, anxiety, fear. I slept, fully dressed, with my keys and wallet in a pocket and my glasses in my boots. The army cots had been requisitioned by the Red Cross, who apparently needed them more than we did, so now we had only foam mattresses to sleep on. Among the other refugees there were punks, there were the homeless, and there were people who, let's say, nobody would mistake for lawyers or doctors. According to the organizers, the room had 179 people in it. The ventilation was lousy. Beside my mattress was a big weasel of a guy who began the conversation by saying that he hadn't slept in four days. Which didn't prevent him from reciting his life story until 2 A.M.

A woman in her forties suddenly became hysterical. She was talking so loudly that everyone in the room was looking at her. The health-centre people spoke to her but they seemed discouraged. Finally they left her alone and she calmed down.

I changed my place to get away from Blabbermouth. The room was becoming so hot I had trouble breathing. My neck was hurting too, probably from stress. I could hardly sleep.

Most people stayed lying down until 7 A.M. They gave us muffins, coffee, and fruit juice, and I took the elevator down to the ground floor to see if I could buy a newspaper. When I got back up, the TV was on and the announcer was saying that all over Montreal people should boil their water for five minutes before drinking it. If this wasn't so serious, it would be downright funny. People were afraid of freezing to death – how were they supposed to boil water?

I spent part of the morning looking out the window. A beautiful view from the thirty-eighth floor. I noticed the lack of cars on the Jacques Cartier Bridge and then heard the TV announcer say that all the bridges to the South Shore were now closed. I went to the washroom and found someone vomiting – he had eaten fish in a restaurant the night before.

But the Metro was working again. I went home in search of my prescription. It was a slow journey home, but finally I got back to my street. The scene was incredible – all the trees were damaged, and broken branches lay everywhere. The street was blocked off by a red police ribbon, but I walked along it anyway. A big wire, which used to connect two apartment blocks, was lying in the middle of the road. One huge branch had almost fallen on the little credit union, and another branch was hanging over the wire that led to the building next to mine. My cedar had buckled under the weight of ice. I didn't exactly feel safe there.

My apartment was so cold I could see my breath. I gathered everything I needed, and took the Metro back to Place Ville-Marie. I called my parents from there, and found that my father had managed to install an old oil furnace he had in storage. On the news, people were talking about the danger of burst pipes, and because the bridges were closed, my father couldn't drive in and turn the taps on in the two small apartment buildings we own. So I decided to use the Metro once again and deal with the taps in all the apartments I had a key for. That done, I returned to Place Ville-Marie and phoned my father to say that I couldn't stay another night in the shelter. As soon as the Mercier Bridge was open again, I would chip the inches of ice off the car and make my way out to the country.

In the shelter, they served us submarine sandwiches for dinner. All the time, people continued to arrive. The very old were the saddest to see. Looking at them, you wondered if they'd survive the next five minutes, let alone the many days they might well have to stay here. They were given a special area, away from all the rest.

I was exhausted, I needed a shower, I needed some sleep. The air still smelled awful. But I heard that the Mercier Bridge had reopened, so I left the shelter once again and took the Metro back home. Having de-iced the car, I set out towards the bridge. The streets of Montreal looked like cities after they had been bombed in World War II – an impression the radio also gave. Just before the bridge, I stopped at a supermarket to buy some bottled water. All I could find were three bottles of Vichy Célestin. I got back into the car and headed off, but at the last stop sign before the bridge, I noticed some cars blocking the way ahead. At that moment the radio announced that the Mercier Bridge had been closed again as conditions were still too dangerous.

I made a U-turn. I toyed with the idea of waiting in my car, but I didn't have much gas left and all the service stations I had seen were closed. I was now in the suburb of LaSalle, where everything was shut except for a few convenience stores. My only option was to return to Place Ville-Marie. I was discouraged and nearly dropping from fatigue. I left my car in a secure parking lot and emptied it of my belongings again. When I got back to the shelter, I phoned Pierre-Charles, who said he not only had gas heating, he also had electricity. And he would be willing to put me up. Ice storm crisis? What ice storm crisis?

It took a long time to get through to my father and tell him that I'd found another place to stay. I was afraid that if I quit the shelter and he didn't hear from me, he might decide to come in search of me as soon as the bridge was open. Finally I could leave Place Ville-Marie, letting the authorities know they could give my "bed" to someone else.

The blackness was incredible on Ste. Catherine. When I got to the door of the Metro, I found the system had shut down again. But I saw a taxi, and to hell with the expense – "Verdun, s'il vous plaît." The Atwater tunnel was closed for unknown reasons, so we had to detour through St-Henri, with only the taxi's headlights to see where we were going. At last I reached Pierre-Charles's street, an oasis of light in a black desert.

I took a shower – what joy! Pierre-Charles lent me a T-shirt, socks, and shorts. I went to sleep in a sleeping bag on the floor of the living room, surrounded by books and videos. My first night of sleep in the last three days – I told myself I was saved. I would stay there for the next five nights.

Whatever doesn't kill us makes us stronger. We are millions of Supermen now.

Apart from this little incident, there's nothing much to report.

Daniel Yelle is an office worker in a suburb of Montreal.

URSULA CHAUTEMS

After ten days in a house eventually down to 4°C, it is somehow the little things that seem to remain most vividly in my memory:

– toothpaste too stiff to come out of its tube

– the happiness of finding a forgotten box of matches

– my eyeglasses fogging up when I put them on my nose

– knitting in semi-darkness with icy needles to pass the time

– the butter on my bread too stiff to spread

– being finally sincerely grateful for Aunt Martha's hideously coloured gift scarf – I can breathe through its open weave while filtering some of the cold air

– slowing down physically and mentally; reading the *Gazette* in the waning daylight, and forgetting what I have read

– my scalp itching under three layers of head coverings worn day and night

– watching a favourite tropical houseplant slowly die

– finding that I am allergic to the fuel in our only source of cooking, a fondue burner

– knocking over things while waddling along with a big comforter tied around me

– remembering half-forgotten skills for making shadow pictures on the wall with my hands in front of the candle

– unlearning the modern habit of doing more than one thing at a time; instead, stringing out the few possible activities to pass the time until things get better

– trying to sit down on a kitchen chair and, at the last moment, feeling it pushed away from under me by my many layers of bulky clothing

– the long stretches of complete silence

– the utter irony of my French family name, Chautems, which translates to "Hot weather"!

Ursula Chautems is retired from her job as assistant city clerk of Pierrefonds, a west-island suburb of Montreal.

EMILY URQUHART

The first afternoon it's sort of a novelty: watching branches crash down onto innocent pedestrians, exclaiming in delight that we could see our breath in our own home. And classes at Queen's are cancelled, the feeling reminiscent of those high-school snow days when the bus doesn't show up and you know you aren't destined to go to school that morning.

Ciara and I sit all afternoon bundled up by candlelight in the living room. I am playing fun games with the telephone, which is allowing me to hear not just my own voice mail, but all of Kingston's private messages. I am also swigging vodka to keep warm. Ciara, whose lips have never before touched liquor, sips some every now and then. One sip equals exactly thirty minutes of warmth.

Soon the vodka runs out, and Ciara and I can no longer feel our hands and feet. We take the next logical step, and head towards Kingston's downtown grid, which has power and the promise of food and more liquor. A long night at the bar is ahead.

By the middle of the night I begin to sober up and become painfully aware that I can't really go home. Not alone, anyway. I glance around at the drunken Queen's students, behaving considerably more animalistic than usual. I think back to the large branch that crashed down at my feet earlier in the day. "You all right?" a stopped motorist had called to me. "You should be more careful. You could have been killed."

I think of my car – Tony, the oldest and rattiest car in Kingston – unscathed in the backyard but trapped in a cage of trees.

"Happy State of Emergency!" Cheers ring all around me.

This is the point where the ice storm stops being so much fun. Best to get obliterated under these conditions. You sleep better in the cold, if nothing else.

That night we pile several mattresses onto the floor of the living room, where Ciara, the vodka, and I had sat so many hours prior. There are about ten of us huddled together. My mother later described the room as having the foulest scent she had ever encountered.

The next morning Leslie, a roommate, shows up to check on the house and us. She brings Coltrane, her boyfriend's dog, who is making funny noises. We consider the possibility that his insides have frozen. Our cat, Tigger, has long since up and left, finding his surroundings extremely undesirable.

The army shows up soon after Leslie. I answer the door to a stern young man in full military regalia. To my horror the boys are screaming from the other room, "Is he cute? IS HE CUTE?"

I am paralyzed. He doesn't find this even slightly amusing. He *hates* us. This man has been knocking on students' doors all morning, handing out pamphlets and ordering evacuations. This is not a fun job when everyone considers Kingston's state of emergency a school holiday. He knows that the ice storm isn't funny. He realizes what the students don't: how badly it is affecting the rest of the population.

Ciara finally gets the phone to work and rings her mother to explain her present situation. At the suggestion of heading to a shelter, her mother mentions something about chastity belts. My own mother wants to drive directly to Kingston to pick us up. I assume she hasn't been watching the news, because if she had been she might have noticed that Kingston looks like full-out war has recently erupted, and that car travel is close to impossible.

Day two is spent wandering from coffee shop to restaurant to bar. That night everyone plays board and card games by candlelight. I hate board games, so I watch in dismay. The candlelight begins to make me feel as if I am going blind.

We go to the smoky bar to find light, leaving Alex behind in the cold. He is sitting calmly playing cards and drinking gin. He is found in the same position three hours later upon our return.

I am becoming delirious. We are all becoming delirious.

"How long do you think it will take to get the power back?" I ask before falling asleep.

"Probably a month or so, seeing as Kingston's wiring system is such a hodgepodge of whatnot," a voice answers from the darkness.

This was the engineering student among us.

I awake the next morning to find that Ciara and my parents have been in cahoots, and that my mother will be arriving in the next few hours. Usually when one's mother arrives, there is a frenzy of cleaning activity. This time I do not care. I leave the house in disarray and head to the warm student centre to wait for our rescue.

The boys jeer at the four of us who decide to go with my mother. "Wussies." "Can't handle the ice storm?" At my mother's arrival they all regress to the age of six, and get in their own cars to head home.

While we are packing up the Ford, Leslie and Coltrane appear again. They have both been running circles in the park to keep warm. Unfortunately, Leslie can't leave the dog or its owner behind. As the car pulls away, our waves become frantic motioning. Leslie is standing under a dangerously precarious phone pole. She glances up, shifts position, and keeps waving.

Emily Urquhart came to Queen's University from Wellesley, Ontario. Her mother's story appears on p. 312.

RON ZINN

Sunday, January 4
It's been a wonderful Christmas vacation and I'm looking forward to a few extra days off before I go back to work on Wednesday. Freezing rain is in the forecast, and I try to explain to my twin daughters, Erica and Michele, what it is and what happened in 1963, when we had a freezing rain storm and were without electricity for three days.

Monday, January 5
As forecast, the ice storm hit. It rained all day, and as soon as the rain touched down it froze onto everything it touched. It was kind of beautiful; everything was sparkling under the moonlight.

Tuesday, January 6
Hmm. This morning when we woke up, we discovered the power had gone out during the night. Later we discovered that the power was out almost everywhere in the Montreal area, and getting worse. By supper hour, Hydro-Québec was saying some homes could be out for a couple of days.

Wednesday, January 7
The power is still out, but what the hell, I decided to go to work anyway. It was my first day back.

The power was on at work but went out at two-thirty, so they told us to go home.

On the bus ride over the Champlain Bridge, it looked like the entire South Shore was blacked out. But as the bus got closer to home, I could see that our little section of Brossard had power. I danced all the way home from the bus stop, and called my wife, Louise, at work to tell her the good news. I then pumped up the heat, full blast.

Louise's sister Danièle called at around 7 P.M. She couldn't take being cold any longer and asked to stay with us. She was into her fortieth hour without power. Minutes later the doorbell rang. It was Jacques Pouliot, our neighbour and local handyman. He's like, "Tabernac, l'arbre de votre voisin est cracké et pret à tomber sur votre maison! Viens aider nous autres – maintenant!"

This tree was split in half and ready to fall right on my house. I put rain gear and hard hat on, and went out to help the neighbours. It was raining hard and freezing solid on everything, but we had to cut that tree down.

Danièle showed up while I was outside. Her husband was away on a business trip. She was frightened and very cold. She had a hot shower, and we talked till 1 A.M. before deciding to hit the sack. Just then, there was a loud crash outside. One of my maples in the backyard had succumbed to the weight of ice and fallen to the ground. Shit, that was a nice tree! Again I put on my rain gear and hard hat and went out to inspect the damage.

Thursday, January 8
Freezing rain all night and the power has gone out again. I really didn't want to face the day. I got up at ten and didn't even call in to work. I knew no one would be there. Jacques and I worked most of the day to cut up my fallen maple. We also started to cut another tree in the backyard – it was split really bad and was going to fall on my new toolshed.

I found the only open restaurant, a Kentucky Fried. I waited in line for almost an hour and bought fifty-four dollars' worth. Mmm. My family and I ate by Jacques' warm fireplace and played cards with his grandchildren after.

Louise freaked when I said it was Thursday night and nothing could stop me from going to Sudsey's with the boys, even though I had to scrape three inches of ice off the car. Big John had eight candles going and it was still surprisingly warm in his apartment. Bentley and Ken were there too. Big John said that Sudsey's had been closed nights since Monday, so we hit the only tavern in the area that was open, Chez Vincent in old Longueuil. The place was almost empty. Bentley and I won fifty dollars on the slot machine, so on the way home I filled up the tank in the car.

Friday, January 9
The power is still out and the freezing rain has started again. Hydro-Québec is now saying that 1.3 million homes are without power. Louise decided to take off with the kids and her sister to her brother René's

place in Sherbrooke. I had to stay. Nothing would take me away from my home. I worked all day cleaning up trees and branches in the yard and then had supper over at Jacques': chicken pot pie, cooked in the fireplace. I went home right after. The house is now at 10°C.

CJAD is off the air because their tower collapsed – there's only CIQC, broadcasting emergency news. Nothing to do but drink beer and walk around to keep warm. Army helicopters fly over continuously, and army trucks rumble down my street. I walked from the back door to the front door, front door to the back door, looking for some action. Beer, chips, CIQC, candles, front door, back door, front door, back door. More beer and more pacing.

Saturday, January 10
Still no power, so I worked all day long in the yard cleaning up the mess. The temperature in the house is 8°C.

At around midnight, after about six beers, I heard all kinds of yelling and noise in the front yard. When I went to check out what was going on, it was the Canadian army cleaning up all the fallen branches and logs! I put on my coat and safety equipment and went out to help them. What a buzz – we worked and talked for more than an hour. They were really good guys and it was quite an experience. They told me they were all from the Quebec City area and had just returned from six months in Haiti. They said it was strange having to work in Canada, helping some of their own, but they felt proud helping fellow Canadians. I had them all in for Cokes while they waited for their CO to return. I will never forget this as long as I live. The Canadian army helped me!

Sunday, January 11
Same old thing. Still no power, so I worked outside. Peter Ross and René Bergeron showed up in the afternoon with a truckload of firewood from Sherbrooke. What good guys – they just gave the wood away to any of my neighbours who needed it. They said, "It's okay, there's no charge, you're a friend of Ron's."

We heard on the radio that some places in Longueuil might have power, so Jacques and I headed out to see. There was unimaginable devastation everywhere. Thick ice was on everything, roads were closed, and it was extremely dark except for the lights from cars. We noticed a Petro-Canada that was operating with a generator – the cars were lined up for more than a kilometre to get gas.

Back home, listening to the radio by candlelight, drinking beer and eating chips. At around 11 P.M., after six beers or so, Louise called from Sherbrooke. I'm not 100 percent because of the beer, but Louise thought I might be suffering from hypothermia because my speech was a bit slurred. She sent her brother to pick me up and take me to Sherbrooke.

René arrived at 1:30 A.M. Together we closed the water main and emptied the pipes and hot-water tank. We also put antifreeze in the toilets and drains. I plugged in my old answering machine, so I could call home to know when the power was on. What a weird feeling. I had said I would never abandon my house, and here I am leaving.

Monday, January 12

My first day as a refugee. Life for people in Sherbrooke was almost normal. They were not really affected by the storms. I had a good breakfast, and a visit with Louise and the girls, and then got ready to head back home to Brossard. I just had to check the house. I was concerned about looting, fire and flooding.

René, John Barrington, and I loaded up the car with candles, fondue oil and lamp oil, and headed back to the "war zone." Every tree along the highway was damaged, rows and rows of telephone poles were down. It looked like World War III. Near Granby we saw a convoy of 120 Detroit Edison trucks who had come to help out. I figure the convoy was five kilometres long.

When I got home I found a large 'X' taped on my front door. I later learned this meant the house had been checked and secured by the Armed Forces. It meant the house had been abandoned, there were no dead bodies inside, and nobody was in there suffering from hypothermia. When I looked down the street, I saw that almost every house had an 'X' on the door – they were all abandoned. It was quite eerie.

Wednesday, January 14

We heard that some people in our area had their power back, so we decided to head back to Brossard to check it out. My friend Nurhan

Papucciyan had power, so he invited us to stay with him and his family. This was convenient because Pooch lives only four blocks from us. We played lots of Nintendo and I called home every half hour. Still no answer.

Friday, January 16
I decided to go to the office today. I had worked half a day in the past three weeks, so it was kind of strange being there. Everyone had a million stories to tell and so did I. After noon I did manage to get some work done, but there wasn't a lot to do. I had expected more.

Saturday, January 17
Still no power at home. It's very frustrating, because people around me have had their power for days now, but not us. While out for an afternoon drive, I saw a convoy of Connecticut hydro trucks headed for our area, but they seemed to go right past my house, so I lost hope.

I decided to try one more time, and it worked! The answering machine picked up! The power was back on! I ran all the way home from Pooch's. I passed some neighbours on the way and yelled, "Oui, on a du courant!"

I was pumped. I ripped the 'X' off the door and set the thermostat at ten degrees. Thermal heating from the sun had kept the temperature on the ground floor above zero, but the bedrooms and bathroom upstairs were freezing. Some of the plants had died and the girls' aquarium had frozen solid. The fish were all dead, frozen in the thick ice. They looked like they were in suspended animation.

It seems the girls liked their fish more than I thought. They cried in harmony when I told them the fish were dead.

Sunday, January 18
Louise and I cleaned the fridge and freezer and threw out all the spoiled food. We filled six garbage bags with stinking, gooey, dripping food. It was horrible. The house took fifteen hours to warm up completely, but everything worked fine – no problems with the pipes and hot-water tank.

Life is slowly getting back to normal.

Ron Zinn works as a purchaser for Batshaw Youth and Family Centres in Montreal. He originally wrote this diary for friends in Scotland.

SUSAN CARPENTER

"This must be what it's like in the Bosnian refugee camps." That was my first thought as my nine-year-old daughter and I waited in the reception line of the shelter set up at Centennial High School, in Greenfield Park on the South Shore of Montreal. We'd toughed it out at home since the ice storm hit – my husband, daughter, dog, four cats and two parrots huddled in one room, barely moving. That day, however, we bowed to the inevitable: we had to leave. My husband elected to stay in our flat with the pets, a decision that would prove to have serious repercussions later on, but Martine and I packed hurriedly, called the police command post, and waited for a ride to the shelter.

When our ride came, we drove down blacked-out Taschereau Boulevard – a surreal, depressing experience. Once in a while, through the inky darkness, a tongue of blue flame would spiral out of a blown transformer. The implications were fearsome, but to the ear and the eye, it was quite pleasing. At least at first.

The shelter, an oasis of light and warmth, was packed. I couldn't help but make the inevitable comparisons between this shouting, dishevelled mass of people clutching pillows and suitcases, and what I had read of the reception centres at camps during the Holocaust and in other war zones. "If this is just a hint of what those folks went through, unendingly," I thought, "how will I cope?"

The chaos looked and sounded worse than it actually was. In relatively short time, we were registered and shown to an upstairs classroom to deposit our belongings. Already, five sleeping bags were stretched out on the carpeting. By the time we went to sleep that night, the number of people in our room would total thirteen.

Martine and I went to the cafeteria to line up for supper. The wait was long, but that truly didn't matter in the least to us. We were beginning to thaw out, after having felt the numbing cold creep into our bodies, slowly, insidiously at first, then settle into the very marrow of our beings. I don't remember what we ate that night, but it was hot, unbearably delicious, and sustaining. A TV blared and children were playing organized games in the gymnasium. One would think, at first glance, that this was a convention of some sort. At least the kids treated it like an adventure. My two older children had attended this high school; now we were seeing it in a whole new light. The light of the generator, as it were.

The hot meals, the steaming showers, the reassuring hum that told us heat was coursing through the building: all came to an end that night. The generator failed, worn out from its efforts at keeping the elements at bay and upwards of eight hundred people (that particular night) warm. In a matter of hours, the picture had changed drastically. For one frightening meal, food was rationed. Some people's tempers flared repeatedly. Others, too numb to make much of a fuss, sat miserably and stared blankly, exhibiting what came to be known as "ice storm stare."

The sky was leaden grey – never quite light. Daylight and twilight became blurred, and a sense of timelessness prevailed. I stepped outside for a smoke, shortly after the last freezing rain hit, and was struck by the absolute silence. Not a bird could be seen or heard, and that was a chilling experience. "If the birds have abandoned this place, this blasted landscape, what is to become of us?" I thought. The bridges that had linked us to the city were closed. We were isolated and inaccessible. I feared, for the space of two breaths, that it would always be like this. It is a curious thing when one experiences total loss of hope. That loss marked, for me, the worst moment of the crisis.

It passed quickly, and in many ways things did get better. The army came in with two huge generators, and order (along with electricity) was restored. My husband eventually joined me at the shelter, but not before he had contracted pneumonia. His state of mind was not the best, either. We were blacked out for nine days, and Centennial High School was where we remained all that time, except for daily forays to the old homestead to feed and exercise the family pets.

Martine spent the entire time with me at the shelter. At first she was excited about the whole experience. She engaged in the organized activities and made quite a few friends. Like her mother, she is a voracious reader, so she read all the available material, age-appropriate and otherwise. After a while, however, she did succumb to boredom. Even the most entertaining company and games become mundane in time. She had no problems sleeping, but mealtimes became of paramount importance to her. She was not alone in this; we all looked forward to being fed. I have observed that same preoccupation with food in hospitals, jails and psychiatric facilities – all places in which I have worked.

I wasn't just a victim of the storm; I was a volunteer. Being fluent in both French and English, I worked on the registration desk at the Centennial High School shelter. People who were not staying would come in to visit friends or relatives, and I would take their names, find out whom they were visiting, and send runners (usually teenagers) to track down the friends or relatives.

In the end, the stress got to me. On the last day of my stay, I started to experience stabbing chest pains, and collapsed in a hallway. I was given nitroglycerin spray and taken by ambulance to Charles LeMoyne Hospital. After much hullabaloo, it turned out that my heart was fine. When it became obvious that I was going to be okay, the Greenfield Park police were called, and they returned me to the shelter. It was just another little blip in the whole adventure.

Susan Carpenter is a writer and teacher living in Greenfield Park, on the South Shore of Montreal.

GILLES CHARETTE

The cold
Bevie and I stayed in the house and did not go to the shelters, so we could keep an eye on the pipes and fend off burglars. We managed to keep the house from going below the freezing point, but overnight it would drop to 5°C until I got up to prepare the house, light the candles, make the tea over the candled fondue dish. . . . Then we would sit in our chairs, fully winter-dressed, with ten candles burning at all times. We would encourage each other, and listen to the little transistor radio, and keep each other from falling asleep – forever, perhaps. A couple of times we both felt drowsy and the fear of falling into hypothermia was real. I would wake her up after five or six minutes. She would do the same for me.

I remember thinking how good it would be to be constipated during the seven days of cold in the house. It was hell to go. Worse for Bevie, of course.

The propane heater
Pete Beaulieu called us repeatedly and even came in with a propane heater, which allowed Bevie to take a shower after six days. I took two showers in the cold and one wonderful one when Pete was here. The trouble with the heater was that we did not have enough ventilation and I thought we would all faint. I opened the doors and kitchen windows but that was not enough. Pete had to take his heater back and the house went back down to 7°C after we had peeled off our clothes at 22°C. We woke up still wearing our light night-clothes. But I thanked him profusely and sincerely for his care for us.

Friends and neighbours
I'll never forget Robert Ratelle running over, once with a pot of coffee, and another time to offer his barbecue, which we used to heat up a teapot full of water. We used the water to make soup.

I remember telling Jacques Masse to calm down and take it easy as I struggled to help him put his garage-door pieces back together. I remember playing his piano when his house was 2°C and I had just filled his toilet bowls with windshield washer.

I am a good friend of Alex Belanger, now. We have known each other for thirty years, almost. I told him to call me "tu," not "vous."

Married life
Bevie was wonderful and never complained. With those big brown eyes, she looked so sweet, but shivering and courageous. We comforted each other. I tried to be sweet and tender and reassuring. I lost my cool and felt discouraged a couple of times, when getting up and being unable to pull the wick up on a candle, etc. But on the whole, I felt calm and in control of the situation. Bevie said I was wonderful during the crisis, and that is my priceless reward. I managed to do a pretty good job of keeping her safe and loved. It was cozy at night in bed, under triple blankets and with long johns and pyjamas and tuques – and each other.

When the power came back
We will have to clean up the smoke and smell from the candles. The hydro system is very fragile so we are using the power very carefully. One light bulb at a time, and I turn the computer off after each use.

The car started, after twenty-five turns. But I still haven't tried to drive it out of the garage. Our driveway is four inches of pure ice.

Canadiens vs. Flyers tonight on TV. But I can't get interested in hockey and I don't know how long it will be before I can again enjoy seeing young millionaires play a game for money. Not while our people, so many of them, are still suffering from the cold and darkness.

Bevie is enjoying toast after toast, my baby is. With strawberry jam. She missed that so much. Bills can wait – still. Too tired – still.

Gilles Charette is a retired railway employee living in Pierrefonds, a west-island suburb of Montreal.

STEPHEN EAST

Some of my most memorable experiences during my sixteen years of driving a taxi at the Ottawa Airport occurred during the Ice Storm of '98. The flight schedule was the first casualty. In a situation of weather problems, we usually don't get many fares from passengers off their flights; we get them from people who've gone to the airport only to discover to their horror that their flight has been cancelled or delayed to another day. The first couple of days, the ice storm didn't affect things much more than many other weather problems. I'd been through it before: fog, snowstorms, and freezing rain (the scariest of them all). By the third day, the situation became unusual. The weather forecast was calling for even more freezing rain, and this news scared off a lot of business travellers. The flight arrivals became even more sporadic. Normally we'd wait an hour and twenty minutes, on average, for each fare at that time of year, and the airport would rarely run out of taxis. But during the ice storm, everything changed.

We'd wait for three to four hours in the holding area for a fare. Then, all of a sudden, a huge unmanageable number of flights would arrive within minutes of each other, causing chaos for the baggage handlers and overwhelming the taxis. Even though we have 128 dedicated licensed taxis for the airport, we would run short and people would have to wait. Most people were quite reasonable. However, we all got our share of angry, grumpy creeps.

The road conditions slowed us down. The main roads had been salted, but most of the side streets and parking lots were very icy. It's much scarier to drive during freezing rain when you don't know where you are going to be forced to go – like when you drive a taxi!

I live in Ottawa on the fifth floor of an apartment building on Springland Drive. The electricity went off on the third day of the ice storm. There are no windows in the stairwells or hallways. It was pitch black, and of course no elevators were working. Even in the daytime, the only way to find my unit was with a flashlight. The temperature gradually dropped, but I didn't get alarmed because I thought it was only temporary.

The fourth day of the ice storm was wild. It was all over the news, and the forecast was shocking, calling for even more freezing rain. I had been warm under the covers, but when I crawled out of bed, it was cold. I decided to take everything out of my freezer and put it on the balcony outside. With no way to heat food, the only appealing things were canned beans and sardines with bread, mustard and butter, along with raisins for dessert. It was so cold in my apartment that I decided to go to work (my car) to get warm. It was very irritating not to be able to have a hot shower, but at least the water was still running – though getting colder and colder.

At the airport I got a fare right away. The people lived in a residential area in Elmvale Acres. On the way, the scenery was unbelievable. Trees fallen very dramatically everywhere. Major intersections with no traffic lights working. Ice-covered branches in the roadway had to be dodged. When we got to the destination, an older street with huge mature trees on either side of the road, the extreme weight of the ice was making the branches hang very low over the road. I could plainly see that my car, even in the middle of the road, would barely clear the lowest branches, but it looked like I had a chance. The address was at the end of the block, so I proceeded very slowly. About a third of the way, I could hear the branches scraping the roof of my car and my heart started pounding. The last thing I needed was to get my car damaged. At first I was just worried about my car, then – *crash!* – a branch got caught on my taxi roof-sign and started a chain reaction of branches breaking all around. I no longer cared about what happened to the car, I became worried about my life!

*Bicycles with icicles: Carolyn Molson noticed
them on an Ottawa street.*

My passengers screamed. I stepped on it and bombed all the way to
their house and swung into the driveway, out of harm's way. The only
damage to the car was a broken power antenna and some small dents
and scratch marks. However, as I was helping to bring the luggage to
the door, I did a super wipe-out and landed on my forearm very hard.
I was so glad to get out of that situation in one piece, I decided I
wouldn't press my luck and would head for home. I couldn't handle any
more fares.

On the way home I decided to buy more batteries for my transistor radio, and candles for light. There were no more D-size batteries any-where, they were sold out completely. I tried many stores. I finally found some candles in the most unlikely place: the old Christmas decorations section of a drugstore. The candles were in the shape of little houses; that's why they hadn't sold out. When I got home it was utterly boring: no TV, no Internet, no heat. I read the newspaper from cover to cover by candlelight.

The next morning, my arm was hurting like hell and I had a monster-size bruise on it where I had fallen. Utter misery. I decided to spend the rest of the day under the covers, listening to CFRA on my ever-weakening radio. The ice storm ended about 2 P.M. on the fifth day and my power came back on. I was one of the lucky ones.

Stephen East continues to drive a taxi in Ottawa.

KURT JONASSOHN

My apartment building is located at the western edge of downtown Montreal. My own apartment is on the twenty-third floor and faces east, giving me a panoramic view of downtown, from the mountain on my left to the South Shore on my right. There are several layouts avail-able in this building, and I deliberately chose one where I can look through the apartment and out over the balcony as soon as I open my front door. This choice was very important to me because that view does wonders for my morale, no matter what happens before I get home.

When the ice storm started, it didn't particularly worry me. After all, similar events are part of our winters here most years. We take snowstorms, freezing rain, icy streets or power outages in stride. They add spice to life and confirm our ability to cope with adversity. Freezing rain, in particular, has its enjoyable aspects. When trees, bushes, poles and wires are all covered with a transparent coating of ice that reflects light, Montreal becomes a fairyland. We ignore the dangers of icy streets and come out with our cameras to record this miracle before the inevitable thaw makes it all disappear in a day or two.

Only this time the thaw did not come. After a few days, the miracle became a serious menace.

For myself, I did not worry too much. My lifelong Boy Scout habits would finally prove their worth. I found a use for the candles that had never seen a match. My battery radio kept me in touch with the world outside. There was enough food in my kitchen to keep hunger at bay, even if it could not be cooked. I filled some bottles with water in case the pumps that raise it to the twenty-third floor should stop working. And I did not worry about the lack of heating, because it would probably take several days for this large apartment building to cool down enough to be a hardship. In addition, the building has an emergency generator that would keep one of the elevators going.

I belong to a generation that always prided itself on being able to cope with whatever happened to come along. Although I was only a teenager at the time, I remember the Great Depression only too clearly – with its shortages of food and money. I also remember the war in London, where blackouts were taken very seriously. Although we had lights inside the house, no glimmer was allowed to escape to the outside. Seeing London completely black made a lasting impression on me. The first air-raid alarms after the start of the war forced us into our dank and badly equipped basement. Shortly afterwards we acquired an Anderson shelter in the backyard, which was little more than a very small tin shack half-buried in the ground and covered with dirt.

After the first few days of our ice storm, we stopped enjoying the sparkling glitter of the ice that covered everything. Instead we started to listen to the news in the hope that the weather would break; but all we heard were stories of the increasing hardships of people deprived of heat, light and cooking facilities. I felt increasingly fortunate to be able to remain in my own apartment with minimal discomfort.

Ordinarily my apartment is never very dark, because of the myriad lights from the downtown buildings that sparkle in the night. After a few days, some buildings had lights in them while others next to them were dark. As a result, the night illumination was reduced. Then, suddenly, one evening my apartment went dark. Looking out at my view, I saw nothing. There was not a single spot of light anywhere. Perhaps it was due to the memories of the London blackouts during World War II that this blackness really shook me up. Nothing brought home to me the seriousness of the situation so much as this complete blackout of Montreal. My wonderful and glamorous city was dying!

Kurt Jonassohn is a retired sociology professor at Concordia University. He is the co-author of Genocide and Gross Human Rights Violations in Comparative Perspective *(1998).*

CORINNE FIELD

This is a sad story with a happy beginning and happy ending. Now that it is over I prefer to look at the scarred trees when I want to mourn the ice storm's damage. But the losses go deeper. . . .

We had returned to Montreal on Sunday, after two weeks in Vancouver in the company of octogenarian parents. We were not in great shape. A day spent putting life back in order was not enough, thought I, until the phone call roused us Tuesday morning to put my work life on hold. Snuggling into the covers for a second go at conquering jet lag seemed heaven sent.

The next call was out of this world: Toronto's head office of my husband's service organization phoned to say that he had won an airline ticket worth $1,700. As he sleepily took the call, I checked the digital clock. Blank. It would be weeks before we even remembered that morning phone call. Only then could we afford the luxury of considering the puzzle: one ticket?

By that evening, the shape of things to come was chillingly clear. The next morning we called Mia to ask if she could take us in. "Of course you can come here," was her expected reply. After all, she called me her "sister," and her apartment in the Golden Mile had everything we needed. I had often been a weekend guest at her country home up north, just the two of us. After decades of mere acquaintanceship, we had become friends when her marriage came apart. We had shared the grief and the intense need to talk out the pain.

Arriving with our hastily packed bags from our tree-lined N.D.G. neighbourhood, we surrendered gratefully to the elegance of her apartment, with its '20s grace and its enormous rooms where antiques and paintings nestled alongside the grand piano and pale silk upholstery. Our room was the serene grey study in the bedroom wing. The *en suite* bathroom and the distant view of Sherbrooke Street, happily illuminated, seemed assurances that our creature comforts would not suffer.

That evening, dinner was served with the usual elegance. The eight-foot-long mahogany table glittered, as did the silver; the orchid blossomed for us; the graciousness of the room and the cordon bleu cookery of our hostess enveloped us. As always, she seemed glad of our company – perhaps an inevitable craving for a woman ambushed by fate to be single at the end of a long, successful career as a consummate professional and wife.

We returned to our own home every day, and blessed the fact that Mia's apartment and our house were each a reasonable – though progressively more nerve-racking – distance from the Metro system. One day's visit had us step out of the Metro just as the power went off. Another day's visit saw us barely able to tow our abandoned car off the street. One more day, we were told, and it would have been there for the duration. It went into underground parking, and we returned to Mia's for the rest of the deepening crisis.

It soon became imperative to arrange the emptying of the hot-water radiators in our house. That, it turned out, was the beginning of emotional temperatures rising in our home-away-from-home. Leaving telephone messages for the plumber was fraught with frustration. Mia stayed home from work and spent hours on the phone; in spite of having won a complimentary month of call waiting, she refused to use it, or even listen to how to use it. Being interrupted mid-sentence was not an indignity she was prepared to countenance. My stomach knotted in silence. I left messages for the plumber, knowing that if he called he was unlikely to get through to us.

On Friday, the power failed at Mia's and in the rest of the city core. My suggestion that a bathtub full of water might be essential on the tenth floor was ignored. Mercifully, the reservoir on the side of the mountain spared us, and we had water. The immense, black six-burner gas stove in the tiled kitchen promised us a continued supply of elegant meals, even though I had begun to resent the focus on fine cuisine. Why, I fumed, had my question upon rising – "What's been on the news?" – been answered by the keeper of the portable radio: "What do you think of this as a possible menu for tonight?" Why, I fumed, did my suggestion that the fridge door not be held open too long find its answer in the door being reopened to check the thermometer? And why, I fumed, did we have to dine in unreal splendour so that other single friends could marvel at Mia's unstoppable gourmet tastes?

The silver candelabra was polished and did yeoman service. Friends trudged gratefully up the many floors. Mia's wine cellar was bottomless, and we added to it. But my admiration for her serene competence was eroding by the hour.

My panic had grown with the days, and with it my husband's depression. Having been an apartment dweller all his life, he had always relied on my knowledge of our house and its workings. Now he felt helpless and useless.

Our trips to the house had been cranking up the anxiety with each passing day. I left the taps dripping, as the advice on the radio suggested, only to hear, the moment I returned, other radio voices warning of accidental floods. Windshield-washer fluid in the washing machine and all the sinks – was that enough? Wine stored in the fridge, to keep it from freezing. Fears of every sort, fed by the daily thermometer checks. Finally, as the house reached 3°C, the plumber was called in. As he unhooked the washing-machine hoses, he smilingly pointed out that they would surely have burst, since the taps had remained open and the machine stood under a basement window. This momentary relief was followed by radio voices warning of freezing ground beside vulnerable foundation walls. We were fraying. And the dinner parties went on.

Sunday. The radio warned downtown residents not to walk outside. Sheer ice was cascading off the walls of tall buildings. Mia insisted that wild horses would not get her to risk her life outdoors, until a friend called at about eleven with an invitation to meet for coffee at Westmount Square. She was gone inside half an hour.

How my husband and I savoured the luxury of being alone together. The power was still out, but the rising heat kept us relatively warm, at the expense, I reckoned, of the apartments lower down. I vaguely registered the tension leaving my shoulders.

Mia did not return. At three o'clock I found the telephone number of the building's concierge, and was able to confirm that she had indeed returned, some hours earlier. Had she collapsed, I fretted, trying to mount the flights of stairs? I remembered the heart problems that had beset her when we had bicycled on a shared Caribbean vacation. As we were about to set out with candles, the concierge called, telling us that she was visiting within the building. I fumed. Yes, she was as narcissistic as her children had accused her of being. Why had I denied it when she'd asked me if it was true?

At five we were together again. She had visited Chantal, one of the dinner guests of the previous night, and then Pierre, and . . . Mercifully, dinner was whatever could be salvaged from the warm freezer, just the three of us and (finally) informally, at the chopping-island-cum-table in the kitchen. Had I remembered the fleeting moment last night when Chantal had told my husband something about not starting to eat until we were all ready? Probably not. But as the hot meal in the chilly kitchen arrived at my husband's placemat, he fatally reached for the salt.

"For God's sake, don't start eating until I'm ready to sit down with you! Don't you realize you make me feel like a servant? Surely you have enough manners to know . . ." As Mia went on with her diatribe, my cheeks flamed. My eyes were glued to my plate and my heart sank for my poor spouse. A man of Mediterranean pride, I knew he indeed did know – at least, when manners were on his mind. The drubbing went on. "I know I shouldn't be lecturing you" was followed by a long lecture on how at her table, "five children, guests, no one lifted a spoon until I was seated, no matter how long . . ."

The next day, Monday, Mia informed us that her maid would be in on Wednesday and there were other guests expected on Friday. We took the hint and arranged to join West Island friends in the home to which they had just returned. Alone, I traversed the oriental rugs in the elevator hall for the last time, to pack, and to try to salvage a friendship. In the waning hours of the afternoon, awaiting my husband's arrival, Mia and I sat in the sitting room, sipping wine.

"Why," I asked, "if it was so upsetting to you, didn't you just whisper something in my ear?"

"When I spoke to Chantal yesterday, she told me she had scolded him for just that same thing. She told me about it because she wanted to apologize for being rude to my guest. You know, that night was the first time she had been to my home. She's a very elegant woman . . . and I intend to have her over again." And so it went.

We caught a burger and fries on the way out to the West Island. The welcome, when we got there, was warm. The company was good. So were the drinks. The squishy sofa cushions received my stiff back with a sensation akin to what it must feel like to have a corset unlaced.

Much later, I knitted together a theory that made sense of it all for me. For Mia, Chantal's disapproval of her downmarket guests – and the likely lost chance, as a result, to enlist Chantal in her stable of lady friends – was what had fuelled her rage. What Mia had reported to me, but failed so utterly to understand, was Chantal's delicate message: "Please apologize to him for my rudeness in scolding him. One does not do that to guests, let alone someone else's guests." Lost in all the pretense of what is "refined" was that selfsame delicate message – the ultimate sticking-point, for a Mediterranean man – about guests and hospitality.

My mind returns again and again to the mysteries of friendships. In our few contacts afterwards, Mia and I agreed to talk. But we have not.

Oh, and the prize of flight tickets. Somewhere out of the mess of papers – if only people-messes were as easy to restore to order – my man found the original notice of the prize. Two tickets. Our summer was very bright indeed. Voilà, the happy ending. The middle lingers, much as our memories of the storm itself.

Corinne Field is the pseudonym of a high-school teacher living in Montreal.

ELMER ANDERSON

On Sunday, January 4, we had not an inkling of what was in store. Penny-Sue, our health-care worker, came as usual and cooked some food for us. The next day our lights were still on, but the streets and sidewalks were almost impassable. It took me about fifty minutes to walk to the bank, a trip that usually takes eight minutes. Some of the power lines were down, but as there was no electrical power, the wires were dead. The only live wires that I could see were the work crews and the pedestrians, and each of these two groups was having a hard time. As there was only a narrow path in the centre of the street, now and then I got out of the way to let others go by.

On Tuesday, our lights went out for the first time and stayed out for roughly thirty-five hours, so Virginia and I then knew firsthand what millions of other people were going through. Our apartment became cold, which forced Virginia to stay in bed. She was suffering from a severe cold, and I encouraged her to take care of herself by spending as much time as possible in bed to keep warm. We dined by candlelight (no wine). During the days of the power failure, our only source of heat were eight candles that were lit only during breakfast, lunch and supper.

When the power was off, we had three cold meals every day. I went to the shopping centre three blocks away to buy sandwiches at the restaurant, and I took along a Thermos bottle and had it filled with hot soup. This one cup of soup each was our only hot food during the ice storm. I also bought Spam, chocolate bars, etc., and anything without salt, to give us some energy. To keep the soup as warm as possible, I always came home in a taxi. As the shopping centre had generators, it was ablaze with light while everything around it was in total darkness. A strange, eerie sight.

On the subject of keeping warm, we had every blanket to our name on our bed. We even used a padded bedspread, which made our coverings very heavy, but they kept us warm. We wore woollen socks in bed, and for the first time both of us wore thermal underwear, the kind worn by lumberjacks and construction workers. I had kept the thermal underwear in a trunk for years, and never dreamed of wearing them again. One never knows. As there was no hot water, I wore rubber gloves while washing the dishes. I almost froze my hands trying to wash or rinse dishes.

Wednesday was just like Tuesday. The temperature in our apartment dropped to 12°C. During the early-morning hours, two large limbs fell from the tree in front of our building. One limb, while falling, scraped against the side of the building, and it sure made a racket. The building shook when the limbs hit the ground, or at least I thought it did. Maybe my imagination was working overtime. The other ice-covered limb fell over the sidewalk near the entrance to the building, and for two days we had to clamber over it to get in and out of the building. After a while, a work crew came along and used a chainsaw to make the sidewalk passable. The sidewalk was covered with nine inches of solid ice, which the caretaker of our building took his good-looking time (three weeks) removing.

The power came on around 4:50 P.M. That afternoon I had an

appointment with my doctor, so when I left, the building was in darkness. The traffic lights were working, the Metro and buses were running, but many of the stores were closed. I bought some sandwiches at a restaurant for supper, and was pleasantly surprised to find the lights on at home. That evening we watched TV, and saw some of the havoc created by the ice storm. It was strange to find out what was happening to us.

On Thursday the power was still on, so we had a normal day of sorts. As the furnace had not been functioning for thirty hours, the apartment was still cold. Penny-Sue came by, and we were glad to see her. She cooked a tuna casserole to last for three days. It was a pleasure to have some warm food, but this treat did not last too long.

The next day there was a power failure at 7 A.M., so it was back to square one; i.e., eight candles at a time for heat and light. I had a business appointment downtown that morning, so I had a change of scenery from freezing to death in the dark. I bought some chocolate bars and cookies to eat with our Spam at noon.

On the days when there was no power, we got up around 7 A.M. and went to bed around 5:30 P.M. In other words, out of bed at sunrise and back to bed at sunset. We went to bed early to save our candles, which to my surprise did not last very long. For recreation, I read the newspaper in the living room by daylight. I raised the blind to take advantage of what little light was available. Unfortunately, Virginia was bedridden, and thus had no recreation at all. To keep warm while reading the newspaper, I wore my overcoat. I took it off only while preparing and eating meals. I also wore thick corduroy pants while outdoors and around the house, but not in bed.

Saturday, January 10, was a day like every cold day in our apartment. I went to the shopping centre for the usual: Thermos full of hot soup, sandwiches, Spam, candles, chocolate bars, newspaper, and home by taxi. Because of the condition of the streets, every day I had to take a longer route home than before the ice storm. Instead of paying five dollars for a short trip, I had to shell out ten.

On Sunday the lights were still out and Virginia and I talked about going to a shelter. As one would expect, she was becoming quite despondent and I was not too far behind. She was more or less a prisoner in her bed, with the only change of scenery being provided by trips to the dining table and the bathroom. I promised her that if the power was not restored by Tuesday, I would try to get a place for us in a shelter. Admittedly, it was rather late to be thinking of a shelter. Also on Sunday, Virginia wondered out loud if the young man in the apartment directly below us was keeping warm. As he was living with a lady friend, I assured Virginia that keeping warm was likely not a problem.

On Sunday night, around 8 P.M., the police came calling. They knocked at our door for a few minutes while I got out of bed, found my flashlight and put on my overcoat. I opened the door and was greeted by two burly policemen armed with flashlights. One policeman was bilingual, and the other one spoke only French, and I spoke both languages while they peppered me with questions. I assured them that despite the cold in the building, we were both doing well, had plenty to eat, etc. During this crisis, the police had been given special powers to remove people who were in serious trouble from their homes, by force if necessary. In certain parts of Montreal, when the water mains collapsed in addition to the power failure, the police emptied entire streets. Because of this, a man we know was forced out of his home, and he and his family spent twelve days at a motel. One expects this kind of thing on a summer holiday, but not in the dead of winter. It cost him around three hundred dollars a day. His kids enjoyed the swimming pool.

On Monday, January 12, at 2:30 P.M., the lights finally came on and stayed on. Oh happy day! Our ordeal thus came to an end. As the temperature had dropped to 8°C, and it took the building a week to warm up, we did not have a great deal of comfort, but the electricity was most welcome. Two days later, we were able to do our laundry for the first time in two weeks.

Fortunately, Virginia and I never had to go to a shelter. Even with heat and light and warm food, life in a shelter was no picnic. Because of our health problems, we stayed home. We go to the bathroom quite a few times, both day and night, and going to the bathroom at a shelter would have meant standing in line. At one point the city of Montreal was only hours away from running out of water. Apparently there were plans afoot for a mass evacuation.

Who knows, you might have had Virginia and me pounding on your front door.

Elmer Anderson is a retired high-school teacher living in Montreal.

SUSAN BROWNRIGG

When the lights went out on that January day, we had no idea what would be in store for us during the next eight days. It was romantic at first, terrifying towards the end. My husband, Cary Smith, and I live in Dollard des Ormeaux (a west-island suburb of Montreal) and we had no idea how bad the situation was until the day after the power went out. I work for Kruger Inc., a Montreal newsprint and recycled-paper company that was not affected by any power outages, so I had access to a radio and the stories of my co-workers. We use millions of dollars' worth of electricity every year and were asked by Hydro-Québec to shut down the paper mill (located in the same building as our offices) in order to save electricity for residential areas. Still, we were able to keep the offices up and running. Everyone came to work every day and we all tried to support each other as best we could.

The most difficult part was going home each evening. The streets around my home were basically abandoned, as most of my neighbours had left to stay at friends' or relatives' homes. We stayed in our house because most of our friends and relatives did not have power either. My parents, Gordon and Micheline Brownrigg, live not too far from us, and we were able to go over to their house for Mom's great home cooking the one night they had power. Luckily we have a woodstove and were able to cook and have a bit of heat. The food was not gourmet – eggs, canned spaghetti, black coffee and the like – but at least we had something. And since we use natural gas, we were able to take showers (a very small comfort because even though the showers were nice and warm, getting out was pure torture). The whole family – my husband, myself, our dog and two cats – huddled by the stove each night with mounds of blankets and layers of clothes to keep us warm. We talked, read by candlelight and froze every night. Our dog is a husky-shepherd mix and was the only one not suffering through the cold.

By the evening of the eighth day, though, the romance was gone. We had nothing left to talk about, we must have read about six different novels, and I wanted my power back! The temperature in the house registered 8°C; the low-temperature warning on our alarm would not shut off, along with the low-battery warning, so we had to turn off the complete system. We decided to go and stay with my cousin and loaded up our stuff in my husband's car. Sleeping bags, clothes, toiletries, the cats and dog, cat and dog food, people food, we had it all – and then his car wouldn't start.

We unloaded everything and put it into my car. By this time the cats were in a complete panic and were howling. As I was backing out of the driveway, we noticed the house looked strange. It took a few moments to register that the lights were on. We had power!

Susan Brownrigg is a paper buyer for Kruger Inc. in Montreal.

LAURIE LEWIS

It's an icy fairyland here, but dangerous. We hear trees crashing, electrical sparking. I'm frightened. From my window everything I see is covered with ice, a crystal world, a Norse legend. The birch tree in the front yard is looped over the hydro wire, its tips frozen to the ground. Across the street I see bare tree branches like giant toothpicks poking into the sky. The sound of the trees snapping is terrifying, a crack like a rifle shot. Our electricity keeps flashing off and on.

While we are having lunch our black-walnut tree comes down. It turns slowly as it tears apart down the centre of the huge trunk – one giant limb in the driveway, one on the back deck, the rest sprawled on the garage and into the garden. But we are lucky – not a window broken, no damage to the house. The weather is outside, where it belongs. The car is trapped in the garage, but we don't want to go anywhere anyway. We need to stay inside while the storm goes on.

During the night our power has died. The house is cold this morning. I start scribbling in my Grand and Toy steno notebook. I don't know who I'm writing to, I just write. I need to let someone know what's happening.

I'm in Kingston in the great ice storm. Today – so far – all is well.

It's Thursday. Our second day without electricity has begun. In the newest suburbs the power lines are underground and still functioning. I have to move my mother into a motel and I'm fortunate to find a room. On the telephone at 9 A.M. the motel says they have only one room left – with a king-size bed and "two-man jacuzzi"; I say I don't need the two men, it's for my mother and she wouldn't want them. I think I've already gone goofy with tension. I take the room. They tell me they might have something else later, with two beds. They do. Not only two beds but a microwave and a small refrigerator. The taxi driver is a hero; he knows how to make my frail mother feel safe – as safe as possible – on the slithery ride to the motel. Past the broken trees lining the roads. Green Acres Inn, under mounds of white. She wants me to stay with her at the motel, but she knows I have to leave. I'll be back tomorrow, I tell her. I'll phone in the morning. Blessedly, the phone service endures.

We are lucky. In the little house where we live there is a fireplace, built in the early '50s, in a time of good fireplace technology. Out in the garage is a stack of firewood that I piled up when I was cleaning the yard six years ago, old and dry wood even then. We have used a little of it since, on the occasional festive evening when we lit a fire only for its charm. The wood is not merely dry, it is severely dehydrated.

My husband and I are having – for the most part – a lovely holiday. He tends to be very serious – studious – and we've never holidayed together in our disjointed lives. But here we are, camping out, with none of the inconvenience of a tent or outdoor toilet. We're at home. We have fresh water. No heat. No light. But beyond that, we are in no danger. We have a flashlight and a radio with batteries. A box of candle ends; we are using the shortest ones first. My husband begins to remember all his Boy Scout skills. He builds a good fire.

I am mastering fireplace cooking; a metal plant-stand over the wood makes a stove. We eat chili and chicken stew and spaghetti on our big oak coffee table in front of the fire. A red-check tablecloth, candles every evening. I am cooking things from the freezer as they thaw. The refrigerator is useless, of course. But my mother's granny flat is now a walk-in cooler where we keep milk and salad makings and some cold beer. With my mother tucked away safely in a warm motel, our focus becomes more intimate.

But the cold begins to creep in through the bricks, up from the floors, down from the roof. The outside is getting in. During the day we take our duvet into the living room to warm it for the cold nights. The arthritis in my hip aches in the cold; every muscle is tight; my knees hurt.

In the mornings I stay in bed, cozy in the lingering warmth under the duvet. I have learned to wear a hat in bed. It's surprising how much it helps. My husband wears his black beret. I wear a white one. He lights a fire and I hear the crackle, smell the smoke. He practises Zen, and I am aware then of his quiet morning sitting, when the house is still. Without electricity the stillness is astonishing, no hum from the refrigerator, no furnace noises. Even the cat is soundless these mornings, and I am cling-ing to sleep, not yet thinking about the day ahead. I know my husband has water heating for morning tea.

He's something of a pessimist. He's worried that the old dry wood may burn too quickly, worries that the situation here may last a long time. I'm an optimist. I think, Ah, well, a couple of days, maybe three or four, a week at most. He thinks we'll be lucky if it ends in a week. It may last a very long time: two weeks, three, a month. We'll have to con-serve candles, wood, kerosene, he says. He thinks this may be forever, this now. He learns to bathe in a pot of warm water heated in the fireplace. In the bathroom we set up one candle end in a saucer. A book of matches.

We have tended to live very separate lives, my husband and I. He's a writer – hard at work on a major biography. It's well into its fourth year, this book, and I sometimes think it will never end. My time is filled with my old mother – eighty-seven now – also a writer. I'm helping with revisions on her new book, a memoir of the Depression years. But here, now, suddenly, my husband and I are sitting together night after night in front of this fire, living a life together in a small space.

Beneath our cozy fireside nest, the sump pump is not working and the waters are rising in the basement. Into my husband's office and mine. Into the bookcases and stereo, the couch, his favourite old wing chair. I have rescued my computer and shoved its components upstairs here, under the bed. My husband's computer and all his papers have been moved up into the dining room. He's working on chapter eighteen, making notes by hand. As long as he can work, he feels we have some control over our lives. He wears his beret, and a large red Mexican poncho over his down jacket. The black beret is perfectly colour-coordinated with the large eagle on the poncho. A fashion statement. What the well-dressed scholar is wearing.

I phone my mother every morning, and now that the tree has been removed from the driveway I go every afternoon to see her at the motel. To ensure that she is safe, I think; perhaps to try to reassure her that she is safe; to be company for a couple of hours. I take her a lamp, a teapot, china cups and saucers, food to heat in the microwave. More books. Her computer. I have a shower in hot water, a great luxury, letting it beat on my back to ease the tension in my muscles, to release the tight chill that accumulates during the hours at home.

I give her progress reports: there's a foot of water in the basement; a friend brought a generator all the way from Hamilton, we're sharing it with the neighbours; the cat is fine, she misses you. I can't seem to focus on her, I can't see what is happening to her. I don't notice that she is getting weak, moves very slowly, has a cough. Until suddenly I do. Suddenly I hear what she has tried to tell me. I phone her doctor, who comes to the motel in the afternoon to listen to my mother's crackling lungs. Our neighbourhood pharmacist, Robert, has kept his small store open for days in the darkness and the cold, just in case people need medicine. And he delivers the antibiotic to us at the motel, riding like a knight to the rescue, we say, wearing a black leather jacket.

Power is finally being restored through most of the city, but I have to tell my mother she can't come home yet. The sump pump is sucking the water out of the basement; the furnace is driving out the cold, but the house is still frigid and damp. You mustn't come home yet, I tell her, and I abandon her in the warmth and safety of the motel for one more night.

In the morning my daughter says she's coming with her husband from their icy home north of here, where they are still without electricity or water but have the luxury of a propane stove. They bring food, love, smiles and helpful hands. I drive my mother home at last. I open the front door and my daughter scoops an arm around her grandmother's back and takes her inside, where pots of chicken and dumplings wait in the warm and crowded room. My husband has moved the woodbox away and is cleaning ashes from the fireplace.

Laurie Lewis is a writer in Kingston.

3

SURVIVING IN THE COUNTRY

remember talking to a woman who lived alone in a big house west of Montreal, and who went to stay, during the ice storm, at the farm of a friend. For two weeks the woman slept on a mattress in the barn, which she shared with seven horses, four dogs, and a cat. Neighbouring farmers brought barrels of water up the hill so that at least the farm's toilets could be flushed. The woman was safe and relatively warm. But she couldn't wash her hair, and as the days passed she became desperate to do so.

Finally she drove to a big school in the town of Rigaud that was serving as a community shelter. She climbed several flights of stairs, the elevator having ceased to function, and joined a long lineup for the shower. The hot water and the shampoo came as an immense relief – until the woman remembered that she'd left her towel in the car.

She began to cry. Her tears mingled with the rushing water. She had to dry herself with her dirty clothes – at least she'd remembered to bring a clean set of clothing up all those stairs.

An unimportant incident in its own right, perhaps. But it became a defining moment, one of those events around which memory coalesces. After the ice storm was over, I doubt the woman could again take hot showers and clean towels for granted.

The stories in this chapter from people living in rural areas often mention some such item. It could be water, it could be music, it could be telephone service. In each case, the item becomes a kind of symbol of the storm's deprivations, and its eventual return brings an exhausted joy.

Country people tend to be resilient by nature. They endured a lot in the ice storm, and some of them suffered terrible losses. But they know, more readily

than city-dwellers, that – as Emerson put it in his great essay "Self-Reliance" –
"Nothing can bring you peace but yourself." These stories are the work of people
who, having come through an onerous time, seem at peace with themselves.

JAN GEDDES

I have no place in a collection of experiences like this. I didn't watch,
baffled, as yet another cow held in metal stocks in my dairy barn suddenly dropped dead, only to discover after a number of such incidences
that a live electrical wire lay on the barn's metal roof. I didn't freeze to
death beside a spluttering fire because I refused to leave my home with
its seven dogs. I did have a generator stolen. They were being stolen
even from railway crossings, and from telephone-line terminals that had
to be guarded twenty-four hours a day. I did go without the benefit of
hydro at a time when the temperature dropped to thirty below. My
water pipes did freeze. But I had three fires going, and a lot of support
from friends and neighbours. The situation tended to emphasize the
sometime chill of living alone, but if I was dirty and cold I was also dry
and fed.

I remember small things most vividly. I have a wonderful bronze
sculpture outside my entry door. It's a duck on wheels by artist Peter
MacElwain, and as a result of the storm it grew a carapace of ice. When
the weather warmed slightly, the carapace shifted sideways, so there were
two ducks on wheels, both with nasal drip. The east wall of my 1840s
farmhouse developed a sheet of ice with tiny icicles along every vertical
piece of siding, which reminded me of a modest version of the stun-
ning ice palace in *Doctor Zhivago*. And the light on the ice everywhere
was liquid and concentrated, repeatedly shifting the mind's numb focus
on the destruction.

On the Highland Road, which runs north and south a few miles from
my property, so many of the hydro poles broke that the upper portions,
with their branches and insulators, hung suspended directly over the
road in a dense hammock of wires, a deadly canopy illuminated by a
car's headlights. Another memory involves the local supermarket –
generators hummed and provided sufficient light to make the space

foreign, to see that most of the shelves were bare. There must have been a great deal of panic buying, and D-sized batteries were worth their weight in gold. And I remember a neighbour who responded to my question about where to find oil-lamp wicking by giving me half of the only length he had. My neighbour, Bob, came daily to hook up his generator to my water pump, or to help cover a broken window, or to bring food.

I remember a constriction in my throat as darkness descended, the growing acknowledgement of my vulnerable condition, and my rather bizarre stubbornness about staying at home to care for it. I remember realizing that my feeling of vulnerability was yet another version of my normal state of puzzlement about the world and its workings. I remember how it seemed that in the pulling together of the local community, there still lay a further confirmation of my sense of individual separateness, of rural isolation even in the sheer distances over ice from the house to the road, as well as of continuing privilege to be living in a country that had the resources and inclination in times of need to provide help.

Although I don't belong in this collection, I represent many not particularly robust souls who carried a sliver of pride when it was over, because the silence had been endured. I missed music most of all.

Jan Geddes lives in Dunvegan, Ontario. She is the publisher of Cormorant Books, one of Canada's finest literary presses.

CONNIE McDIARMID

The ice storm proved to be a major and costly inconvenience for dairy farmers. We live outside the village of Osgoode, along a dirt road about half an hour's drive south of Ottawa, and we survived twelve full days without hydro. But we were fortunate – others were without power for three weeks and more.

We were faced with our first power outage at about 7 A.M. on Monday, January 5. Most farmers were partway through their morning milking. My husband, Jim, fetched the tractor, hooked it up to the hydropole switch, and presto, *power!* We have a switch that has to be specially ordered and installed by Ontario Hydro, so that when the generator is hooked up, power is restored to our house, barn and shop. We have to be careful, however, not to run too many motors at once, because the generator can only put out 50 kW of electricity. Most generators owned by farmers are meant only to get the milking done.

We managed to complete our morning chores, but at a much slower pace than usual. We have about 140 head of cattle, about half in a heifer barn and half requiring milking in a cow barn. We also have three silo unloaders, two stable cleaners, five fans, a milker pump and a cooler. With the generator, only two of the motors could run at the same time, in addition to the water and fans. So chores that would take two hours were now taking four. We weren't complaining, though. We were grateful to have the generator. By noon, the phone started ringing.

Neighbouring farmers without a generator began trying to locate one so they could finish their morning milking. Their cows were becoming quite uncomfortable and really needed to be milked. Four neighbours called us, wanting to borrow the generator. We loaned it to the first two callers, and by the time their chores were done it was 4 P.M. and time for us to begin ours again. Neither of the neighbours had pole switches, so it meant calling an electrician to hook up the generator properly into panel boxes. Some farmers had three different panel boxes for the barns, then a separate box for the house. Every time they wanted to do something different, it meant moving the generator and hooking it up again.

Luckily the power was restored that day by 4:30 P.M. Everyone could chore normally and put the whole experience behind them. In many cases, farmers were milking for the first time that day! (Barns do *not* need to be heated, as the media incorrectly reported. They need to be ventilated by fans to remove stale air and keep temperatures cool, or else cattle will develop breathing problems and pneumonia.) Cattle that miss being milked on time become very engorged in their udders. Their milk leaks out of their teats, they are in a lot of pain, and infection can begin in the udders if prolonged. Dairy cows produce large amounts of milk these days – it is not uncommon for good cows to produce over a hundred pounds of milk in a twenty-four-hour period. One can imagine the stress placed on this animal when it is not milked. Women who breastfeed their babies know how it feels when a feeding is missed.

Top it off with the fact that these cows have not had any drinking water either, and we now have a very unhappy group of animals. They start to bawl continually until their needs are met.

Farmers dealing with this situation become extremely frustrated and their patience wears very thin. They cannot do a thing without electricity. People might suggest getting out the buckets and milking the cows by hand. But with herds of fifty cows and more, one cannot begin to milk by hand. It would take probably half an hour for a top-producing cow, and after one cow the farmer's hands would be cramping and sore. Farmers are not used to this and neither are the cows. Some cows wouldn't even co-operate with hand-milking. Then there is the question of what to do after hand-milking. Throw it in the already full gutters? Milk has to be cooled to 37°C or it will spoil, and without power the coolers were not working.

Another question commonly asked was, "Why don't dairy farmers all have generators?" I agree we all should, but the generators required are not little ones that people can afford easily. The ones we need cost at least five thousand dollars and a pole switch is another three thousand plus insulation. Not a lot of farmers can afford the luxury of owning a generator that might be used once a year for a short power outage as a result of a thunderstorm.

Rain continued throughout that Monday night, and the next day the power was off again. Farmers without a generator were now frantically trying to make arrangements with someone who had one. Our phone was ringing once more, but we were unable to share with anyone else besides the two farmers who were the first to call.

As we listened to the news reports, it became clear by Thursday that the power was going to be off for weeks, not days or hours. That night hydro poles snapped, transformers blew, wires broke and trees crashed down. By Friday it was still raining – thundering with lightning, actually – and I remember thinking, "When will this end?" The answer was that day, but temperatures would be dropping drastically. Friday was the day that most phones stopped working. Things were going to be terrible for the rural folk now. With the mild weather, basements had flooded but with the cold, houses needed heat. People had to decide whether to evacuate. Farmers of course could not leave, but some of their families did. We had enough to cope with in the barn – now we had to worry about freezers thawing, pipes freezing, bored children, making meals and all those things that the townsfolk were dealing with.

There were just not enough generators around. Farmers were not getting their sleep for worry, and they were working around the clock – they could not keep milking six herds of cows with one generator for much longer. Milking times were staggered so that everyone had their turn with the generator. We had the morning and early-evening shift, one neighbour the noon and midnight shift, and the other neighbour the 3 A.M. and 3 P.M. shift. We would feed between shifts as we had the biggest herd, so we would feed at 2 A.M. and let the cows have some water. The generator would be back at 6:30 A.M. when we would milk.

Saturday morning dawned bright and sunny – the first time we saw the sun in over five days. Warm temperatures prevailed, and miraculously the ice was melting! What a welcome sight. We got out the tractor with the front-end loader, stood in the raised bucket with a long pole and started knocking the ice off the power lines. The power lines in our yard were coming dangerously close to collapsing and it was imperative that we get the ice off. Personal-property hydro damage was the lowest priority for the company – you would be the last one repaired. We couldn't deal with that. By Saturday afternoon all the ice was off the lines and a good portion of the ice had melted from the trees. Everything was dripping! It was a tremendous relief, as we were well aware that cold weather was coming that night.

At this point one of the most frustrating things was not being able to communicate. Without telephone or radio, we remained cut off from everyone. You had to drive to talk to anyone, and the roads were glare ice, so that in itself was a daunting task. When we had use of the generator, we had the radio on for news about what was going on. We were so surprised to hear about the state of emergency and how the army was moving in to help. Also that the outage went as far as Kingston and all the way to Montreal. We were not alone!

Some farmers by this time had yet to clean the stables. When there is a short-term outage, you do only what has to be done: feeding, milking, cooling the milk. But when things begin to drag on, cleaning the stables *has* to be done. Stables are cleaned by running the gutter cleaners at least once per day to remove the cow manure and liquids. If the gutters are not cleaned, they may overflow onto the cow stands and alleys. Soon, inevitably, the entire barn is full of you-know-what, and along with that comes the smell and buildup of ammonia gas, which can cause animals to get pneumonia. Appalling conditions for man and beast.

Another problem we faced was getting rid of the milk. Milk trucks pick up most farmers' milk every other day. In order to empty tanks, power is required. The trucks had to time the milk pickup for when the farmer had a generator. Sometimes the generator had to be fetched from someone else's farm for the fifteen minutes or so that it took to empty out the tank. This created confusion, of course, but it wasn't so bad until the phones stopped working. Then we didn't have a clue when the truck was coming. Things also got tricky when we found out that the milk-processing plants weren't processing because of the power outage, so there wasn't even any place for the milk to go. A number of farmers ended up dumping their tanks or portions of them because there was no room in them for the next milking. We were so glad to see the milk truck when it came!

Saturday night arrived and so did the cold. After days of temperatures hovering around the freezing mark, this was a real shock. I milked with my husband every milking, so we would be done quicker and the generator could move on. On top of everything else, then, I had to arrange babysitting for my four children, aged two to eight years, while I milked. Luckily we had great neighbours who always volunteered to come over. Of course the house had power so they could take a shower and watch TV and have something hot while they babysat, so it was a fair exchange. Unfortunately, my husband and I were always choring when we had power in the house, and we never got to enjoy it. Jim went seven days without bathing.

That Saturday evening we got the generator around 6 P.M. and the worst possible thing happened: it broke. Not just a little break, it was major and it would be weeks before it could be repaired. We and our two neighbours were devastated. We ourselves had 140 head of cattle that hadn't been fed or had water since 10 A.M. The stables weren't cleaned, the milk was getting warm in the tank, the barn was filling up with steam, seventy cows hadn't been milked and every one of them was bawling at the top of her lungs. We could not hear each other's voices over the noise that those cows were making. Even from the house we could hear them, and we were totally helpless to do anything. We had no phone to call anyone, we were totally stressed out due to lack of sleep and the sheer pressure of everything that had happened since Monday – and now this.

My husband went to find his father, then tell the two neighbours what had happened. I went with another neighbour to see the army in Vernon, a few minutes' drive away, and find out if they had any big generators available. There weren't any, and there was such confusion – generators were supposed to be coming, but no one knew where they were or when they would arrive. Someone offered to notify the Ottawa radio station CFRA and say that we needed a really big generator. With no phone to take calls, I didn't hold out much hope for that plan. But it was worth a try.

I did have a cell phone that plugs into the car lighter, so I managed to call my dad, and miraculously his phone, having been out, just happened to work at that moment. I told him my plight and he knew of a generator belonging to my cousin that we *might* be able to use that night only. It was close to South Mountain, so it would take well over half an hour for Joe to get to our place, but he arrived around 10 P.M. The generator wasn't the same as ours and we had to get hold of an electrician to hook it into the panel box at the barn. By midnight the milking was done. We fed just hay, so there was no need to run the silo unloaders. We were exhausted but relieved to have a quiet barn.

When we got to the house it was getting cold, as the furnace hadn't run since 10 A.M. We covered the children with extra blankets and we ourselves slept in our clothes. It was a worrisome night, and we really didn't get much sleep. The wind was howling, it was bitterly cold, and we had no idea how we were going to get through the next two weeks without a generator. Little did we know that the CFRA distress call had been heard, and help did arrive for the two farmers that we were sharing with. They both got their milking done.

Sunday dawned bright and cold. The house was 10°C and the children were wondering what had happened. The neighbour who had been babysitting for us took the children to his house to get warmed up, as he had a woodstove. My husband and I drove to Winchester to visit the army and try to find a generator to use for the next two weeks. Nothing was immediately available, but they took our name and added it to the list. We went home and to our amazement there was a generator hooked up to the pole, and running! Another neighbour had just bought this generator on Friday, and would share with us until ours got fixed or the power came on. It was like heaven.

We shared with him until the following Wednesday when his power returned. Then we could have his generator full time. Imagine, power full time! During that time, one of my relatives took three of our children for a couple of days to give us a break. Other neighbours got in groceries, took the children to a gym, brought us hot meals from the Vernon shelter and helped to do errands for us. We were truly blessed to have such kind neighbours. People from the towns were wondering, "If the farmers were having such a tough time, why weren't they coming to the shelter?" It was simply because we had no time! We were spending all day choring.

It was the first five days that were the worst for farmers. After that, there seemed to be lots of help. Truckloads of generators arrived from southern Ontario; money was promised; a disaster-relief fund was set up. The army was still in town, but they were not a whole lot of help to farmers. All we needed were generators. We could handle the work.

Only a few of our cows got sick, and luckily none died. We had one with pneumonia and she recovered nicely. Two cows had bad mastitis and lost a quarter of their production permanently. We had one birth during that time, and the calf was a girl that we named "Storma." No cows were bred, so we knew that unlike among humans, there would be no ice-storm babies. We use artificial insemination, and with no phone to contact the technicians, nothing was done. With the cows and farmers being so stressed, it was a low priority. As a result, in October '98 most farmers failed to fill their monthly milk quota, as there were no cows ready to calve at that time.

It was on the sixteenth of January that our power finally came back. The first thing we did was turn everything on. It was so nice to clean stables and feed at the same time. Chores went so quickly! We had a life again. It was ironic that the first night we had power all night, the automatic water dispenser failed to shut off and flooded the entire heifer barn. Wouldn't you know?

Connie McDiarmid lives on a dairy farm outside Osgoode, Ontario.

HAZEL RYE

I remember first the sound of silence as the freezing rain came day after day

even the birds fell silent

the sound of creaking and groaning as trees struggled to survive the weight of ice

the hissing of oil lamps and their friendly glow

the sound of my heart pounding as I waited, unsleeping, in the night for the expected crash of trees outside my window

the terrible sound as so many lost the fight and surrendered to the ice

the reassuring sound of a generator with its promise of heat and light

the awful sound of a chainsaw finishing what the storm had started

then on the ninth day I remember the purring sound of a furnace, never again to be taken for granted

the joyful sound of birds singing once more

and the final sound, the great sigh of relief, that it was indeed over.

Hazel Rye heard these "Sounds of the Storm" in Ingleside, Ontario, about 20 kilometres west of Cornwall.

RENIE MARSHALL

The ice was here, the ice was there,
The ice was all around:
It cracked and growled, and roared and howled,
Like noises in a swound!

– Samuel Taylor Coleridge, "The Rime of the Ancient Mariner"

Wednesday, January 7, 3 A.M.
Another crash against the house! I shiver and shrink down further into my little warm bed, hiding my head under the covers to shut out the frightening noises outside my tiny cottage . . . branches cracking and falling on the roof, and a howling wind blowing full force against the windows, determined to push them in upon me. Emma, the cat, meows and jumps up on the bed. I let her sneak in between the sheets and cuddle her close. She purrs and somehow I feel comforted. It is just like one of those bad moments during World War II in London, when I was in my late teens and fear of the unknown struck terror in my young heart.

Wednesday, January 7, 8 A.M.
A dark dawn is breaking. Bundled up in a blanket and blurry-eyed, I look out upon a scene of incredible, unforeseen devastation. I catch my breath. Memories hit hard again . . . memories of over fifty years ago, of coming off duty from the fire station in North London to be confronted with devastation wreaked by landmines dropped by parachute during the dark nights.

My mind wanders for some unknown reason to the years between then and now. The joy of getting a job in Switzerland, where I spent many happy years. Then emigrating to Canada, meeting and marrying a widower, and raising four young stepchildren who were ready for a mother again. We had a cottage too, on Crooked Lake, far into the Laurentians, where we spent weekends and holidays. I remember I always liked it better than the rambling old house where we lived in Montreal West.

The children grew up and left for good jobs abroad. Some years later, my husband died suddenly of a heart attack. Three years ago I moved to Wolfe Island, the largest of the Thousand Islands, a place I had come to know and love. I had the good fortune to find a cottage to rent – my little "gingerbread cottage," as I call it. Not only is it cheap, but it sits happily by the water, water that I now realize is a sea of ice.

I switch on the light. No light. I turn on the taps. No water. I pick up the phone. No phone. But praise the Lord and the old gentleman who built the cottage years ago, I have an old-fashioned oil furnace and my stove is roaring away. I have heat! I cuddle Emma and we purr happily together. At least I can stay home. It turns out that hundreds on the island have to leave their houses and seek shelter elsewhere.

A bang on the door and my neighbour, Chris Kane, barges in. She is dressed as though about to go into outer space. She is my landlady, but now, as she says laughingly, she is soliciting temporary tenancy with her tenant. She is a cheerful and kind lady and, at eighty years of age, is a darn sight more energetic than I am at seventy-five. There is no heat in her spacious, modern bungalow, and she has had to ask the help of one of the volunteer firemen to pump out her flooded basement. He has promised to do it every few hours.

Friday, January 9
Chris has had to sleep on my settee, but it is comfortable and she is grateful to be warm. It's a wonderful community we have on this island, and I benefit even though I am not a born-and-bred islander. Every morning people bang on my door to see if we are all right, if we need anything or if I want them to do something for me. They keep me sup- plied with drinking water; big plastic containers of it have been donated, with food supplies, by sympathetic companies on the mainland. I use this water sparingly. Farmer Jim, who lives next door, turns up early every morning, blue with cold, with a bucket of water taken from the bay (and he has to break the ice) to flush my toilet. Then, shivering, he goes back for a second bucket so that we can wash dishes and wash our- selves (the dishes get priority). To economize on the water, I clean my teeth with 7-Up.

Saturday, January 10
This is the fourth day we are without the telephone, electricity and so on. Now it has snowed heavily, and the harsh icicles everywhere are hidden under a soft whiteness. Longing for a little fresh air, Chris and I venture out with our canes and, treading carefully and cautiously, slowly make our way to Chris's car and inch our way over the ice to the village. (It's too slippery to attempt the ten-minute walk today.) Only the two grocery stores are open, lit and warmed by oil lamps. We are looking for candles, fondue fuel and lamp oil. So is everyone else. The stores are completely sold out! But it is nice to see a few other people and chat and laugh with them, and catch up on the news.

I am lucky to have Chris staying with me. She is cheerful and adaptable. We heat water on the stove in a big, black, heavy iron kettle that I bought once at a garage sale for five dollars. We use lake water for washing ourselves and washing up. In the morning I heat a little drinking water for breakfast with my fondue set. It takes a long time, but never has warm instant coffee tasted so good! I make stew in a big saucepan on the stove. It takes all day or all night to cook, depending on when we need to use the stove to heat water. The recipe is new, and mine alone: pork chops, lamb chops, chicken legs, liver, kidney, spare ribs, all grabbed from the slowly defrosting freezer, bunged together into the one pot, and flavoured with every spice I can lay my hands on. It is tasty and lasts for days with reheating.

Chris and I are both enthusiastic card players, so we play two-handed euchre for hours. It is a good mental exercise and helps to make the time pass quickly. We both like to read and, since we are quite "senior" seniors, we also enjoy a little snooze in the afternoon. It has become a habit to retire to our respective armchairs and candles after lunch. My faithful stove throws out a good heat and I keep it on high. It is something like -18°C outside.

Sunday, January 11
More and more I feel that I am reliving days of the past, days of no water or light, days of huddling in a small kitchen around a small fireplace, but managing somehow. It was the same then – people helping people, people caring, people sharing, people opening their hearts and

homes to friends and strangers alike. Even the words they spoke are the same as now: "It could be a lot worse! We are lucky to have what we have! We are lucky to be alive!"

Tuesday, January 13
The unused food in the freezer has finally gone bad. Like everyone else, I'll have to throw it all away.

Wednesday, January 14
A sickly winter sun shines bleakly but the wind is bitter. Chris and I struggle to the fire hall, which has been a haven and a source of food and cheer to many in need. Prime Minister Chrétien is going to drop in, and he does, literally, by helicopter. He shakes our hands and assures us that everything possible is being done in this declared disaster area. And we are reminded that in Ontario and Quebec, hundreds of thousands are suffering from the ice storm.

Wednesday, January 14, 4 P.M.
A thump at my door and the beaming face of Farmer Jim. We will have power in thirty minutes, those of us in the village area. We give a cheer, Chris and I, and do a little rheumaticky jig. Our thankful hearts lighten at the thought of a hot shower and a hair-wash. And cleaning teeth with *real* water. Just how lucky can you be?

"Trust not one night's ice," wrote the seventeenth-century poet George Herbert. I agree, George, and we are not likely to forget it either!

Renie Marshall is a writer living on Wolfe Island, Ontario. This article was originally published in Cottage Life *magazine.*

DONNA RICHARDSON

We are your typical baby-boomer family: three teenagers, two working parents and a house full of pets (a dog, two cats, a bird and fish). We live in a residential pocket of about fifty homes, just off the island of

Montreal on a dead-end street. We are by the lake, have lots of trees and live in a hundred-year-old home. It is so peaceful and quiet. You hear nothing but the sound of the birds, and the wind through the trees. Country living at its finest.

Before the ice storm struck, we had plans to go on a ten-day cruise. Then, everything changed.

When I think back to the ice storm, I remember feeling totally isolated, frustrated and out of control. My five closest neighbours left. We had to stay to try to prevent our hot-water radiators from freezing up. The first days of the storm, we made the living room our home (all of us, including pets). The fireplace was there, but we cooked our meals on the barbecue. The temperature in the house ranged from 2°C on the cold days to 10°C on the warm days. My husband and I took turns being next to the fireplace, only to have the responsibility of keeping the fire going all night. Believe me, there was nothing romantic about the blackout.

We kept the fire going for nine days straight. Of course we were not prepared and ran out of candles, batteries and fondue fuel. We allowed ourselves only one hour of radio a day. Luckily we were able to raid my neighbours' homes for candles and the odd bottle of rum. We used two propane heaters in the house to help keep the pipes warm. The bird was our gauge for survival. If we woke up and she was dead, then we would not be far behind.

After the fifth day, our kids bailed out for a warmer home. Everyone was on everybody's nerves. The daylight hours were spent cleaning up the mess from the night before. Candle wax everywhere, wood splinters, black soot covering everything.

We had to prepare for the darkness. I don't know when you stop caring about yourself, sleeping in five layers of clothes, full of dirt and ashes, wrinkled and dishevelled. Keeping warm was the priority. Keeping clean was not. I remember looking outside at the stillness. I was blinded by the darkness of the night. There were no shadows. I thought that if the world were to come to an end, it would be like this.

On the fifth day, we had our first shower. We were fortunate enough to have friends who allowed us and others to use their facilities. It was a quick shower, as you are grateful but not greedy. Then we got the dreaded hardware-store phone call: "We have a generator, but you must be here within ten minutes." So off we raced, only to have to turn the generator down, as it was really too small for practical purposes.

I remember going out in public to get a cast-iron fry pan to cook with. Normally I wouldn't go out without makeup on. Yet here I was in Canadian Tire, desperately seeking cast-iron pans, grabbing the last two, and thinking how I would fight with my life for these pans. I'm glad that my picture was not taken as I would not have recognized myself.

Depression and desperation were overwhelming. I remember being angry with myself for "letting" the ice pile up in front of my car and now being trapped as well. My husband and my two boys were frantically chopping the ice away from my car to keep me from snapping. Who was this person? One morning, no water came from the faucet. Nothing like being hit while you're down. Now I was frantic to buy water, and food that looked "not too spoiled."

Somewhere in that time, I had stopped living. I was merely existing. Like the birch tree in my yard, I was being bent into an abnormal shape. How much more weight could it take before it broke? How much could I?

Day nine, we got a generator. With a quick-fix wiring job, we finally could keep the radiators warm and no longer had to take a chance with the propane heaters. On day eleven, it was over. As quick as a light switch, the power was back on.

I couldn't repair my broken spirit as easily. I was angry that all of a sudden I was expected to return to a state of normality as quickly as the power had been turned back on. How do you start living again when your lives have been put on hold? The enormous cleanup. We lost some fish. Burned ten cords of wood that winter. The trees looked as if a bomb had hit them. Our cruise vacation was lost.

I never thanked my newspaper carrier. He was the only constant I had throughout – my only contact with the rest of the world. I feel badly that he never knew how much I appreciated him.

Now, a year later, my memories are vivid of that time. We are better prepared, as is everyone else. One long-lasting effect is the need that I have to be warm. I get cold more often, do not hesitate to put on layers of clothing, and don't have to look perfect to go out in public. I am enjoying the stillness of my home again, the peace and quiet, the birds and the sound of the wind through the trees. Country living at its finest. My spirit is no longer broken.

Donna Richardson is an emergency-room nurse living in Vaudreuil, Quebec.

DEBBIE McAULEY

Living through the great ice storm has changed all our lives in many different ways. This is how an Ontario farm family in the township of North Dundas, south of Ottawa, coped and survived.

It's Tuesday early morning, 5:15 A.M., when our power goes off. We go ahead and feed the cows their hay and ration for breakfast. Mom and Dad start the woodstove in the kitchen – the warm fire really feels great. The dogs are slipping and sliding around the yard. There are no birds flying. When the power comes back at 1:15 P.M., the order is to water the calves and hens and clean the stable. Waste no time – with this weather, the power could go off any time. Freezing rain is still falling and everything is covered in a thick crystal crust.

This evening we chore early. Pails are filled with water, Thermoses are filled in the house. We are preparing for the worst. But little do we know how bad everything will get.

On Wednesday morning there is no power and the house is chilly. We have a long lane and the pole at the road has snapped off at the ground. The big ash tree my dad so lovingly planted over forty years ago is almost destroyed by the heavy load of ice. The lilac bushes which stood so graceful with their blooms in spring are reduced to the ground. No matter where you look, there is destruction.

Mom and Dad start the woodstove again. Heat feels great. We have breakfast, Mom puts a huge pot of coffee on the woodstove, and we spend the morning assessing the damage. Dad cleans the small calves as I pail water out of the puddles in the yard to water the calves and hens, and also to try and get enough water for the cows to have a small drink. The noise in the barn as you measure the water out to each cow is deafening. It brings tears to your eyes when you see them fighting for a drink. The stakes creak under the strain of them reaching for your pail of water. All you can do is turn your back, walk out and try to get some more water any way you can for them.

We leave for the other barn down the road that has the young cattle. The roads are slippery and unploughed. We wonder why the county hasn't been up to salt and plough yet. The wires are hanging low across the road. Trucks can't go under them, so Hydro comes and cuts the line. The lines are broken at the other barn – no power and no way of watering. But we clean the stable as always. We never need electricity for that, as we have an old-fashioned, push-powered, litter-carrier bucket and track.

When we get home, Mom tells us the power lines are all down in Winchester and still more lines are crashing. Evening is coming on fast, darkness seems to come really early now. We feed and ration what little water we have to the cows, calves and hens. Milking has to be done by hand and feeding by flashlight.

Winchester Fire Department comes to check on us and see how many people are in the house. Everyone who comes into the kitchen heads for the front of the woodstove to get warm. It seems funny to go to bed at 7:30 P.M. No matter where you look, everything is in darkness tonight. Mom and Dad get up several times in the night to keep the fire going. You wonder how much worse it can get – the radio only gives news about the city and very little about outlying areas.

Thursday is another dark day. We chop a hole in the ice-covered gully west of the house. We use a toboggan and set two milk cans on it and pail the water from the gully into the cans. Slowly we pull them to the barn to give the cattle another small drink. As we are loading the full cans of water into the back of the truck, the sky lights up with a great crack of thunder and blue lightning. We stand and look at each other and say, "Did you see blue lightning?" It's weird. Little did we know that it was more towers and lines crashing down.

As we water the heifers at the other barn, they fight and bawl for more water. This has to do for this trip – we clean the stable and head home. As we sit at the dinner table, we decide to see if we can get a neighbour to come in and pump some water for the cows and maybe clean the stable. Dad and I leave. We go to a few farms, and when we get to Bobby Mattice's, Dad says, "Could you come and pump some water for the cows?" "Yes, I'll be up in half an hour."

The devastation of the rural landscape, as captured by Jo-Ann Safruk of Alexandria from a bridge in Kenyon Township, Ontario.

It is great to see Bobby and Linda come. We take the switch on the wall apart and put a plug on the end. Then we run an extension cord to the generator with fingers crossed. The generator pumps the water. We turn the tap on at the barn, the water bowls begin to fill, the cows fight with each other for a drink, and after an hour passes, all are watered. I had decided to wash my hair, but as I wet my hair, the water is so cold I begin to think it was a bad idea. Even worse, I think the shampoo has frozen in my hair. But I manage to get it rinsed. Boy, does that feel good, even though it is ice-cold water. As we sit in the kitchen talking, we decide to set up times which are convenient for us all. He'll come each afternoon and we'll tank up his generator with our gas, so our cows and heifers will be watered and he'll have power for his sheep.

Friday morning it starts all over again. Our friend Kevin brings groceries for Mom, and more people check on us today. We have fallen into a routine, but the days are so short, the nights so long. Sleep doesn't come easy with all this crashing. Sandy, our house dog, barks and cuddles in closer with each loud bang.

Saturday morning the turning point comes. The military are setting a generator up in Winchester Springs and we are next. We are all excited – help is on the way. No one can describe the feeling when the generator and trucks come in our lane – it is a godsend.

The main priority is to get the cows water. In half an hour, the barn is up and running, the cows are all drinking, the stable cleaner is started up, and three days' manure roll up the chute. The electrician, Roy Tubman, had never been on a farm. He said no one in the city has any idea of the devastation the farmers are facing. Mom is allowed two things to run in the house. Roy says we have to get a television running and get back in touch with the outside world again.

Our next problem comes in the evening: the generator won't start our milker pumps. So back to milking by hand – at least we have lights tonight. Sunday morning we take the motor off the milker pump and phone Ralph Behler to see if he will look at it. His answer is, "Bring it down." We have to get the car out of the garage, and chop eight inches of ice to open the door, but finally Dad gets the door open. As we put the motor in the trunk, he tells me to be careful. I hate driving alone. As I drive down to Crysler I can hardly believe my eyes: huge towers all bent and twisted out of shape. I don't meet any traffic at all.

I get home and we put the motor back on the pump, but the generator still can't handle it. The army works at the generator most of the day, then late Sunday afternoon they decide to take the motor back to Ralph. This time I have company with me, three army men. Ralph checks the motor and sends an extra motor back with us. It is dark again when we try: no go. The army works into the wee hours of the morning. Monday morning, the Ontario Department of Agriculture sends a small portable generator in to pump water at the other barn. The army men set to work again and finally they solve the problem. We all sit in the house and talk and enjoy hot tea and fruit cake. Tonight we can milk with the milkers for the first time in a week.

Thursday evening it is colder out. Bobby and Linda come in just at suppertime – their generator went out last night and they have tried to get help all day with no luck. Bobby asks Dad if he could borrow ours. "Certainly," my dad says. They stay for supper. Now there is a couple going home happy. This is what makes friends and neighbours – we all work together in a time of need.

Our hydro line has been fixed and we are waiting for our road to come on. Friday evening, the hydro creeps up our road house by house, farm by farm. But our power doesn't come on – the breaker hasn't been closed on the pole. It is so close but yet so far. We have gotten used to sitting in the dark with only a lamp.

Saturday morning, the generator is shut down, wires disconnected, fuses returned in panels and switches turned back on. Morning passes, afternoon passes, and suddenly, at four o'clock, a Hydro truck stops at the pole. Power is on! The chores start. Clean the stable, turn water on for the cows, we're back in business. Everything is great tonight – the first nice warm bath since the storm hit.

During the storm we asked for help and received it. To help others out, we gave sixty dozen eggs to food shelters. We have many people to thank, but most of all, we thank God for giving us all the strength to cope.

Debbie McAuley is a farmer who lives a few kilometres north of Winchester, Ontario.

CARMEN STACKPOLE

I know mine was not the only household without power during this awful storm. We were without hydro for eleven days. That was bad enough, but my phone was out of order for three weeks. My husband works shift work and I am left alone at night. I found this extremely difficult, and I was unable to sleep well. We were in contact with both utilities several times to restore the telephone. Each one kept saying it wasn't their problem.

After talking to all the supervisors who finally showed up, I told them that I could get by without power, I could do without heat, I could live without sex . . . but *I could not be without a phone!*

They, of course, thought this was very funny and enjoyed themselves at my expense.

But they repaired my phone immediately.

Carmen Stackpole lives in Greely, Ontario.

WINNIFRED BOGAARDS

No sane person could ever love a Canadian January, but January '98 gets my vote as the worst on record. The great ice storm coincided with the first week of classes at the University of New Brunswick in Saint John, where I was teaching Tuesday night and Wednesday and Thursday afternoons. On the Tuesday around 11 A.M. I went outside to find my car encased in a full inch of ice, which took an hour to remove. When it had returned to the same icy state by 3 P.M., I gave up and cancelled the class. Wednesday was sufficiently better that it was safe to drive, but Thursday repeated the same awful conditions of Tuesday, forcing a second cancellation.

At 5:30 P.M. the power lines came down in the Kennebecasis Valley north of Saint John, where I live. Most of us in these river villages have wells. No power means no water, as well as no heat or light. Most of us have hot-water baseboard heating. If the power stays off for any length of time in very cold weather, the entire system has to be drained to prevent broken pipes. I was luckier than my neighbours across the street in that my telephone lines stayed in place and I could consult with various other afflicted friends about the dreaded decision to drain the system, but they were luckier than I in having a fireplace which kept their entire house warm. Mine heats only the room it occupies. However, I did have a large, full woodbox inside, the legacy of the loss of power experienced more than twenty years earlier during Saint John's Groundhog Day hurricane.

By morning the temperature had dropped to 3°C. I toasted bread over the fire and boiled a cup of the precious gallon of water I had on hand, for instant coffee. As I used two tablespoons of water to brush my teeth, I wondered how my prairie forebears endured such conditions every winter in a sod shack and how they ever had time to plough the soil when it took twenty minutes to boil a cup of water.

At 11 A.M., to my amazement, Canada Post delivered the mail. I laughed out loud when I saw the first gardening catalogue of the new year. Sitting in my kitchen dressed in my winter outerwear, I relished as never before the glorious colour photos of flowers in bloom. By 4 P.M. I had called the firm to place an order for about a hundred dollars' worth of plants I didn't need, none of them bearing icy white blooms.

After the candles were lit (bless my Scots mother for teaching me to save everything, including two-inch candle stubs) and the evening soup heated over the coals, I tried to read. I soon gave up. No wonder Milton went blind reading for hours by flickering flames. I called my friend Anne to see if she had yet taken the great decision to drain. No she hadn't, being entirely preoccupied by the explosion into flames of the transformer at the foot of her property, which then set alight a great tree overhanging her house. I went to bed cheered by the knowledge that others had problems worse than mine, but longing for the comfort of a hot bath and change of clothing. Wearing the same clothing twenty-four hours a day for two days reminded me of a young boy at my prairie school whose mother sewed him into his long johns in the fall and didn't remove them until spring.

I was saved from his fate Saturday morning, when the only neighbour intelligent enough to install underground power lines when he built his house called to offer me a warm bath and bed. The battery-powered radio informed me the temperature was due to drop to -8°C that night. I called the plumber to drain the system and moved up the hill to civilization.

In a house with a working TV I discovered the storm had made international news. Once my numbed brain had been restored by hot water and food, it occurred to me that my Dutch sister-in-law would be worried about my welfare. I called to tell her I had survived, only to find she had no idea my region had any problems; her news focused solely on the misery of Montreal, on the millions in Quebec rather than the thousands in New Brunswick. Suffering, and ignored to boot!

But indeed we were much luckier than Quebeckers. Power was restored at my home by Sunday afternoon. The plumber got the system running on Monday, and I was able to concentrate on the masses of snapped trees around my property. We were told to pile the broken limbs and branches along the road front, where the army had been recruited to pick them up. It took the crews many weeks to complete the cleanup but they had no wood from me. I used the remains to build a brush fence to protect my garden from marauding deer. Happily I now have an ice storm fence and a golden ice-storm rose (appropriately named "Alchemist") transmuting base weather and technological failure into objects of utility and beauty – not to mention the six gallons of water now permanently stored in my basement.

Winnifred Bogaards fights nature in New Brunswick's Kennebecasis Valley.

OAKLEY and DOROTHY BUSH

Oakley: The power went off on a Thursday morning, about eight-fifteen, and the following day when we got up there were several inches of water on the basement floor. So we started to bail it out with a little dustpan into buckets. We'd carry the buckets up the stairs and out the back door, then dump them into other buckets on the toboggan and haul them away from the house. By three or four in the afternoon, we were really tired. Dot was doing the scooping and I was doing the carrying. Two buckets of water is a heavy load for somebody of my advanced years – I was eighty-two at the time. It was a cold, windy day and I decided that we needed help. But I didn't know where we could get it.

I put on whatever clothes I could and started walking, because I can't drive the car any more, towards the Fassifern General Store, hoping that if I got there I'd get a ride into Alexandria and maybe see some of the policemen I know. I was in pretty desperate straits at that point. Anybody who would give me help, I was willing to accept it. And Barry Lucking, who lives up the road and has an audio business for television commercials, came along in his car and saw me walking and said, "Where are you going, Oakley?" I said, "I'm going to the police department, I need help." "Get in, I'll take you!" So we drove into town, which is five or six miles, and we went to the police department. But my friend there, when I asked him if he knew anybody who would help us, said, "Gosh no – everybody's in the same situation. Everybody needs help."

"Well," I said, "I guess I might as well go back home." So we got in the car and Barry drove me back here. He didn't say anything, but he went home, unknown to me, and got his wife and three teenagers to come over. They moved in, took over the bucket brigade and spent the night here, taking turns on the buckets, playing cards, and sleeping occasionally.

Dorothy and Oakley Bush, in the kitchen of Fassifern Farm.
Thanks to the portable generator, their basement remained dry.

Dorothy: I have a daughter, Holly, in Toronto. But we didn't think of leaving and going to stay with her because we had the five horses here. And the chickens and ducks and peacocks. It didn't bother me staying here. On Saturday morning we were able to buy a portable generator at the co-op, and Barry helped us start it up. That solved the bucket problem. And once the driveway was cleared of branches, I was able to drive into town. I learned where to put the generator because my husband can't see very well. But he would still insist on telling me where to put it, even though it was the wrong place.

Oakley: The problem with the generator is that it is so overloaded that the lubricating oil in it breaks down. You fill the gasoline tank and it operates for half an hour. Do that three times and the oil is finished, it's all separated, so you have to change the oil in the oilpan. You have to drain out the old stuff and put in new stuff. When you drive your car, the oil is good for several weeks or months. But with the generator, you'd hardly get it started when you'd have to change the oil again.

Dorothy: You have to put the gasoline in outside. And the wind's blowing and it's minus thirty. And your fingers are frozen . . . oh dear. So we just used it enough to keep the water down in the basement. Once it stopped raining, we weren't being flooded as much.

We managed. We have a little airtight stove in the living room. But you had to stay awake all night to keep putting wood on it, almost every hour, because otherwise the fire would go out. We were afraid to put too much wood on it because of the danger of a house fire. Too much wood, and it really gets hot.

Oakley: So that's what heated the house in the eighteen days that we were without electricity. But the other thing is, before the power failed Dot filled the bathtub with water. We used it for washing and flushing and quite a few things – we even took it out to the chickens and the horses.

The ground was totally frozen. Most people would fall, but I didn't. I didn't lift my feet off the ground, I just slid back and forth. We've had ice storms before. I have rubber boots with cleats on them.

Dorothy: I thought he was going to fall a couple of times! We had to chop through several inches of ice to get the barn doors open. We left the horses in for several days, but then we got some snow on top of the ice, and that pebbled the ice up. Then we were able to put them out during the day, and they were able to go down to the spring.

We were scared when we were taking the horses out. They were pretty much in the dark for days. We let the mare go out first, she's the smartest. And she had shoes on. Then we took the other horses out. The horses were excitable – you had to keep them quiet. The little ones had never been on ice before and they had no shoes, so we were holding on to them – you didn't know whether to let them go. We led them out slowly, and then they got their feet and realized they were sliding. We didn't know what they were going to do. It was an anxious moment.

Oakley: It's good to have a watchdog. One day Dot was helping serve lunch to residents of the local nursing home, so there was no car in our front yard and the garage door was open. A little red car drove up our driveway, went around the house to the backyard where the generator was operating loudly, and turned in readiness for a quick getaway. But

Zak, the watchdog who saved his family's generator.
His reward was an extra sausage.

Zak, our husky-retriever, started barking in the house and I wondered what he was barking about. His ears were sensitive enough that he reacted to the sound of a strange car. I ran to the front window in time to see the car speed down the driveway and turn onto Highway 34. We were lucky – there was one day in all of this when more than sixty new generators were stolen. Zak received an extra sausage for lunch.

By then Holly had bought a pump for us in Toronto, and she sent it on the bus. It was supposed to be unloaded in Lancaster, but it went all the way to Montreal. They unloaded it there, but they didn't know what it was and stuck it to one side. It took us four days, with phone calls back and forth, to find it. Finally they put it on another bus going back to Toronto, and it was unloaded at a motel along the 401 in Lancaster.

Dorothy: Holly also sent a courier package of candles, flashlights, and batteries. And then she came herself to provide support and company, and to help tend the stove. On her suggestion, we rented a room for three hours at a motel in Alexandria so that we could have hot baths. But when I walked with her out the back of our property, you couldn't even find the trail. It was such a mess.

Oakley: The woods reminded me of an overgrown tropical jungle in West Africa. I was out there during the war, as a supervisor in the reduction works in what was then the Gold Coast – Ghana, now. On the way back, our ship was torpedoed and I was adrift in a lifeboat for ten days.

Dorothy: In the ice storm I was the one who stayed up most of the time to mind the stove, but towards the end, he stayed up a little more. And then when my daughter came to stay, there were three of us. We told her it wasn't necessary – she has asthma, and we were doing fine. Except when Oakley starts telling me to put the oil in the wrong place.

Oakley: Someone on our battery-powered radio advised, "If your marriage can survive this ice storm, it can last forever." I agree. Before Holly arrived to reduce the tension and deadly monotony of our long, dark nights, we were having shouting matches over such important matters as whether the big boots should be parked at the top or bottom of the cellar stairs.

Oakley and Dorothy Bush live on Fassifern Farm, about ten kilometres north of Alexandria, Ontario.

AMANDA LEWIS

Water. That was the real crisis. We had heat, because of the woodstove, and cooking facilities, because of the propane stove. But the days revolved around water. Water for drinking, for washing, for flushing toilets, for feeding chickens. Every day began with the gathering of buckets full of snow. A pot to heat on the propane stove, two buckets to melt beside the woodstove. Every day ended with fresh buckets of snow left in front of the fire to melt during the night.

The first three days we boiled snow for drinking water, pouring it through coffee filters to try and filter out the worst of the detritus. By the third day we all started to feel pretty sick. It was a year later that I read about all the various parasites and bugs that live in snow. Oh, well. At the time it seemed better than nothing.

By day four we were able to get into town and buy bottled water, or fill up at friends' houses where there was still a water supply. But we kept boiling water for washing. Washing is very important to one's mental health. Nowhere is this more evident than in the mental health of teenagers. We had two teens in the house and it seemed that the loss of proper washing facilities was somehow even more critical than the loss of television. The minute they could locate someone with power (and there were many odd, hidden pockets of power), they would lobby to spend the night there, whether that person was a friend or dire enemy. Somehow hot water broke down all barriers.

We kept buckets melting in front of the fire for the chickens and the toilets. The chickens of course were not sympathetic to the crisis and still needed two buckets of water a day. Slipping across treacherous terrain with full buckets of water is harrowing enough at the best of times, but the fear of spilling any of that hard-earned liquid added a sickening tension to every step.

The toilets were another matter. Toilets can be "flushed" by pouring quantities of water down them, but of course, with a water shortage, we did this sparingly. Our daughter took to singing around the house "It's Beginning to Smell a Lot Like Urine" to the tune of a formerly favourite Christmas song. After about a week, I realized that a distinctive odour permeated our clothing and skin.

It was about then that a friend with power brought over a large camping container full of hot water, wrapped in an insulated blanket. I poured it into the tub and bathed by candlelight. It was the best bath of my entire life.

Amanda Lewis is a calligrapher, writer, theatre director and teacher who lives outside Perth, Ontario. Her mother's story appears on p. 48.

4

LIFE AMONG CHILDREN

his chapter includes stories of two very different kinds. It contains memories of the ice storm, as written by children; but it also contains memories of the ice storm's effect on children, as written by adults.

The children, as you will see, calmly recount what they saw and did. "We were all right," one of the children says, "so please don't worry." "After a week," another remarks, "there was still no power. But I got used to it." Even if it was scary at moments, the ice storm appears to have struck children as more of an inconvenience than an actual menace. They may not have relished the storm, but they seldom bothered to worry that it would cause them any long-term harm.

Which is what a lot of parents worried about, all the time. Even when their stories have a humorous overlay, these are still tales of care under duress. The children could live in the moment; their mood could change within a few seconds. It was harder for parents to get rid of their anxiety – the underside of protectiveness – because parents, virtually by definition, think ahead all the time. In the ice storm, both their anxiety and their protectiveness were magnified. "We're running out of milk again? Is her bedroom warm enough to sleep in? Is it safe for him to go play with a friend?"

Decisions, decisions; the storm, or more accurately the power outage, demanded so many of them. Parents often pretend to know the answers to kids' questions, but these answers were harder to find in the dark. After a while, they wore thin ("Don't cry, darling, I'm sure the power will come back soon"). Nobody had all the answers. Nobody could be entirely secure. Perhaps this, as much as the physical disruption of their lives, was the hardest thing for small children to accept. The best that parents could do was offer comfort and steady love.

And as usual, that was enough – more than enough.

JANE BARCLAY

Tuesday, January 6, 6:30 A.M.
I woke to the sound of the phone ringing. This was almost immediately followed by a minor stampede as our sons came charging up the stairs. They stood at the foot of the bed – Geoff (fourteen years), Tom (twelve years) and Steve (seven years) – the Three Stooges, poised to deliver a public-service announcement. "School has been cancelled," they announced gleefully. The news had the desired effect and I sat up in bed, only one question on my mind: "Why?"

As if in answer, a tree crashed to the ground, a transformer exploded, the wires caught fire and the power went out. In the eerie orange glow, another sound: the snoring of my husband as he slept beside me, oblivious to the beginning of what would be a generally bad week.

Tuesday, January 6, 9 A.M.
It is right about now that I wish I wasn't in the habit of turning down the thermostat to 17°C and opening the bedroom window every night. It is 13°C in the house, even with the fireplace going in the living room. It seems to be adding atmosphere, rather than actual heat, and I am beginning to have suspicions about my two cords of "dry" firewood. The last piece I burned had barnacles on the bottom.

Tuesday, January 6, 10 P.M.
Got fireplace in the basement started, so have settled in for the night with three boys and two cats. Husband and large dog are upstairs in the living room, keeping an eye on the fire up there. Have strong doubts about the success of this plan as I can hear them snoring already.

I can't sleep. Maybe it's the adrenalin from what's now being referred to as a crisis. Then again, maybe it's the hot dogs and Bailey's I had for supper.

Wednesday, January 7, 10 A.M.
A friend who still has electricity dropped in with a Thermos of hot water and a kerosene heater. She was the bearer of bad news. It went something like this: "Hey, guess what? Now there's millions of people

without power, the government is calling in the army and you wouldn't believe what's happening on the Weather Channel! Oops, gotta run before the muffins burn and the kids finish watching their movie."

I head back underground with my heater and my Thermos. We have become the mole people.

Wednesday, January 7, 3:30 P.M.
The monotony of the afternoon was broken by the sound of the furnace. We had power! I raced around the kitchen frying bacon, heating ravioli, boiling soup and brewing coffee. We ate, showered, ran the dishwasher, blew dry our hair. We have gone from moles to pigs – energy pigs. We are wallowing in electricity.

Later that night
We crawled into bed with the thermostat at 21°C and the window shut. My husband was too hot and couldn't sleep, so he headed downstairs. There was a loud pop. It was the energy weasel, and the house was once again in darkness. My husband climbed back into bed and we lay awake and listened, as outside Mother Nature unleashed a few more bulls in the china shop.

Thursday, January 8, 8 A.M.
Back down to the basement. Starting to rely on survival instincts. I have sectioned off our living area by hanging blankets from the ceiling. It also acts as a barrier from the cat-litter boxes. (I wish I'd cleaned them pre-crisis.) My husband has designed a tool from a coat hanger that enables him to toast bagels without burning the hair off his knuckles. I'm so proud.

We finally got the kerosene heater going. It really throws quite a heat, which is great because the window's wide open so we don't die from toxic fumes.

On a fashion note, I believe I may be dressed in the ultimate ice storm outfit. Besides the obligatory T-shirt and undies, I'm now wearing a polar fleece "muu muu" with pale blue trim to match my lips. To complete the look, a pair of knee-length red stockings that on December 25 were hung by the fire stuffed with little gifts from Santa.

Thursday, January 8, 6 P.M.

In an act of poor judgement, I warmed two cans of baked beans in the fire. Let's look at this from a mathematical point of view: 2 cans baked beans + 3 boys + 1 enclosed room + 1 kerosene heater = disaster! There was enough gas in the room to run a small generator, if only we had had one. To add to my misery, there was a knock at the door and there stood my neighbour handing me a covered platter. "It's not much, but it's the best we could manage under the circumstances." I thanked her and peeled back the foil on a chicken dinner complete with mashed potatoes and gravy. I flung open the door and yelled, "Yeah, well, we have a bagel toaster!" Showed her.

Friday, January 9, 5:45 A.M.

Another sleepless night. We were up early for an eight-fifteen appointment downtown. We'd decided to turn it into a family outing, the lure of lights and warmth being the deciding factor.

As we rolled down the highway, all that was missing was the theme song from *The Beverly Hillbillies*. We were sooty, our clothes were wrinkled and, as the heater in the car kicked in, we were starting to smell like smoked ham.

After the appointment, we headed to McDonald's for breakfast, then trudged back to the car full-bellied, warm-nosed and in much better spirits. Suddenly, it happens – a huge flash of lightning followed by the unbelievable sound of thunder. Then down it comes. Freezing rain, hail, ice pellets – a smorgasbord of weather served from the heavens.

When we're finally safe inside the car, I look in the back seat at my three sons. Their hair, tossed by the wind and frozen by the rain, stands in all directions, framing their grime-streaked faces. I have only one thought: We are the proud parents of the Back Sleet Boys. . . .

Friday, January 9, 10 P.M.

I had to bring the guinea pig down to the basement after I went to check on him and he was banging a frozen carrot against the bars of his cage and squealing for the warden. Now for sleeping companions we have one guinea pig, two cats and one huge dog. I spend the night shining the flashlight on the guinea-pig cage and hissing at the cats to get down from the top. Then I use the flashlight to hit the dog on the head and tell her to lie down and leave the cats alone. Then I just make obscene shadow puppets on the ceiling because I can't sleep. I wonder how Mrs. Noah managed. If it had been up to me, we'd definitely be missing a few species.

Saturday, January 10, 10 A.M.
The Hydro crews have arrived! We rush from our dwellings to greet them, forgetting that the outside world is one big skating rink. When they climb out of their trucks, they are greeted by a bunch of babbling idiots, floundering on their backs like overturned turtles.

Saturday, January 10, 2:30 P.M.
Power is restored.

Saturday, January 10, 2:31 P.M.
Friends who don't have power arrive to share ours.

Later that night
I am reading the newspaper and it is filled with stories of families brought closer together by the Ice Storm of '98. Ha! The way I see it, our family was already so close, the storm pushed us over the edge. I click off the lights and toss a dry log on the fire. It spits, fizzles and finally goes out.

Jane Barclay is a children's author. She wrote this "Diary of a Mad Housewife" in Pointe Claire, Quebec, where she lives with her husband, Alun, and their three sons, Larry, Moe, and Curly.

MARY OPOLKO

I feel awful, because I know I caused this mess. Don't laugh, it's true. The day before the ice storm, my mother and I went cross-country skiing. It was a beautiful day, with the sun high in the sky, but one thing troubled us. The snow had an odd greenish tint to it and there weren't any birds in the sky. We were sure something was going to happen.

Coincidentally, it was the last day of the Christmas holidays. I really did not want to go back to school, so I wished with all my heart for freezing rain. At first I only wanted a few days, but then I thought if I could get a few days, why not several weeks? Three, to be exact. Little did I know I made a huge mistake and wished for what some call the storm of the century!

Even though we had to take showers at friends' houses and at the gym, we were far luckier than most other people. At night we slept with extra covers and we kept the woodstove burning twenty-four hours a day. The roads were like skating rinks, and sliding down the hill was great fun.

We also went from house to house, giving people food and bringing them to the emergency shelter at the parish church. Unfortunately, patients from a mental institution also arrived at the shelter. It is quite scary to be in the dark with people who can get violent if they don't drink enough water per hour. All in all, we were all right, so please don't worry.

Mary Opolko lives in Morin Heights and attends Laurentian Regional High School in Lachute, Quebec. She was twelve years old at the time of the storm.

ALI ISMAIL

I am from Boroma, in northern Somalia, and I came to Montreal in 1988. My wife, Basra, joined me in 1993 with our four children. Then we have two more children born here. Amira, my youngest child, was eight months old when the ice storm began. It was Ramadan, the month of fasting. Amira was the one who had the seven-hour heart operation – the one who had the medical problems.

When my light went out, I stayed with my friend Muhamed Amin – he has five kids in just a two-bedroom apartment. And then when his light went out, he and his family came and stayed here, because we had the light again although it was very, very cold. He stayed one night, and then another friend came with his wife and sister for two nights. So we had eighteen people, all here in my apartment. We're lucky to have five bedrooms and a big basement.

My little baby, Amira, had had the heart operation the previous October. She had had a hole in the heart. After the operation she needed an oxygen mask for her lungs. Every four hours, Amira had to have the mask. Six times a day! Basra was taking her wherever there was power, because you need electricity to use the oxygen mask, which is attached to a small machine.

Sometimes me and the other kids went to the shelter on Atwater, in the Alexis Nihon shopping centre. It was crowded, there was too much noise, but the people were trying their best. Some people complained about the food, but there was no fighting. I would go there with my children to get warm and get some food in the evening, but I did not stay there. I came back here to sleep even when it was cold.

In Ramadan there are not only the usual prayers, five times a day, but also special prayers. The first three nights of the ice storm, I was not able to say those prayers. This was very sad for me. I was taking a French course for immigrants at that time, and the school was closed.

My wife was too scared for the little one to trust the shelter. When there was no light at Muhamed's house near Van Horne Avenue, fortunately the light would come on again here. All the time, I was driving back and forth! To Muhamed's, to the shelter, to my home. The day and the night, the day and the night. My wife would also come home to help with the other children – Mumin, the second-youngest child, was not yet two years old – because even though I am a good father, there are some things I can't do.

The police were helpful. At the beginning they were going from door to door, giving out papers with information about shelters. And they asked us if we wanted to go there. We were given special attention because we had a sick baby.

It wasn't only the oxygen mask for the lung problem – Amira was also taking medication. This was the worst part. We had to throw out the liquid medicine because we couldn't store it properly without electricity. So then I had to find a pharmacy that was open, and buy more medicine for the baby. It was expensive: each bottle costs fifty dollars. I was afraid because we only had two hours of supply left. In two hours, we would have run out. We were not expecting the ice storm, so we were not prepared.

Before the storm, the kids were excited to be going back to school. Then when this happened, they were sad and frightened. They would ask me questions I couldn't answer – "When will the power come back?" "Where will I sleep?" "Where are we going to eat hot food?" When it was over, they were very happy. Happy not just to have the light again, but to be back in their home. Only, when we came back, all the food in the refrigerator was rotten. It took Basra and the children two days to clean up.

My main concern was the fate of the little one, Amira. And she is fine now. My faith helped me. This storm was sanctioned by God: it was something that was going to happen.

Just in case it happens again, I have three days of candles and flashlights and supplies.

Ali Ismail and his family live in the Little Burgundy district of inner-city Montreal.

LORRAINE AUERBACH CHEVRIER

My story takes place in Pointe-Fortune, Quebec, a rural town of about 350 people, located on the banks of the Ottawa River. This is how we, the residents of Pointe-Fortune, and those residing in Chute-à-Blondeau, on the Ontario side of the interprovincial boundary, braved the storm.

My husband, Normand, who is a municipal councillor in Pointe-Fortune, had just returned from a council meeting at 10:30 P.M. when he remarked that the rain had turned into ice. The roads had become slick while the wind had picked up. We live about two kilometres from town. Normand suggested we store some water, presuming we were going to be without electrical power at some point during the night. Out here, no power means no water.

By 3 A.M. the winds were wicked, the power had gone off, and we were unable to sleep for fear that a tree might fall on our roof. We awoke our two sons, Jonathan (aged sixteen) and Marc (aged fifteen), and had them move with us into our unfinished basement. The boys

Branches from this tree hit Lorraine Auerbach Chevrier's bay window on the first night of the storm. The tree was later cut down.

slept on two single mattresses on the cement floor, while Normand slept on a sectional sofa around the fireplace. I camped out on another couch. Sleep was fitful, seeing that the fireplace had to be fed constantly, every two hours or so. Not until the following morning did we realize how much damage our property had sustained from fallen branches and trees.

During the first few days, we managed relatively well at home. We spent most of our time in our dimly lit basement, reading or playing cards. A portable kerosene heater, which we placed in the kitchen on the main floor, provided localized warmth and was used to heat up water and soup and brew coffee.

Perhaps the hardest challenge for my husband and myself was having our two sons keep their tempers and testosterone in check. After three days in the house, cabin fever started to set in. My older son, Jonathan, being a party animal, felt very confined and spent most of his days being miserable and making sure that we were aware of his discontent. He wanted to be in Ottawa, where several of his friends live, while we, the parents, were putting a damper on his social life. We wanted the family united at that time, an idea which did not sit well with him.

Soon both kids had had enough of reading, checkers, board games, and Scrabble. Tempers were short and emotions ran high. This togetherness was starting to wear thin. One evening the boys got into a fight and had to be physically separated. How to make them realize that we had to pull together? And then, the silver lining. . . .

The person I most admired during all of this was the mayor of Pointe-Fortune, Denis Labonté. On the second day, Monsieur Labonté and his son set out on icy roads and uncertain conditions for Quebec City, a three-and-a-half-hour drive from here under optimal conditions. When they had safely returned with a generator, our town hall was converted into a makeshift shelter. Pointe-Fortune welcomed nearby Ontario residents as well, because their municipality was doing little. The Red Cross brought in cots and blankets, and Roslyn Karp, the president of our local Citizens' Committee, was put in charge of meal planning. She called me, saying that she needed volunteers to help prepare meals. It was then that I realized why I truly enjoy country living.

The first day I arrived at the hall, an elderly lady was seated alone at a table. I was told that for the past two days, she had been seated there doing nothing. Seeing that we had lots of bread, I approached her and asked if she'd like to make a bread pudding. This broke the ice – figuratively speaking. Everyone who had come to the shelter was invited to play a role. The next few days were spent planning meals, washing dishes, playing cards, chatting, dozing, whatever met your fancy. People were jovial and conversation was animated. French, English and even a smattering of German were heard. Everyone got along well. Children and teenagers alike – including my two sons – were now able to be with their peers.

I should add that the police played an important role: they went door to door to ensure that all residents were accounted for. Anyone wanting a meal, or those without any heat, were invited to come to the shelter.

Only one elderly man with several dogs refused to leave his home. The following spring, he died alone in his house with his pets.

Lorraine Auerbach Chevrier works as a medical secretary and lives in Pointe-Fortune, Quebec.

SAMANTHA WHITE

I was writing a letter to a friend of mine when the lights started flickering. It had already started to rain, but not just any rain – it was freezing rain. My mom was at work and my brother, Chris, was watching TV. When the lights stopped flickering, I threw down my pencil and ran for candles. I was crying as I lit them – I'm afraid of the dark. I called my mom and begged her to come home, but she couldn't. I didn't know what to do. My brother's biggest concern was what was going to happen to the red Power Ranger – he's so immature for a twelve-year-old. I ran to him crying and he just burst out laughing. So I called my mom again and she asked me why I was being such a baby. She told me that the lights would be on in no time.

A week and about a hundred candles later, there was still no power. But I got used to it. A lot of people were evacuated from their homes to the church across the street, which was being used as a shelter. I went to the church to see my friend Britt. I slowly walked down the crowded aisles, and found her sitting on a bench in the dark. She had popped out of the shadows and scared me. I invited her to stay the night at my place by the warm fire, but she didn't want to leave her family.

Samantha White lives in Morin Heights and attends Laurentian Regional High School in Lachute, Quebec. She was eleven years old at the time of the storm.

JENNIFER WEI

We immigrated from Taiwan five years ago. That is a place with no snow all the year round. The whole family – my husband, Robert, two sons, Rickey (nine years old) and Rockey (four years old), and myself – always were anxious to see the snow when the winter came. Then the disaster arrived. When the freezing rain began to fall, my husband left for Asia for his business trip in the morning. Luckily he took an early flight, as many flights were cancelled later. But three of us did not have his luck following.

In the first morning, I was still optimistic the power would be reinstated any minute. The longest time we experienced without hydro in Quebec was three hours maximum. I told the children to get into the blankets. We live in Brossard, on the South Shore of Montreal. The house was getting colder and colder as time passed. My friend Mrs. Chang called me to see if we had power yet. Of course, the answer was negative. She said she and four children were fine for the time being, because of keeping the fireplace going with wood logs. They were fortunate, they had a gas stove for cooking. I had nothing, neither wood logs nor battery-operated radio, but cold bread and a freezing house.

She invited us to go over and have something warm to eat, and she said my children could stay there for the night. It was getting dark and I rushed to the store to buy some logs. There were not many people lining up at the cashier and I took four boxes of the fire logs left on the ground. Coming from a tropical area, I thought the fireplace was only for decoration and romantic; I never took it as a heating device. I was so naïve that I told a guy behind me not to worry, the power would be back soon, probably tomorrow.

It was an endless night for me. I was solitary in a freezing room, surrounded by darkness and quietness. Only the flame and a book accompanied me. I had to keep watching the fire to avoid it burning down. I thought of my sons, especially Rockey, who was only four and never left me. I missed them in such a lonely night. I fell asleep with tiredness and was awakened by coldness continuously, as the flame was almost dying out. Then I put another log to keep the fire going.

The next morning Rockey cried in the Chang family and I brought him back to our cold home. He was very tired and took a nap with two big comforters and a blanket in the basement, because he did not have a good sleep without me the night before. It was getting darker. Another friend, the Tsim family, came knocking at my door. The bell did not ring any more without electricity, and they pounded the door so hard I almost thought it was a bad guy trying to break in. They told me it would be more than four to five days without hydro; I was astounded.

Then I heard Rockey crying and calling me in the basement, as he was scared of the darkness. My tears were in my eyes and I felt so helpless. I ran out of wood logs in the first night. A father of Rockey's preschool classmate brought me fire-starters, which was the only thing he could find in the store (no more logs). The first thought I had was how I would survive the next few days, with the room temperature already down to 7°C.

Mr. Tsim asked me to move to downtown Montreal where they still had power in his wife's parents' apartment. I rushed to throw clothes and necessities in a luggage bag, using a flashlight in the dark. Mrs. Tsim helped to wrap the sleeping bags which were in front of the fireplace where I had slept alone the night before. She also shut down the water valve for me and released the water in the taps. Gripping my hand tightly, Rockey was not aware what I was doing and seemed in panic in the dark. Meanwhile, using the screwdrivers, Mr. Tsim locked the automatic garage door which could have been easily pulled up without electricity.

After packing I called my friends in Toronto and I also called Mrs. Chang's house and told Rickey I was picking him up. They were so lucky that they still had logs and the room temperature was approximately eleven degrees. After picking up Rickey, I was trembling when we were heading for the downtown, as it seemed we were refugees and running away to a safer place. We were six people packed into Mr. Tsim's car. Mrs. Tsim drove another car. The road was slippery and the freezing rain was so heavy that one of the windshield wipers broke. Mr. Tsim could not help but drive very slowly. The whole of Brossard was like a dead city in the dark. I was whispering to our abandoned house: "Bye, my home. I'll be back soon, but don't know when."

Mrs. Lee, the mother of Mrs. Tsim, welcomed us at the door and the supper was already prepared. I saw another two families there. We had sixteen persons at supper that night. I had not watched TV for three days and after watching TV news in the apartment, I finally realized how bad the damage was in Brossard. Before the Tsim family came to rescue us, I still expected the power would come back the next day, and planned to endure one more cold night in front of the fireplace. Finally I accepted the reality that nobody would know when we could go home.

That night Rockey held my hand and fell asleep in the living room, just like a baby. Poor Rockey had had a long day and was exhausted. Rickey seemed to understand after I told him why we had to leave home. Although we lived in a house of seven thousand square feet, we did not see any crowd in the two-bedroom apartment when it was filled with warm and kind people. Mrs. Tsim was very thoughtful, she brought toys and books for her two sons, aged four and thirteen. All the boys got along with each other and were happy at such an extended winter vacation.

Three days later, we had to move again because Mrs. Tsim's brother lost electricity and his family moved into the apartment. So we went to the Holiday Inn. Saying goodbye to Mr. and Mrs. Lee, I held Mrs Lee's hands with tears and told her how much I appreciated what they had done for my family. The kids were excited that they had a place to swim in the hotel and more space to play.

I watched TV news every day and night to see if the power was reinstated in the street of my house, but I was disappointed. During our stay in the hotel, we had meals in the different restaurants every day and got bored. All I could do was watch TV and nothing but endless news reporting all the sadness and despair. For me, it looked like rootless plants floating on the water surface and not knowing when or where to settle down.

It was the twelfth day when we could go home again. I stepped into my house and the first thing I told myself was that I was lucky there was no break-in. I was thankful for those policemen's and soldiers' patrols. But I felt so miserable when I found water coming down from the ceiling in the family room after I turned on the water valve. I was staring at the water like a shower coming down and I almost forgot to get a bucket. It was so bad and I had to take care of everything by myself to repair my home, and throw away the dead interior plants including my favourite tree, eight feet tall. Thank God that two good friends, Mr. and Mrs. Jonker in Toronto, sent a package by courier to cheer us up: a book of goodnight stories for Rockey, and a pair of flashlights with batteries for Rickey. Rickey called Rockey: "Come and hurry, look what Uncle and Auntie sent us." It was the most sweet feeling I had after going through those problems.

I appreciated all the friends who helped us through the ice storm. Without any brother, sister or relative living in Canada, I have the most precious friendships in the world.

After the ice storm, Rickey always put the flashlights beside his pillow. He told me he was ready for any blackout, just in case.

Jennifer Wei lives in Brossard, Quebec. She and her husband own a business that exports Canadian products to the U.S. and Asia.

JESSICA FINCH

My name is Jessica Finch. I live with my older brother Jacob, my mother and my father. It was the first week of January, I was ten years old and I took a week off school to go skiing in Sutton. We stayed in a condo which had two bathrooms, two bedrooms, a kitchen and a TV with no cable. The skiing conditions were wet and foggy but we didn't hear about the storm until Monday when my father was back in Montreal.

The storm was on the news for a long time. Lots of people had no lights and no power, but in Sutton we did till Wednesday, when we lost it. On Thursday we had to go back home, but that's where the storm was. We listened to the people talk about the storm on the radio all the way back. My brother got very annoyed with that.

As soon as we got back, my brother phoned his friends who had power and he left us (he abandoned his family!) for his friends. Me and my parents stayed at home with candles. We slept in the basement because we had no heat and it was cold upstairs where we usually sleep. Every night we invited our neighbours to dinner because they could not cook anything. On Friday I went to Ian and Claire's house, they had power until 1:30 P.M. After, I went home and played cards with the neighbours. We had lots of fun even though we had no power.

Saturday we still had no power, it was sort of a bit of a boring day, not much to do, so I went to the neighbours and played a little with them. There were some branches on the wires and a lot of ice. My friend Lorna was glad to see me because she was bored as well.

Amazingly, on Tuesday, we got power back for about ten minutes. My dad was putting water back into the heating system (a plumber had drained it the day before) as he thought we would have our power for the rest of the day, but he was wrong. I got to go to my friend Kate's house for a sleepover. My mom during all this time was working very hard at her job as a physiotherapist. She was already a basic full-time cook for us as our gas stove has never worked so hard!

My poor fish must have been a little cold, but they give you valuable information about what to do about pets on the radio. And the cats, well, they were meowing a lot about not having enough food.

When I came back from Kate's house, we did have power, thank God. We were luckier than other parts of Canada. The Ice Storm of '98 was like a week back in time.

Jessica Finch is a student at Willingdon School in the N.D.G. area of Montreal.

PAUL STEJSKAL

For most of the ice storm I was in Lennoxville, doing the last year of my education program at Bishop's University. Lennoxville had no freezing rain, as I remember. But I'm also a volunteer firefighter in Baie-d'Urfé, a suburb on the West Island of Montreal, and I had been calling home to find out what was going on. By Thursday things were getting really bad, so on Friday I came back home and spent the weekend working. We were pumping basements, responding to downed-wire calls, checking up on people who didn't want to leave their homes, and bringing other people to our shelter in the curling club. It was a relief when the army came in – until the lieutenant asked if they could borrow our chainsaws. They only had one chainsaw, believe it or not. One of our guys, under the stress of it all, said, "When you go to war, do you bring your own guns?"

Later in January, one of my professors, Duffie van Balkom, called a few of us in and told us that the principal of Hemmingford Elementary School, in the Châteauguay Valley, had requested extra help. The staff was under a lot of stress because the area was still blacked out. I was one of three people selected to go there. I had no idea what I was getting into. Prior to teachers' college, I'd been an integration aide at a high school, and my training was in high-school level physics and math. The assignment was to show up Monday morning and help out in whatever way we could. Duffie briefed us that the community felt there was a need to get the school back on its feet. The regular school building was still closed, but they had set up a makeshift one-room school, powered by a generator, in the community centre behind the church.

I was paired up with a teacher called Glenn Faucher. He's a great guitar player. He had brought his guitar in, and the students were making up their own songs and doing writing exercises about the ice storm. Age groups were being kept together, because the room was split up by temporary dividers, and there was some learning going on. Glenn asked me to do some science activities, and so I started doing rudimentary science – again involving the storm.

Later I found myself reading a story to Grade Three kids. I'd never envisioned myself doing that! A class of students were sitting on the floor, listening to me. It was a First Nations story, and somehow I was able to tie it in to the ice storm as well. The whole room was extremely loud – I remember the kindergarten class was up on stage, doing their thing. Some of us sat back for a minute and asked what it must have been like back in the days when most schools were just one room.

We were there for a couple of days, and then they were able to reopen the school – it had been used as a command post for the police and other emergency services. It was a little crazy going back there. But I was able to teach the kids a little science. I remember doing an acid-base indicator by using lemon juice, cabbage juice and baking soda to work these magic potions that would change colour.

Even after being in Baie-d'Urfé, my first day going into Hemmingford was unbelievable. Trees were toppled over like I'd never seen. Power lines were still down and lying by the side of the road. Makeshift power lines were being held up with two-by-fours. But the kids' mood was pretty upbeat. When they went out to play at recess, there were no problems. It was kind of like a big adventure.

Paul Stejskal is now a high-school teacher working in Châteauguay, Quebec.

NIKKI WOODWARD

It is so hard to live for a week without power. When you have to go to the bathroom, you hold it for so long that your stomach hurts, because you have to wait until you can go to someone's house. I missed the phone so much – I already hadn't seen my friends for two weeks, because of Christmas break.

I was hungry as well as cold. We were living off canned food – canned ham didn't taste so bad any more. One day Mom went down to Grenville to the bakery and bought all the bread he had, which was only ten loaves. When the storm was over, I didn't like bread any more. Usually I drink water a lot, but in the storm we needed water for everything.

I wished I had batteries so that I could take pictures of this disaster. But we needed batteries for other things. I never imagined that where we lived, there would actually be a natural disaster. I always thought that where we lived, we were away from all that. I was thinking of moving to San Francisco when I'm older – no way, this ice storm scared me so much that I don't think I could stand an earthquake.

One night, near the end, we went down to my aunt's house. It was such a relief to eat food that wasn't canned, and to have the lights on, and to go to the bathroom when you have to, not an hour later.

Nikki Woodward lives in Harrington, Quebec, and attends Laurentian Regional High School in Lachute. She was thirteen years old at the time of the storm.

TIM WYNNE-JONES

We live twenty minutes out of Perth, Ontario, in dense bush country, where the gunshot-like report of tree limbs snapping became so frequent during the ice storm that one could easily imagine a merciless pack of John Wyndham monsters, Triffids or what have you, advancing on the house from all quarters.

We are a relatively self-sufficient bunch in Brooke Valley, heating our homes with wood, cooking on propane or wood stoves, for the most part, and used enough to power outages, being on a branch line of the hydro grid, so to speak. Many of us have a back-up kerosene lamp or two on hand and a stock of dried food. We are also quite proud of being a community, able to help one another out. It was clear, in any case, that trips into town should be kept to the bare minimum, since the roads were far from safe.

But trips had to be made and, now and then, you were on your own, community or no community. One neighbour, a single mother, desperately short on supplies, found herself in just such a position. She was loath to wake her newborn baby from his afternoon nap, but as the light dwindled, and there was still no one around to help out, she bundled him up, against his will, and headed off. By the time she pulled into the parking lot of Home Hardware, he had cried himself to sleep in his car seat. She wasn't sure what to do. She hated to disturb him yet again.

Looking around the twilight lot for a familiar face, she noticed that she had parked next to a busload of soldiers. One soldier at the window of the bus caught her eye. He had noticed her, it seemed, and had accurately assessed her dilemma. Through sign language he was able to convince her that she should go get her shopping done and leave the baby to him. The store was minutes from closing; she had run out of options. She rushed into the hardware store, never having actually spoken to the man. She wasn't gone long before she became frantic. How could she have done such a thing? Left her newborn, like that, in the care of a complete stranger? She hurried back out with her supplies to find her subcompact surrounded by a veritable platoon of beefy soldiers, their arms crossed on their chests.

"Not a hair on his head was disturbed, ma'am," said the ringleader. Her baby, in his car seat, dozed peacefully.

Tim Wynne-Jones, a winner of the Governor General's Award, is one of Canada's best-loved writers for young people.

LOUISE McDONALD

It was a warm, sunny day in May 1998, and I knew that I would have to make my lesson hum if I had any hope of keeping my Grade Nine geography class on task. However, I never expected the following situation to arise.

We had been doing a unit on the water cycle, and the day's topic was the conservation of one of Canada's most valued resources, water. The topic was close to everyone's heart, because our area of eastern Ontario had been hard hit by the ice storm in January. The storm had coated Vankleek Hill and environs in approximately ninety millimetres of freezing rain, leaving it without hydro power for up to three weeks.

The project involved a simulated contamination of the local water supply. Residents would be rationed to twenty-five litres a day from a supply at the local community centre. Students were asked to develop a plan to cope with the rationing situation, and to decide on possible safeguards and solutions to problems which might arise. The spokesperson for each group gave a summary of its proposed plan, and it was now Phillip's turn to make the last group's report. Their proposals were similar to those of all the previous groups – until he announced their last solution.

His group had decided to forego their shower rations. Instead, they would bottle the resulting surplus and sell it at black-market prices to the local population.

Pandemonium broke out instantly. Students from the other groups began shouting, hissing and jeering. Rachel screamed out at the top of her lungs that this suggestion was more despicable than the actions of a store owner who, during the ice storm, had sold his last six loaves of bread at five dollars apiece. Lindsay reminded us all of the two men who had stuffed the trunk of their car with free firewood and then sold it to an elderly couple isolated in the countryside.

I banged on my desk for their attention and reminded them that they were simply role-playing and this was a pretend situation. Phillip yelled back at the others to "get real" and remember that such things happen in the mean and nasty real world. Ferguson, a student from another group, immediately bellowed out the story of the guy who had sold an extra generator for three times the normal price, just because of the emergency.

I sat at my desk amid the din and recalled how little controversy the identical assignment had spawned with the previous year's groups. This year's class was different. They had survived Ice Storm '98. They had experienced compassion and unselfish behaviour in their own families, in emergency shelters, and in the entire community. But since they had also lived through some guilty exploitation, nobody was going get away with selling water, imaginary or not.

These students had the experience; they now owned the knowledge.

Louise McDonald teaches at Vankleek Hill Collegiate Institute in Vankleek Hill, Ontario.

5

GIVERS OF HELP

later chapter in this book is entitled "Enjoying the Storm." I mention this only because it occurs to me that this chapter – about helping others get through the crisis – could easily have a similar name. The stories in it are ones that evoke satisfaction, fulfilment, and the kind of giving that turns imperceptibly into receiving. The contributors were of service to others; they also enjoyed themselves.

I wouldn't want to draw grand sociological conclusions from this, but it's worth pondering for a moment all the same. Of course, not all efforts at generosity in the ice storm were a success. Recently I came across a short story by the Quebec writer Monique Proulx, "Banana Chaudfroid," which describes one woman's lurch into generosity: her rescue of a family of strangers from a crowded shelter. After a few days in their silent company, Proulx writes, "She wants to say to them: Go away. Please go away." She won't force the family to leave – they have nowhere else to go – but for a time, she comes to regret her large-hearted impulse.

The voices you will hear in this chapter have no such regrets. For most of them, the chief importance of the freezing rain was the transformation it brought about in human relationships. The warm fronts and cold fronts in the quivering sky had their counterparts here on Earth, in the way people gave or held back. Likewise, the sense of quiet triumph that many people felt at the end of the crisis arose in large measure from a knowledge that even if the electricity pylons had snapped and shattered, the lines of human generosity had remained intact.

Is there an element of self-praise in all of this? Possibly, but no more than a tinge. None of the contributors to this chapter is nominating himself for a medal. Each appears to feel, in retrospect, lucky to have had the chance to serve. It may *be true that crises bring out the best – not just in individuals, but in a whole society. The cheerful selflessness that was so prominent during the ice storm is not exactly rampant now.*

ROD McDONALD

The eastern Ontario ice storm lasted two weeks on the calendar but will last decades in the minds of some of its hostages. For the old and infirm, and especially for shut-ins, the storm evolved into a bitter test of willpower that had some people hanging on by their fingernails. Fortunately, the town of Hawkesbury avoided a prolonged power failure because of its hydro grid location, and so became an oasis in a desert of ice.

My brother, Bruce, had been living as a virtual hermit for the last thirty years of his life, and the storm presented him with a massive wall of challenge which seemed unscalable. He lived with my mother in an old house in Alexandria, a small town approximately forty kilometres south of Hawkesbury, where I reside with my wife. Bruce was born with a congenital defect which left him partially deaf, and as a result, his speech is peculiar and readily understandable only to my mother. The only sounds he can easily understand must come through an earplug or headphones. After an excruciating time in high school, where adolescents teased him about his appearance (he has a neck deformity) and his speech, he resolved never to set foot outside the house unless it was for medical reasons. Even then, he had to be extricated by my mother.

So the crisis of the ice storm was worsened by the fact that my brother was painfully shy. Over the course of many years, he had learned to live by himself with hardly any social interaction except for his tentative relationship with my mother. At forty-five years of age, Bruce, suffering from diabetes and overweight from inactivity, knew that he would either have to leave the security of the old house and face a public which he had refused to confront, or stay in the drafty, poorly insulated wooden house and slowly freeze to death in his own deathly silent world. His amusements had been rendered useless by the power outage: no television (used with an earplug), no taped novels. Furthermore, the army would be by to remove him to some sort of shelter, eventually. Hydro poles were snapping like matchsticks under the weight of over sixty millimetres of ice, and the prognosis was bad. With some luck, and an abatement in the ice buildup, the power might be returned within a week. There was no option for my mother and my two sisters, Diane and Linda, who also lived in Alexandria, in a condominium. After a long discussion with Bruce, they managed to squeeze my brother and themselves plus Do-Do the rabbit and his cage into their tiny car. They left for Hawkesbury in driving freezing rain, as I busied myself draining the pipes in both their homes and making sure that all the power switches were in the "off" position. I then got into my car for the slippery ride back to Hawkesbury, where I would be meeting Bruce for the first time in years. I did a great deal of soul-searching on that trip, and I prayed that Bruce would be able to cope with so many instant changes to his protected lifestyle. I asked the angels to help him adjust to the turmoil of the ice storm, but I remained skeptical.

When I arrived home and opened the front door, Bruce was there with the others, awaiting me. He was obviously anxious as he shook my hand, gave me a cursory glance and looked down to study his feet. A world of thoughts raced through my head as I tried my best at small talk and Socratic questions (something I am quite at ease with, being a high-school English teacher). Fortunately my wife, Louise, had made some inroads and seemed to have established a rapport with my brother. And so our adventure began.

The most difficult times seemed to be in the morning, establishing a contact for the day. One can imagine how difficult this must have been for my brother. Sometimes when I think of the effort it must have demanded, I am awed. Bruce stuck to my mother like a small child; on occasion, however, he would look up at me and establish a long-lost contact which humbled me and at the same time elated me. There is something about eye contact which disallows any attempt to avoid the issue. My brother was in front of me, and he was open to some form of communication.

As the wind screamed and the ice pelted our windows with machine-gun tenacity, we would sit by the glowing fire and talk about the small things in life, the things which don't matter. And as the week passed, I could see that Bruce was indeed coming out of himself, bit by bit.

Louise was exceptional at getting him to try new food he had never even heard of. His diet was radically changed for that week, and he seemed to delight in it. On one occasion, we asked him if he might like to try a glass of white wine with his fettucine and he acquiesced. He downed the large glass in several great gulps and put the empty goblet down on the table as if it were his custom to quaff wine daily. I knew that this was the first glass of wine he had ever tasted. I remained calm, but I caught a look in Louise's eyes which seemed to say: "Am I glad we offered him that! Let's try another." And we did, and Bruce seemed none the worse for wear after two hefty glasses.

The ice storm continued to bring my brother out of his shell, and when the time came for the inevitable return trip to the old house, we felt a turmoil of emotions. How would he do at home? Would some of the feelings he experienced cause him some confusion later? Would he try to maintain any of the contact he had so painfully and methodically established? Television broadcasts advised us that power had finally been restored in Alexandria, and we planned for the trip back.

On a frigid sunshiny day in January, the surviving maples were flashing prism reflections of the sun at us from their ice-coated branches. Ice fragments hailed down at us like silver bullets as the sun did its work, and the road looked like a winding skating rink. Our guests packed themselves into the car, and as I leaned down and looked through the icy back window, Bruce gave me a look which was comforting and frightening at the same time. The angels had indeed come through to bring Bruce out of his interior. And as I looked out over the Ottawa River towards the devastated but glistening Laurentians on a magical afternoon, I truly prayed that the angels of the ice storm would take up residence with Bruce for years to come, warming his heart with confidence and letting him know that he was not alone.

As their car left our home and crunched its way down the hill on its way back home, I saw my brother's hand pull up to the rear window and wave a salute. I am not quite sure whether he was waving at us or at the angels hovering in the diamond-covered trees. Only he and they know for sure.

Rod McDonald is an artist who teaches English in Vankleek Hill, Ontario. A story by his wife, Louise McDonald, appears on p. 101.

CHARLY BOUCHARA

At our place, the blackout only lasted about thirty hours, no doubt because we're surrounded by hospitals. Like everyone else, I was listening to the radio fifteen hours a day, and I heard mention of shelters that had opened up. There was one of them not far away in the neighbourhood, at the Côte des Neiges Community Centre. I thought we had room enough to welcome three or four people – this was well before Premier Bouchard made his appeal for Quebeckers to take people stricken by the disaster into their homes – and I went to see if a family would like to come and stay in our apartment.

But pretty soon I realized that for these people, the centre was a safe refuge they were not keen to leave. Most of the ones I spoke to – Vietnamese, Yugoslavians, Russians, Latin Americans, North Africans – expressed a fear of finding themselves in the street again if the electricity were to fail at my place. Giving up the idea of having guests, I became a volunteer at the centre.

There were close to five hundred people of about forty nationalities scattered through the gymnasiums and in all the rooms that were big enough to install camp beds and mattresses. For a couple of days, I lent a hand in the kitchens, I helped to empty trucks that were pulling in with food supplies and equipment, I welcomed the new arrivals. . . . Then, and for the rest of the ten days or so that I spent there, I looked after the small "welcome café" near the entrance to the centre. Residents of the neighbourhood could come and warm up there, have a hot drink, watch television. Before they were assigned a bed and a place to stay, people who had just arrived would wait there too. My shift began at seven o'clock in the morning and when I left, around six at night, I was exhausted but happy.

The organization of the centre was exceptionally good, given the conditions and the fact that everything had been improvised in just a few hours. Regular employees, nurses, Red Cross workers, volunteers, the few soldiers who were posted there: they all displayed a patience, enthusiasm, graciousness, and humour I will remember for a long time. There were so many things to do, so many problems to resolve, so many solutions to find – everything had to be organized so that people would feel welcomed, not merely parked there. Thought had to be given to nursing babies, to children, to old people, to pregnant women, and to those who had psychological problems that were sometimes very serious.

If I was, from time to time, aware of exasperation brought on by sheer fatigue, I never saw anyone – either among the volunteers or their "guests" – become irritable or lose their temper.

The children and teenagers were the first to adapt, making friends, getting together, and running all over this new playground when they weren't being called upon to do some cleaning up, or to help carry food into the huge dining room. Some of them had labels pinned on their clothes – "Russian," "Spanish," "Vietnamese," "Chinese," "Romanian," "Serbo-Croat" – so that they could, when necessary, serve as interpreters for adults who spoke neither French nor English.

When the police and the army began their door-to-door visits through the streets of the city, we saw people arrive who had been without heat and electricity for three, four, or five days. They were famished and numb with cold. There were many elderly people, and also a large number of immigrant families who could not understand the messages broadcast by radio. I remember, among others, Russians who had been in Montreal barely a few weeks and who thought this situation was normal. Others were unwilling to open their door because in their country, nothing good could come from a visit by policemen or soldiers in the middle of the night.

We often gave shelter to old people who had been taken from their homes by force. That was how I saw the arrival of one elderly lady who had not eaten in five days. Her body wrapped in blankets, her small face thin and wrinkled, her eyes frightened, she reminded me of some fragile songbird that had fallen out of its nest. The lady kept on saying that she didn't want to disturb anybody, it was the police who had insisted she follow them. She was visibly in a state of extreme weakness, and had she not been rescued, she would certainly have died.

I sat down beside her. With tears in my eyes, I tried to win her trust. I repeated that we had come to look after her, that a nurse would come to see her, that we were finding her a bed or would take her to a hospital if she needed medical care. In the end, she took her hand out from under the blankets and put it on top of mine. In her eyes, I could see her amazement that someone else would be concerned about her. This aspect of the crisis was, I believe, the hardest to endure for many older people after it was all over with. For five, eight, ten days, or even longer, people were around to look after them! The return to normality, for these excluded ones, doubtless meant a return to loneliness, boredom, neglect. . . .

In the Côte des Neiges Centre, everything was made ready for Muslims whom the ice storm had taken by surprise in the middle of Ramadan. This was not the case in some other Montreal shelters. A family of Moroccans had not eaten for three days because their first shelter did not distribute food after 4 P.M., so that they were obliged to wait through the night hungry. For them, to arrive "chez nous" was a blessing. To find somebody who could understand what motivated them to fast was already a good thing, but to be told that they and their children could have a true meal that evening was almost too much. Weeping, the mother held my hands, thanking me as if they owed it all to me. And I, the non-believing Jew, I discussed theology with them, reminding them that the Koran does not require fasting by children, the old and the sick, or by anyone when conditions are so exceptional that the faster's life would be at risk. . . . All the same, they waited until sunset.

Since then, I've run into them from time to time in the neighbour-hood. We smile and wave at each other. Those moments that we shared, all the conflicts in the world between Jews and Arabs can never take away from us.

Overall, I have mixed feelings about the crisis. I saw Christmas trees lit up in the homes of some who were both lucky and thoughtless. I know that many wealthy people were able to have their houses repainted, or their freezers filled, because they were well-insured – which was not the case for everyone. There were profiteers. There was that stupid radio host who kept proclaiming that we were doing too much for the people in the shelters. And there was, as well, the media frenzy around an event that, if we compare it to recent disasters in Central America, Bangladesh, Sudan, and elsewhere, had nothing of the end-of-the-world quality which over-excited journalists and broadcasters were describing.

Despite all that, I met in "my" shelter people of all origins, social conditions, skin colours, religions, languages, and political opinions – people who reminded me that, no matter what Mordecai Richler and others might say, Quebec society is more fraternal, more tolerant, more responsible, and more open than we are often told. I even took to dreaming about a similar crisis every two or three years, as a good way to meet the stranger next door, the one who looks a bit different, the one we are afraid of – a way to get to know each other, discover each other, talk to each other.

Charly Bouchara is a translator who lives in Montreal. Among his recent work is the French translation, Le Grand Verglas, *of McClelland & Stewart's book* The Ice Storm.

DON E.

Pittsburgh is a minimum-security institution, and I share a house with seven other men. Everyone has a different job. I work for Maintenance, and we were very aware that we might have a major disaster. Even before the power went out, we were organizing a crew and getting the chainsaws ready.

The morning after it went out, my supervisor came knocking at the door to pick me up at seven o'clock. We had to start working inside the institution, because all the roads were blocked and the access-ways to the buildings were full of trees.

The first day was very hectic. All we could hear was the trees crashing around us. We wore safety hats and safety shoes and gloves. The rain was so heavy, we could hardly stand up – we had to be very careful when we went under trees. We had some very close calls. If a tree was leaning to the right, we went to the left side of the tree, to try to pull the branches away from the buildings. Some of the sidewalks we just could not reach – too many dangerous high branches.

We tried to direct the crashes. We'd pull on the branches so they would snap, but away from the buildings. We could not climb – ladders were impossible – and we could not use a chainsaw. So we used axes and bucksaws. You had to be very careful not to hit yourself at the same time, because it was so slippery.

Don E. hauls fallen branches from a street in the historic town of Gananoque.
Other minimum-security prisoners helped out as well. (Photo: Peter Harper)

Pittsburgh Institution does not have emergency generators, so until they got a generator in and hooked it up, the house was dark for a few days. It was cold, too. We had emergency lights that run by battery, so we played cards while the storm was on. We had nothing to cook with, so we used a coffee can, put a roll of toilet paper inside it, and lit up the roll of toilet paper with some oil. We used that for boiling water to make our tea, coffee, soup, and we ate sandwiches and cold beans. We wanted to light a bonfire but that idea was rejected.

The next day, the supervisor got me up at seven again, but it was worse. You could hardly walk. On the sidewalks there were two, three inches of solid ice. We tried to keep the main entrance open for the security guards to come in, because some of them fell and were off for months. The idea was to put a lot of sand down, but this didn't work, because the rain kept falling and accumulating on top of the sand. The inmates were told to stay in their houses.

The third day I was taken downtown, to Gananoque, which is about twenty kilometres away. The Board of Works came and got me in a five-ton truck with sand in it. Most of the time there were four of us from this institution working there during the storm.

I ran a backhoe for the town, trying to get the trees off the roads. We had major-size trees fallen on streets and leaning on top of houses. The big problems were with the hydro system – at Gananoque they have their own company, with their own generator that runs from the waterfall. Ontario Hydro didn't have any power, but some of the cables were run by Gananoque's own public utility. So we didn't know what was alive and what was dead. When we pushed through the ice with the backhoe, we kept hitting live wires and the sparks were flying everywhere.

It meant we were taking chances all the time. We could have got electrocuted. But life is just a chance, right? If you don't take chances, it's not worth living. I didn't mind. If you die, you die: that's the gamble I took. If someone's going to get electrocuted, I'd rather it were me than a child walking on the sidewalk. We had to remove those wires!

The army came later. That first day, there was nobody on the side streets – Ontario Hydro was too busy taking care of the highways and the main roads – and it was important to clear the streets, because people were getting sick and freezing cold. During the storm we were wet: it kept raining and they supplied us with raincoats and hard hats. I wear glasses so I didn't need extra goggles.

I put in the day at Gananoque and then I was brought back here in the evening. This was the routine.

The other guys in my house were envious of me. Very envious! They were doing nothing – just playing cards and complaining. And worrying about their friends and family on the outside. I was upset that I couldn't do anything for my mother. The others in my house were frustrated because they wanted to go and help too. But the system has security rules, and also they didn't want to let people go out without safety helmets and shoes.

It's a great opportunity for us to be able to go out on the street. It's something we talk about and dream about. When you get sent to prison, you know you can't go home, but the next best thing is if you can do your program and volunteer your time to go into town. Prisoners work for this and behave for this – you have to earn it. Because of this program, I feel I can pay back a society that I have wronged. It changes my life totally, knowing that I can give something back to society. And when I go to be released, I'll be used to the outside again.

During the storm we worked on people's property. It's hard work, because the branches we had to remove were frozen in. Push and pull, push and pull, until the branches break, or until you bring the machines in.

You were always fighting the branches. We got hit many times because of the ice in them. They had a whipping action – everything inside was springloaded. The wood was wet, and when you pulled it, it'd hit you.

It was a very touchy process. People complain, "You guys are on my front lawn!" Or they don't tell you they had a tree that dropped on their lawn and they've put other branches on top of it. That means there's a big stump in there which does not move. I got stuck one time pushing at the stump, there was no way it was moving, and the people were looking through the window and wondering why I was digging a hole in their front lawn!

But sometimes the people would come out and help us. They wouldn't know automatically that I was a prisoner, but if they asked me, I'd tell them. There was no problem about that – they were happy I was there. They figured, "The more the better." Saves on their taxes, right? Eventually we got a van down from here with twelve of us in it. Plus some prisoners – when they were approved by the management here – were allowed to work in other jobs, like the Humane Society and the food bank. At City Hall they supplied us with coffee and doughnuts at ten in the morning and two in the afternoon. That was a good thing for us. You don't get that too often.

I'd never seen anything like the ice storm before. But it's all part of nature. To me, it's normal, like a tornado or a forest fire. I don't call it "damage"; I call it nature readjusting itself. It's people that are in the way.

I figure this ice storm might teach people not to depend on electricity so much. We're part of nature. But people don't have wood furnaces, they don't hunt their own food any more, and if they cook anything, it's in a box. Then they feel that the government has got to pay for them!

I disagree with the amount of money the government gave. They call it "ice storm relief." I don't believe in that. I've seen people receive $20,000, $30,000, and they used the money not for anything related to the ice storm but for renovations on their houses. I've seen people do their driveways in interlocking stones, paid for by the ice storm. I've been very disappointed by the way people took advantage of the situation.

Don E. is a prisoner at the minimum-security Pittsburgh Institution, northeast of Kingston. Because of a restraining order, his full name cannot be used.

ANDREW TURNBULL

The storm hit us at midday on Friday, and I don't think anybody could have forecast how severe it was going to be. St. Andrews happens to be on a peninsula of land that juts out into Passamaquoddy Bay – it's a very old town in a unique temperate zone. We've lost a lot of the stately elms, but there're still a lot of old trees canopying the roads. After the storm hit, you could not drive down some of those roads. Just to be out, with the number of wires that were down, was quite dangerous.

I was at work that day, and it soon became clear that parts of the town had lost power. So I contacted the town office and said that if necessary we could provide rooms in the Algonquin, where I'm the manager. At first they said it wasn't necessary, but within a few hours they were sending people our way. The Algonquin is a Canadian Pacific hotel, the last of the famous summer resorts, and for many years it closed in winter. But recently we've been open all year round, on a trial basis. There's nowhere else in town that has generator back-up power.

We just opened our doors, gratis. I didn't seek head-office approval – we just did it. It was the right thing to do under the circumstances. All these people without power were our friends and neighbours. Their children go to school with our children. This is not a heroic story – just one of resources meeting a need.

We already had a handful of paying guests, and people from the community started to arrive by late afternoon on Friday. The mood was sombre at first – people were struggling. Many of them were lugging small children and they wanted to make sure the children were warm enough and had food to eat. Others were quite elderly.

I live in a house just beside the hotel property, and I remember that night we were sitting up on the hill overlooking the town and the sea. I couldn't see another light. Basically the whole town seemed to be without power.

That night we lost power for about four hours, both in my house and in the hotel. But fortunately we're on a different line than most of the town, so the power came back during the night. In the rest of St. Andrews, the power was off until later in the weekend, and in some of the outlying areas, it took up to a week before it was restored.

On the Saturday morning, I was trying to get the dog up the back steps of my house when I slipped on the ice and fell down a flight of stairs. I wear glasses, and as I landed, I must have reached up to protect my glasses. But I landed on my elbow and I managed to put a fingernail through my upper eyelid. I had to be taken to the town of St. Stephen, about twenty minutes away, to have three or four stitches at the hospital. Which is how I came to know that other towns near us missed out on the storm completely.

When I got back to the Algonquin, I found it was filling up. We have fifty-four rooms that are winterized, and by Saturday night, we were down to the last couple of rooms. But the mood had changed. People were sitting by the big wood fireplace in the main lobby, the fire was blazing, and a sense of camaraderie quickly built up. It was a complete mixture of young and old.

I know that some people talk about "the venerable Algonquin." Working here, we don't think of it that way. But it's true that it's a hundred-year-old grand hotel, and I suppose many of the people who came to stay in the ice storm had never been here before. The hotel does allow pets, and I think we had a few, but in my home we also had people dropping off their pets. I remember a dog and a hamster came to stay.

For those of us who work in the hotel, a big part of our focus was just fixing the leaks. There was ice on the roof, there was water under the ice, and we started having a number of leaks around the place.

I remember that one of the women staying here went out for groceries. When she was three-quarters of the way back up, her car got stuck. Then when she got out of the car, she found she couldn't walk up the hill, it was so icy. I went down and I managed to help her up and get in the back door of the hotel.

After the crisis was over, some of the people who had stayed here created a fund. On Canada Day last year, they planted a tree on the lawn behind the hotel, with a plaque expressing their gratitude. It's a weeping beech, quite unique. For the moment, it's just a sapling. But it will grow.

Andrew Turnbull is manager of the Algonquin Hotel in St. Andrews, New Brunswick.

BRENDA AJZENKOPF

I'm a secretary in the social-work department of the Jewish General Hospital in Montreal, and on the second day of the storm, I was at work all day. Our offices are up on the third floor, overlooking Côte des Neiges Road. We could look out and see the buses slithering up the hill. The department was very busy that day – we had lists of places where people could go for shelter. If they phoned up and sounded desperate, we told them to come to the hospital.

At 4:30 P.M. I finished work. My daughter Shari had come to the hospital for a doctor's appointment, and we intended to drive over to my mother's in Côte St-Luc. Her apartment still had power. We walked out of the building and made our way to the parking lot, holding onto each other. By the time we got onto Lavoie Street, it was totally filled with cars. It took us twenty minutes to go a quarter of a block. I said to Shari, "We're not getting anywhere – let's go back to the hospital and help."

We got back there after 5 P.M. I remember it was dark already. A shelter had just been set up in the atrium, near Emergency. The chairs and tables and big potted plants had been moved away, and cots had been moved in. An amazing sight, to see the room filled with cots – it was wall-to-wall bunks.

A lot of elderly people were arriving on buses, mostly from seniors' residences in the area. They looked frail. But they certainly got the attention they wanted! Some of them were fighting over beds – "I saw this bed first, I want it!" These people were *running* for the beds. There were some feisty ladies who wouldn't let anyone else touch their bed. Even though they'd just come out of a freezing building, they refused to lie down on mats and blankets on the floor. They didn't want it and they wouldn't take it. It's amazing how strong they could be.

Some women were there with husbands, and there were a few elderly men on their own, but mostly it was single women. Many of them rested in their clothes, but I saw one woman put on a silk nightie just as if she were at home; it was very cute. We served them a meal of spaghetti and juice and coffee or tea, which they would eat while sitting on their cots. Lots of them wanted more tea, more drinks, more food. Others were very passive, very quiet. A couple happened to wander in off the street with a baby – they were Russian immigrants who didn't speak English very well. Somehow a place was found for them.

Later in the evening I was walking between the cots to see if anybody needed anything, and I heard an elderly woman say in Yiddish, "Excuse me, miss! Could you help me?"

First she asked me to prop her up. There was only one pillow on each cot, and this lady wanted more pillows. I managed to prop her up by putting a coat behind her pillow. Then she said, "I'm not feeling well, dear. Maybe you could find my pills?"

She had this big bag, like a plastic laundry bag, beside her bed. Inside it was a big purse. Inside the purse was another plastic bag. Inside the second plastic bag was a white sock, tied up in a knot. Inside the sock was some change and a couple of plastic vials of pills. She said, "Give me one of those pills – it's for my heart. I don't feel well."

I'm not a nurse, and I thought I'd better double-check that this was okay. So I found a nurse, and when she'd looked at the pills, the lady was moved into Emergency, with her bed and all her stuff. I never knew what happened to her. But if she'd died, I think I would have heard. Bad news travels fast in a hospital.

Shari and I stayed for a few hours, until the traffic had moved on, but at about 10:30 P.M. we decided to leave. My mother was getting very anxious. The roads were quiet by now, and I remember it was unbelievably dark as we drove down Côte Ste-Catherine. There was only the black sky and the shadows of trees.

I went back to the atrium the next morning, and it looked like every-one had settled in. The mood was much better. They were very com-fortable, they were together and they seemed content. People were playing cards in corners or listening to little radios. They ended up staying several days. They weren't anxious to leave.

Brenda Ajzenkopf lives in Laval and works in Montreal.

GRUNIA SLUTSKAYA KOHN

I was born in Poland, near the border with White Russia (Belarus), and I lived there until 1939. I was very young – in Grade Five – when the war started and I ran away from the Germans with a group of girls. We walked for 360 kilometres on the highways. The Germans were bombing us: many were killed but we survived. After more than a month they brought us to Kazakhstan, where we worked in the fields. Then all the girls went to the Ural Mountains, where they worked in factories that made ammunition, and I joined them in April 1942.

In 1943 I started working in the city of Sverdlovsk, in a plant where they were making parts for aircraft. I worked three and a half years there. In the evenings I studied and finished high school. I wanted to be a doctor but it was impossible without help – I had lost my family – and I trained to be a teacher instead. For many years I taught German in a high school and then in the medical college in Rovno, near Lvov in what is now Ukraine. I had gone there to join my husband. He was a partisan in the forests near Rovno.

We had to bring up the youngsters in the spirit of Communism. It was hard; I was never a Communist. We wanted to live in a free country. My husband had found out that one of his brothers survived the concentration camps and was living in Canada. Finally, in 1973, they let us leave the Soviet Union. We came with nothing except our two girls. I had to pay back the government eight thousand dollars for my education before we left, so we sold everything. All our savings were gone. But we are proud. We didn't complain. One of my daugh-ters moved to Israel. The other is in Montreal. She has two young sons, Lawrence and Gregory. My husband is still alive but he is not in good health.

We lost our electricity in the ice storm very early. The neighbour at the next house still had electricity, and I was wondering, how does it come? But I was too shy to ask, so I was freezing here. And the stove is electric. But I had candles and I didn't complain.

My daughter didn't have electricity either, so I called my neighbour, Mr. Bernie Sigman, and he said, "Come over!" I said, "But I'm not alone, I have a bunch!" He was a widower, a good man; he died last year. So the five of us came and he gave the kids his bed. I was the cook: I made whatever I could for all of us.

Later on, there was no electricity any more, so they came and took him to a shelter, because he was a sick man. His heart was bad. I stayed in his house, I wanted to make sure it was safe, and even when we had electricity and he didn't, I still stayed two days there. That's my way.

At his house I was sleeping on the floor and my husband had the couch. My daughter was quiet, she is serious like her father. But I told stories to the boys – cheerful, happy stories – we made fun. I said to them, "Don't complain, it's not the end of the world!" They didn't panic: I prepared them. I always told them it could be worse.

And that's it! I say, in any situation, be an optimist. Especially with my experience, what I went through, I could say to them, "It's not the Holocaust! You have clothes, you can put on an extra sweater. So, you don't have a very fancy meal, but you have food on the table. And be thankful to God, and ready to share with people."

I think that some people who were born here don't appreciate this country. It's a wonderful country, it's a country that cares, it's a country that is always ready to help. It comes to you but it doesn't come to everybody. So, we have to be satisfied with everything we have. I was hungry for seven years during the war and after. When I was studying, we were forty girls in a cold dormitory and the rats were jumping around and I would trade my loaf of bread for a piece of soap on the black market. I say to my grandchildren, even today, "In front of me, never throw out bread."

You are spoiled people – forgive me. Do you know what I would do when I was in the dormitory? I had one pair of underwear, I would wash it in cold water and I would put it on because I didn't have a place to dry it. I was sleeping in wet underwear but I wanted to be clean. So, going through all this, I am ashamed for some people when they complain. It's a pity they are so selfish. I would say: it's a crime.

Grunia Slutskaya Kohn is an internationally recognized writer in the Yiddish language. She lives in Montreal.

MAURICE RAINVILLE

I was born in St-Jean-sur-Richelieu, my family comes from the area, and at the time of the ice storm, I had been the priest at St. Eugène's parish for four years. All my roots are here. It's a relatively young, suburban parish with a lot of children, in a part of St-Jean that is still being developed. I myself live in a bungalow near the community centre where the church is located. During the ice storm, the whole region was without power for at least three weeks. It was truly devastating.

I was unable to stay in my house, but each day I would come back to the parish, walk around it, and see what the needs were and what I could do. I could have left the city – it was certainly possible to do so. But I chose to stay here with my people. All the other priests in the area made the same decision. People would often say to me, "I haven't seen anyone at such-and-such a house – maybe you could go and check up on them." So I would do that. But as the days passed, a large number of residents moved elsewhere.

We offered to let the city use the community centre as a shelter or a daycare, but the offer was turned down because we don't have enough sanitary facilities. Without a generator, we also had no way of heating the building. While the crisis lasted, there were no masses in this or most of the other churches. What we did was to go into the two big shelters in St-Jean – one at the high school, the other in the old military college – and celebrate the Eucharist there. We also asked the diocese to prepare four services that did not involve a Eucharist, and on weekdays we would conduct these services with different groups of people. They were special moments – very contemporary prayers and reflections, with perhaps twenty-five or thirty people at a time, to help them on their interior journey.

The cathedral was closed during the crisis. It suffered a good deal of damage because of its old, hot-water heating system, and in the presbytery, the pipes burst. Other churches in St-Jean were also damaged. But there was one parish, St-Lucien, which stayed open and was put into use as a daytime respite centre.

The ice storm brought about some truly beautiful acts of generosity. There were people who never stopped helping others, becoming real pillars in spite of their own fatigue. But the storm also enabled other people to profit from human misery – selling generators at an exorbitant price, or selling candles for truly incredible amounts of money. In this parish and some others, we offered the church candles to people who were in need.

For the first week, I managed to heat a home with little votive lamps from the church. I remembered St. Joseph's Oratory in Montreal: if you walk down one of the side-aisles, where all the lamps are burning, it's hot! So I took thirty-six lamps and installed them in my mother's apartment. I stayed there with my uncle, my aunt, and my mother, and the temperature never fell below 18°C. But then the army asked us to evacuate – the owner of the building had to drain the water, to make sure there was no freezing in the walls. It was a building with 144 units, and we were the last to leave. We also had a budgie staying with us by then, because a lady who had already left the building had asked us to look after it. But we didn't know where she'd gone! Luckily, we were able to trace her and return the budgie.

In that first week, I spent quite a bit of time driving my car and doing volunteer work for the city of St-Jean. I'd criss-cross the streets, going in search of families or older people who weren't capable of staying in their homes any longer. We would take them to the shelters. And I also had to drive a number of people between the shelters and the local hospital. By the end of that week, my car was pretty beat up – the muffler and the bumpers especially. I took my car to a garage and began to hitchhike. Which is how I ended up catching a ride in an ambulance that had come all the way from northern Ontario to help us out. I found this so beautiful that I started to cry. My stress levels had built up so much that sitting there, in the ambulance, I cried like a child.

After we had to leave my mother's apartment, I drove her, my uncle, and my aunt to Montreal, where they were able to stay with my niece. But when we reached Montreal, the city was blacked out. I found the driving very difficult. None of the traffic lights was working, and to travel a relatively short distance, from the Jacques Cartier Bridge to the Olympic Stadium, took about an hour.

With the family safely installed in Montreal, I came back to St-Jean and arranged to stay in a convent, belonging to an order of nuns called the Servants of the Holy Sacrament. They were advanced in age, these nuns – I think their average age was eighty – and they left to stay outside the area. I was part of a group of five men and four women who stayed in the convent, and we became, if you like, the nucleus of the pastoral work for the entire city.

People didn't call on us simply for religious celebrations. We had a working telephone line that allowed people to get through in the event of an emergency or to make a special request. It also enabled those who were outside the area to get in touch with our community; somebody might phone from Manitoba, for example, and say, "My father's not in his home, can you find him?" Often we could. We could also provide counselling and psychological help. And we worked very closely with the CLSC – the community health centre.

Besides which, we helped put on shows. I have friends who are singers and performers, and we called on them to go into the shelters and old people's homes, and entertain the children in daycare centres. There was a need for festivity, humour, fun. One lady said to me, "Maurice, all my life I've dreamt of sleeping in a really huge bedroom. That's been my dream. And now, here I am, sleeping in a gymnasium with three hundred other people!" I found that so funny. I don't know how much sleep she actually got, because the volume of snoring was unbelievable.

One day we got the bishop, Monsignor Jacques Berthelet, to come and put his feet down in the real world. "Come with us," we said, "we're going to a shelter." And it was incredible, the way that people of a certain age reacted. They wanted to get close, they wanted to touch him, as though he were the Pope! He toured the shelter, and you could tell by looking into people's eyes that he was bringing them hope. Not that he was actually doing much! It was his sheer presence, a bit like when some players from the Montreal Canadiens visited a shelter. In a crisis like this, some people who rarely set foot in church will go back to their Catholic roots.

What hurt people's morale, in many cases, was that they didn't know what was going on. Communication was difficult. At the beginning, people thought the power outage might last for two or three days, and the instructions were to open the taps and let the water trickle out. Nobody was expecting the crisis to last three weeks. But then the instructions changed. At first, people thought, "Great, we'll have a party, it'll be just like old times!" A week later, two weeks later, it was becoming harder and harder to maintain any sense of conviviality. Where you had ten, twelve, fifteen people staying in a single home, lining up for a single toilet, there was an awful lot of friction.

I had a neighbour, the man who lived in the house directly opposite, who'd never spoken a word to me. Even when I said "Hello," he wouldn't reply. But during the ice storm, I discovered he wasn't mute after all. We talked to each other! That kind of thing happened a lot. As time passed, I think this area had a feeling of being isolated and misunderstood, especially since most of the insurance companies are located elsewhere. "Listen, sir, we've lived through an ice storm here!" "Oh, that's right," they would say, "you had an ice storm."

The psychological effects of the crisis have lasted a long time. In the fall of 1998, as winter was approaching, I could hardly have a single conversation without being asked, "So, do you think we'll have another ice storm?" This past winter, a lot of families made sure that they were very well supplied. There's a greater willingness to try and be self-sufficient.

Sometimes we'd hear elderly people say, "What have we done, to make God send us the ice storm?" Obviously it wasn't God who sent the ice storm, any more than God sent AIDS. I didn't find any anger directed against God, but I found a good deal of questioning. "How could God have allowed this to happen?" On a spiritual level, I'm convinced that many people took a real step forward thanks to the ice storm. We're very individualist in this society, we're not especially good at talking to each other, and a lot of our conversations are very superficial. But in many homes, during the ice storm, people really opened up to each other. They were able to express their true emotions. Terrible though the crisis was, it allowed people to grow.

Maurice Rainville moved to the neighbouring community of St-Bruno in the summer of 1999. He continues to work as a parish priest.

PATSY SWITZER

Thursday, January 15, 1998
Woke up this morning to do the usual rituals of making lunches, eating breakfast and getting ready for work. While doing this, we were listening to the radio and hearing how the people in London were rallying to donate time, goods and money to eastern Ontario and southern Quebec. We live in the hamlet of Wellburn, Ontario, midway between Stratford and London. Not a big community, but a community with a big heart.

As I'm listening, I look up to see my daughter Gayle looking at me. She says, "You're thinking, aren't you?" I ask, "Why do you say that?" She laughs, because she knows me so well.

You see, we've been hit by a bug. It's hard work, but the joyful feeling of helping others is contagious. You meet many a new friend this way, just because of the common goal. It started when Gayle went on a United Church expedition to Nicaragua last February, and then five of us were able to go out and help with the Winnipeg flood relief last June.

Now here was another disaster. Gayle headed out the door to catch the bus, and I mulled the matter over while getting ready for work.

Reverend Jean Baker's name popped into my head. She used to be our beloved minister, and she had now moved up to Christ United Church in Lyn, near Brockville. I decided to call her, and sure enough, she's involved. She was lucky and had lost hydro only for four days. But many of her people weren't so fortunate – it could be two to three weeks before some of them were getting any hydro.

I asked what could we do if we decided to do something. She said her people needed small batteries, flashlights, battery-operated radios, candles, matches, canned soups and meats, cereals, baby food (especially Pablum), toilet paper, diapers, sanitary products and personal hygiene products.

Our current minister, Reverend Rienk Vliestra, got the next phone call to see if he had heard of any other groups doing anything in this area. No, he hadn't. I asked if we could use the church if this project flew. He said yes. The next phone call went to Jean McRoberts, one of my close neighbours. Yes, she would do some phoning. We made up a list and the calls started. I put in a call to Ian McKay, who has a truck and trailer we might use. Ian had also made a trip to Winnipeg to help with the flood relief last June. Yes, he said, he would help.

Well, the project has begun. We may have a pickup-full, or maybe we'll fill that trailer. We'll see.

Friday, January 16
Ian and Jean and I were back and forth on the phone all day. It seems that this project is like a snowball, it is getting larger and larger. What have we got ourselves into?

One man phoned and donated about twenty cord of wood. A hardware store donated an overflowing shopping cart of supplies. I was able to pick up fifty boxes to use for packing. A friend of mine has already started collecting in her laundry room. After lunch found me collecting goods and dropping them off at the church. The pile is growing every time I go in the door.

Saturday, January 17
My day starts with a phone call at 7:16 from a man wanting to know if we could take down two small generators. So I phone Jean Baker and yes, the people are still crying for generators.

Spent much of the day at the church collecting the goods and sorting them as they arrived. People are also dropping in with cheques and cash. The cheques are going to the Salvation Army, the Red Cross, or the outreach program of the church where Jean is minister.

Sunday, January 18

My morning begins with a phone call to Jean Baker. Is there anything to add to the list? Yes, there is. We added motor oil, five-gallon gas cans, six-volt and nine-volt batteries, extension cords, and garbage bags. Wood is most welcome. Also salt and pepper shakers, pens and pencils, and coffee-cup lids, as they had run out. Jean told me that the emergency dining room had fed four hundred people yesterday. After talking to her, I called Tim Hortons in St. Marys, and they not only donated a thousand coffee-cup lids, but the cups as well.

We have collected close to nine hundred dollars in cash, so Jean McRoberts and a friend head off to do some shopping. The supplies started to roll in at the church and the sorting began. By the time it was over, we had about two hundred boxes packed and loaded onto the trailer. It was then loaded with wood and filled to the very back. Everyone, I think, was amazed that we as a community could have filled a forty-five-foot trailer.

At 8:35 P.M. we pulled out of Ian's laneway and were off. The weather was mostly good and the highway clear. Around 3:30 A.M. we parked the truck in the churchyard beside Jean Baker's home.

Monday, January 19

After a short chat with Jean, we caught a few hours of much-needed sleep. Ian wanted it noted that he got up first in the morning, and I might add not much earlier than myself.

Jean's neighbours, Jennie and Harold McNish, treated us to breakfast, chatting all the time about the storm and the devastation afterward. They told us how the area was grieving over the loss of a thirteen-year-old boy who died in a house fire trying to save the family dog. How one farmer had ordered a generator from Elmira, only to have the driver stop at a neighbour's to ask directions. The neighbour offered cash on the spot for the generator and bought it, thus creating hard feelings. How a Hydro man was working up a pole with a drill, and when the drill quit, the man thought he had somehow disconnected it. He came down the pole to discover the generator had been stolen.

Around 11:30 A.M. we met some friends of Jean's who led our truck to the village of North Augusta. We weren't allowed to travel down the direct road as about 130 hydro poles were down and workers were busy along that route.

The street in North Augusta was really rough, with potholes that had worked their way into the three-inch-thick ice that layered the street. We were directed to the community centre across from the fire hall. Army vehicles were parked here and there. A huge generator, along with a tall radio-receiving tower, was parked beside the fire hall, which had been turned into a command centre for the reserves.

First we unloaded the wood onto a site beside the community centre. Two-thirds of the trailer was loaded with wood, so it took some time. About a dozen young men helped unload the trailer. We were asked if we had had lunch – no, we hadn't – and we were taken over to the Masonic Hall where a cafeteria had been set up.

I went back into the centre to see what was to be left there of the goods, and to take some pictures. I asked one lady's permission and when people had their backs to me, I took a picture, only to find another lady flying out to me upset that I had taken it. I guess they had problems with photographers from newspapers and magazines, and this bothered the people waiting for food. I assured her that my picture was for personal use only, and that I was with the trailer out front. She calmed down and I put the camera away.

By three-thirty the goods were all unloaded. Everything was going to be used. We stopped for coffee and cookies, and then it was time to be escorted back to the church. We had time for a short nap before supper.

At about six we met for a dinner put on by the church directors and their wives. While we were eating, different people would get up and tell their stories. They told of how the storm had drawn families and neighbours together, how the kids worked just as hard as the parents, how some Mennonites from the Listowel area came in to show farmers how to milk cows by hand. How farmers now have swollen hands from milking that way.

One lady told of their twenty-five to thirty cows having to be milked at midnight and noon, because that was when they would have their turn at a generator that was also servicing five other families. She told of how their six children would automatically get up at the sound of it coming down the lane, because they knew that a lot had to be done while the generator was there. They also cooked their meals in the milk house while they still had power. They were lucky so far: they had lost only one cow.

As these people talked, you could tell that they had been through a lot in the last few days, days that just seem to stretch on and on. There were tears in their eyes as they told of their losses, and everyone there had lost something. Yet they had gained something too. Their community is closer now. They know each other better.

It was 7:30 P.M. when we got on the road. The travelling wasn't too bad and we rolled in home about 2:30 A.M. Seven hours each way, and a good feeling of a job well done.

Patsy Switzer is a wife, mother, and insurance agent living in Wellburn, Ontario.

NANCY BILLARD

It was during those few unforgettable icy days in January that I was awakened. Mother Nature had taken away the warmth and the light, taken it all, every last trimming, and left us to fend for ourselves in the bareness of it all. And so we were bared too – stripped down to our very souls, and exposed to our neighbours for all that we were.

The demons among us were soon revealed, but so too were the pure of heart, for I am sure I witnessed angels at work. Sure as Scrooge was visited by the ghosts of Christmas, this cynic-under-construction was visited by angels.

For years I sat on my moral high horse. A Newfoundlander transplanted to central Canada eight years ago, I seldom witnessed the neighbourly transactions that are a way of life in the remote village where I come from.

I have suffered many growing pains since my arrival here. I have seen eyebrows raised when I dropped in, unannounced, to visit new friends. I saw my co-workers' smiling but puzzled expressions when my mother, who'd never met them, knit each of them a pair of winter socks one Christmas. I sensed hesitation in voices when I called friends to inquire about their downtrodden, faceless relatives.

Because not everyone is subtle, I finally clued in. These people think my behaviour strange!

I quickly learned not to do those things, at least not on a regular basis. I went kicking and screaming, but eventually I did as the Romans. This became painfully apparent when I returned to the island a couple of years later. I had learned so well that you always call before visiting, you always knock before entering, that I succeeded in puzzling a whole other group of people with my new behaviour. "Have you been gone so long that you believe you cannot come without all this foolishness of formality?"

It was like I was lost somewhere between two worlds.

I remember my mother telling me the story of her grandfather, who perished in the cold aboard a dory. He was one of nine men who had left their tiny outport community during the Depression to row to the larger village twenty-three miles away in one small boat, so as to get food from the supply ship. He froze to death before he arrived back home.

My father tells the story of his father's brother, Arthur, who was so full of stones they protruded through his groin. The only medical attention he received was on the rare occasion of the arrival of the hospital boat. Dad said you could always hear him screaming out in pain as you walked by the house. When he finally succumbed to this torturous condition, at the age of twenty-three, they buried him in a child's casket because he died doubled up in pain.

No wonder Newfoundlanders cling so close to each other. Their souls have been linked together through their suffering, sewn together with the sharpest needles and the strongest thread. But the angels I saw were not from Newfoundland. They were seen right here in Brockville in the midst of all our devastation.

One was the wife of a firefighter. I suspect that much of her empathy is a product of the tales she has heard from her husband, but she was obviously, very naturally, full of goodness. She called me at the newspaper where I worked after reading a story about an eighty-three-year-old widow whose nightgown caught fire as she reached over a candle. The lady was now at Kingston General Hospital, suffering from burns to 20 percent of her body.

The firefighter's wife had never met the lady, but had heard through the grapevine that her blind dog, photographed in the newspaper, was

The lady who owned this blind dog died in hospital after suffering severe burns.
She was able to see a copy of this photograph an hour before her death.
(Photo: Brockville Recorder & Times*)*

like a child to her. Very graciously she requested a rush order of the photo so she could take it to the lady.

We gave her the photograph. She took it to the lady in hospital. The burned lady passed away an hour after she received the photo.

I told one of our editors about the Good Samaritan and he called her. She thanked him but refused to have any part of being mentioned in the paper. "That's not why I did it," she said.

And that was that. Just like most Newfoundlanders, she did it without ever expecting to be talked about. It was automatic for her.

Another angel was pumping gas. It was evening and I was driving around town to all the funeral homes to collect the accumulation of death notices resulting from the newspaper going four days without a publication.

The indicator on my gas gauge was in the red as I approached an unlit gas station. Most gas stations were closed because without electricity the pumps didn't work, so I thought myself extremely lucky when I noticed signs of life at this one. There was another vehicle being serviced, and the lady attendant was just hanging up the nozzle. I pulled up as the other vehicle was pulling away.

The attendant looked at me disappointedly and gave me the bad news. "I just sold the last of the gas. I'm completely out.

"But wait a second," she said, after she'd paused to think. She went inside the Mr. Gas convenience store and brought out a little jerry can.

"Here, you can have my gas. It won't get you far but it's all I have."

She assured me repeatedly that she didn't need it and refused to take any money for it, saying she didn't know how much gas was in the container. I told her my name and said I would settle up with her somehow, later, but I don't think she really cared about that.

These were only two of many random acts of kindness I witnessed in this province of Ontario in its time of suffering. It became clear to me that Ontarians, like Newfoundlanders, are willing to help at such times, and that maybe, if they had been exposed to the same conditions as Newfoundlanders, it would be apparent in their daily behaviour as well. It was also clear that Ontarians were excited about what was taking place, and many commented that although the storm was devastating, it brought people together in a way they'd never seen.

I was happy to have been a part of it as well, for it not only restored my faith in humanity, it taught me a powerful lesson in humility.

Nancy Billard is a freelance writer living in Brockville, Ontario.

6

A JOB TO DO

any years ago, I read and was puzzled by a scene in Graham Greene's memoir Ways of Escape. Greene was working as a fire-watcher in central London during the terrible air raids of April 1941, when Nazi bombs fell indiscriminately across the city. He described the Blitz and his own reactions with a sort of passionate concentration not far short of actual delight. "Standing on the roof of a garage we saw the flares come slowly floating down, dribbling their flames: they drift like great yellow peonies."

Weird, I thought at the time. Never having had much experience of danger, I failed to grasp the terror of inaction — the awfulness of merely waiting while life cracked apart on all sides. Fear grows from helplessness. Now, at last, I think I understand how Greene could keep himself going while the bombs rained on his beloved city: he knew he had a job to perform. The fire watch gave a structure, a meaning to his otherwise random observations of London under attack.

When the ice storm came, I was lucky: I could take a day off, as our home was ill-prepared. But I was doubly lucky, for after that first day I had a job to go to: an office with powered computers, hot coffee, and colleagues with whom I could trade rumours and information. Writing news articles and features about the ice storm meant I could tell myself that I was needed. In a larger sense, of course, my words were totally unnecessary: they weren't saving lives or rebuilding power lines. But the job gave me a sense of purpose I will always be grateful for.

This chapter has no complaints in it. The stories it tells are of people who worked through the ice storm, sometimes over brutally long hours. They experienced fatigue and anxiety — but they were never helpless. If they seem proud of their work, they have every reason to be so. But I wonder if all of them realize how fortunate they were.

JOAN FOSTER

I was the head nurse in Home Care at the community health centre – the CLSC, to use the Quebec term – in N.D.G. and Montreal West during the ice storm. Nowhere in my job description was there an outline of how to proceed during this type of event. We had a disaster plan on paper, and had held a few mock events, but the real thing is very different. Both professional and personal stories stick out in my mind. Three are especially vivid, and have really changed the way I function.

I remember when we placed one of our elderly ladies in a shelter and notified her family, who lived out of town, that she was safe and being cared for. After a few days her family braved the elements and drove to Montreal to pick her up, and to return to their Ontario home with her for the duration of the crisis and its cleanup. When her son arrived at the shelter – she was over ninety, and he was probably in his sixties – she was sitting on an army cot, reading a story to a child. Other children were playing around her feet. Her son was happy to see her, and told her that he was there to take her back to his warm and quiet home. She looked up at her son and said, "Oh dear, I wish you had called first. This is the most fun I've had for years! I hope you won't mind, but I would like to stay here. I don't want to go home with you." The son approached the social worker and nurse at the shelter, and together they spoke with the lady, but she was determined to stay. Her son drove home alone.

This event really brought home to us the isolation that so many seniors are feeling today. All the health-care dollars in the world will not meet the need for the friendly touch of a neighbour. If only we could bottle all that community care that developed during the ice storm and sprinkle it periodically on our society, when we appear to be returning to our private hurried ways!

In the first few days, I was working eighteen to twenty hours per day, and my wonderful husband, who is a professor at McGill University, was my driver. Bill was busy driving my nurses here and there, as there was nowhere to park; he was also delivering supplies to the shelters; and he was taking seniors too frail for shelters to long-term centres in the east end of Montreal, where there was power and heat. Around Thursday, when we had a quiet moment together, I asked him how he thought his international graduate students were faring. We really hadn't had a moment to think up to then.

We started to find the graduate students for whom Bill was faculty advisor. Some were in residence at McGill, safe and warm, but there was one student here from Fiji with his pregnant wife in an apartment downtown. The odd busy sound of his telephone told us his line was down (we were getting to be experts with this sound), so we decided to drive downtown and check if they were at home or somewhere safe. When Bill arrived at their apartment – it was a small building, a walk-up of about eight apartments – he found them huddled under one blanket in the middle of the room. There were newspapers on the windows and a tin of tuna open in front of them. It was very cold. Bill asked why they were still there and not in a shelter. Jonah looked at Bill and – without any knowledge that what he was about to say would knock Bill off his feet – replied, "Why would we leave? Isn't this winter?" With an electric radio as their only source of communication, this poor couple had no idea what was going on. When they were leaving Fiji to come to Montreal for the year, everyone had said that they were crazy, considering Canada's winters. Having no concept of a "normal winter," they had no idea that this was a huge gap from the norm.

We bundled them into the car and brought them to our house, where we have a woodburning stove, and they stayed with us for the remainder of the storm and its aftermath. Jonah stayed on to finish his studies but I'm afraid it was too much for Emma, who was five months pregnant; she returned to Fiji as soon as a flight could be arranged. I must add that one of Montreal's top neo-natal physicians came to our house to make sure that Emma and the baby were well after three days of being alone in the apartment before we found them. When I telephoned him, there was no hesitation in his voice: no, we weren't to bring her out to the hospital, he would come to our house. Eventually a healthy baby girl was born, and all the family are well and thriving in Fiji. But I wonder, how many new Canadians had no idea that this whole crisis was abnormal?

The final story shows how much we have come to rely on modern technology. At the health centre there was no generator and we lost all our computers. Keeping track of which senior was where was a nightmare, especially as shelters opened and then closed and people were moved around. Families from all over the world were calling to find out where their parents were, but our normal database was down. Yellow "stick 'ems" on makeshift bulletin boards – our windows – became our source of information. We used one window for each shelter, and moved the papers around. My Girl Guide training came into play as we practised survival techniques and put our sleeping bags into garbage bags to retain our body heat. The final insult on the Friday was when we couldn't find a sharp pencil. All our sharpeners were electric, and we had to resort to kitchen knives to sharpen pencils. I did not think that I was so dependent on technology!

Joan Foster is a nurse in Montreal.

BRUCE WYLIE

The ice storm started on a Monday. It's not unusual to have a day of freezing rain, and the forecast was for warmer temperatures the next day. Day two came, and it was still freezing rain. But again the forecast was that it would warm up.

There's a subplot here, and it's very personal. I'm the host of *The Bruce Wylie Show* on CFJR in Brockville, and that Friday morning, forty-seven of us were going to leave for a weekend in New York City. I'd arranged a bus trip back in the fall, and I'd picked January 9, 10, and 11 as the days. So in the back of my mind as this is all unfolding, I'm thinking, "I don't really care, because the weather's fine in New York City and I'm going to be down there pretty soon."

Wednesday arrived, and it was okay in the daytime but it started to rain again in the evening. By then the ice was building up on the branches. I can remember sitting downstairs at my computer and hearing this sound, like the rain beating against a window. And I thought, "Boy, the wind is really blowing tonight." Outside my window, all of a sudden there was this crash. I got up to look and it was a branch that had come down off one of my trees out front. And I realized what I'd been hearing wasn't the rain – it was the sound of branches falling all over.

I thought, "My goodness sake, this is a lot worse than I thought." So on Thursday morning I got up a little early – usually I'm up at four twenty-five, and at the station at five – but that day I got up about five minutes to four. I just sensed it was going to be a busy morning. Well, I got into work and there were so many messages on our answering machine that it was full.

I was hurt by some of the messages. Hurt because they were saying, "You bill yourself as the information station – well, we've lost our power and we want to know what's going on." About halfway through the messages was one from a school superintendent, calling to say that not only were the buses cancelled, the schools were closed. Now that's really unusual, because schools lose their grant money – I mean, they just don't do that on a regular basis. So we knew we were in a severe storm. But again, the weather forecast was saying, "Warmer temperatures coming."

My show goes on the air at six o'clock and it lasts till ten. The station broadcasts through the night, but from a satellite, so there's no live person in the building. That morning I started giving time checks earlier, from about five-thirty. I wasn't even thinking about the scope of what was about to happen – just that if the power's out, people are going to want to know what time it is. We were fine till about five minutes to seven, and then our power went out at the radio station.

And again, I've got to tell you, in my own heart I wasn't thinking that this is a long period of time. The power had gone out before, maybe for a couple of hours, and then everything was back to normal. The underlying thought in my mind was still the trip to New York City – because I'm the promoter of this trip, and if it doesn't go ahead, I'm going to be out twenty thousand dollars. I'm being very selfish here, in part of my brain.

It was sometime in that hour, between seven and eight, that we got a call from the Brockville Public Utilities Commission. Gord Aimer's words were, "There's lines down everywhere. We could be out for days." I happened to be the one who answered that phone call, and I said, "*Days?* This is a city – you don't go out for days in a city!"

We have a backup generator at the station, and when we got that call, a couple of the guys went out to boost the batteries. It meant scraping an inch and a half of ice off one of the station trucks to back it into the building over the snow and the ice to charge the generator up. It was about twenty minutes after eight when we were back on the air. And thank heavens, CFJR stayed on the air continuously, with our backup generator, until the power came back Sunday morning. We did not lose even a minute. It took a tremendous effort by the engineering staff to make sure we had gas for the generator.

I don't know why our tower didn't fall. We're the oldest radio station in the area – we've been on the air since 1926 – so why did every other radio and television tower go down, when little CFJR's stayed up? Our tower is outside of Lyn, a little village not far from Brockville. The power was out there too, but we have a generator at the tower. So we had to keep two generators going. Our sister station on FM was off for several days, because their tower was damaged.

So that morning we went back on air, but we still didn't understand the severity of it all. From six to nine o'clock, my show is your typical morning show – a lot of information, a lot of weather, the sports, the news – but after the nine o'clock news I do a talk show every day. I probably had a guest lined up who wasn't going to make it in, so we had to fly by the seat of our pants. I asked Dave Hunter to join me – he's one of the guys from FM – and we just opened the phone lines up.

And it was during that hour that I started to sense the severity of what was going on. I asked people to call and tell me where they were, so we could get a scope of where the power was out. And we had the mayor come on, too.

I've been at this station for twenty-eight years, and one thing I'm very proud of is the working relationship that I've established with the civic officials. Call it a trusting relationship. If they tell me not to say something, I won't. Now the mayor, Ben TeKamp, had been in office only since the beginning of December, but he was absolutely incredible. His calming words of confidence really helped to ease the situation. We arranged a regular schedule for him and the police chief to come on.

Normally at ten o'clock I would have gone off the air. But I said to the guy who was following me, "I'll stay on." I wanted to keep the talk show going. My boss came in and he said, "How long are you going to stay on?" I said, "As long as it takes." I would have stayed twenty-four hours that day if I'd had to.

Noon hour came and my boss said, "I want you to take an hour's break." We went to our national news package for the hour while I rested, grabbed a bite to eat and regrouped myself – it had been a pretty intense seven hours. I also phoned home. My wife was sitting at home with our three sons. Her comment to me was, "When are you coming home? We need you here." I said, "Why do you need me? Is everything okay?" I said, "I know there's no power in the house, but honey, I really can't come home. I think I'm needed here more." Then I went back and I stayed on air till six or seven o'clock at night.

When I went back on, I knew we couldn't go to music – the last thing in the world I could picture myself doing if I were sitting at home in a crisis situation is listening to a song. I think people wanted the reassurance of at least hearing a voice. And maybe hearing that others were going through the same thing.

Thursday, Friday, Saturday, everybody was in the same boat. There was no power anywhere. And it was Thursday, as the late afternoon came on, that I realized the scope of what was going on. We got calls from Morrisburg to the east, Gananoque to the west, and north as far up as Smiths Falls and Kemptville. Of course we knew that a good portion of Quebec was out, but now we were getting calls from northern New York State. The radio stations down there had lost power, and we had state troopers calling to give us updates.

One thing that was really interesting were the calls I got from people who'd been phoning their insurance companies in Belleville and areas west. In Belleville they weren't experiencing any of this. So you'd talk to an agent in Belleville and say, "I've got water in my basement, is that covered?" The agent would say, "No, it's not covered." The agents just didn't realize what was happening here. These people were phoning me, and they were angry.

We were getting lots of calls now. One phone call would spark another, and so on. We have ten lines into the radio station, and at the height of the storm I would guesstimate we were taking upwards of fifty calls an hour on each of those lines. The lucky thing was that not many of the phone lines went down. When I came home Thursday night, we sat around and talked, and I phoned the travel agent about the New York trip. They said, "No problem, we can cancel things," and that eased my mind. I mean, nobody was going anywhere.

Thursday was a learning experience. I went to bed early on Thursday evening, maybe seven-thirty or eight o'clock, and I got up at three-thirty or four and headed back into the station. I went on the air at five o'clock and stayed on till six or seven o'clock at night. People think I did twenty-four hours – I didn't, I did twelve- or thirteen- or fourteen-hour days. But I'm not downplaying the feat. That was straight through! Besides, you've got to remember, when I'm talking on the morning show and I break for a song, I've got three or four minutes to gather my thoughts. In the ice storm, I'm breaking for nothing! In essence, we didn't have any ads. I threw the odd public service announcement on, just to give myself a break.

Friday morning, I decided I had to get organized. I went into the control room and I said, "This is going to be the column for people that need wood. This is going to be the column for people that need generators. And so on." Which was great from five o'clock till about seven o'clock. I was only answering two lines, and the newsroom was answering one. But when other people showed up and we opened more of the lines, all of a sudden, there's ten lines being answered. Well, guess what, there's now nine people bringing stuff in to me! I've got my notes that I'm trying to keep, and I'm just having note after note dropped on me.

And this is all while we're talking on the air. People would say to me, "Are you listening?" And I'd have to say, "Yes, I am, but I'm also listening to somebody in one ear talking about some other emergency." People were asking, "Is there a gas station open? Where can we get propane?" I'd throw that out and we'd get calls in on the other eight or nine lines. Somebody would say, "You just passed out a number for propane, can you give me that number again?" Eventually I had to say, "If you didn't get that number the first time, it's too late. Because some-body else got the number."

I never thought of the impact we would have. And if I have one regret, I wish I had been able to step outside and watch what was going on in the community. For example, say the Quickie would phone and say, "We have a shipment of propane tanks coming in." So I'd say, "The Quickie at William and Pearl Street is going to have a shipment of propane tanks at 1:30 P.M." At 1:25 there would be absolute mayhem at the place, and at 1:35 they would phone back and say they were sold out. A hundred propane tanks gone in five minutes! I tell you, I would not want to be a merchant who price-gouged in this area. And I honestly believe none of them did.

For the first four or five days, CFJR went non-stop, twenty-four hours a day talk. That was quite a feat! Monday at noon hour, the power was beginning to come back in the community and we started playing some songs again. In that second week, I went on from five till the noon hour, nothing but talk, just taking call after call after call. After the first four days, we still kept the station going through the night, even if it was just with music, and we did that for the people without power.

My wife and kids stayed at home for the first day. The second day, they decided to work. Eileen answered the phone at the station; my son Danny came on the air with me, he's a student and wants to go into radio; my other two sons went to CJs, where the Hydro headquarters had been set up, cleaning dishes, washing the walls, whatever it took. This house was freezing cold and we're on a well, so we had no water, but basically we were only here for a few hours at a time.

I don't think I ever told my listeners about my own experiences. What I'm most proud of, you know, is the fact that I learned to listen. I accepted whatever people called in with, and I didn't criticize them. Talk-show hosts have a reputation for being pretty rough-edged. Not in a small town as much as a big city – but I could still snap at people if I didn't think they had a legitimate point. In the ice storm, I just felt that people needed an opportunity to talk to somebody.

I remember one lady phoned in from Spencerville. I guess the phone call from Spencerville to Maitland is a dollar-fifty or two dollars, and she said, "I had to phone five times a day for the last few days! Who's going to pay for my phone bill?" Well, I didn't have to answer her. People themselves would answer complaints like that. "That lady thinks she's got a problem? I'm a dairy farmer and I'm throwing out five hundred dollars' worth of milk a day!" I realized what people were going through, and I tried to take everybody as equal. I'm a Christian, I have a strong faith in God, and I think God gave me the extra strength.

The power came back on Sunday morning, both at my house and the station. Saturday, Father Hibbard from the Catholic church came over to the station and wanted to know if we'd announce that they wouldn't have Saturday mass but that they would have a mass on the Sunday morning. I said, "Father, let's go one step further. Let's do a morning service on the air." I had Eileen phone a couple of the ministers I know, and they went on air with Father Hibbard, having very quickly put something together. That was something else that people tell us was really moving and helpful.

The power came on almost immediately after the church service. And even though I'm a religious man, I do not believe for a moment that the timing was anything other than a fluke.

From that point on, over the next few days, was my hardest time. Hardest because I was happy for the people that were phoning to say the power was on – but I also felt for all the others. I felt the emotion of every caller. If somebody called and was happy, I was happy. But I tried not to be overly joyous. If they called and were sad, I felt their sadness. I felt their anxiety.

You see, Thursday, Friday and Saturday, nobody had power. So there were no complaints. People were not expecting anything. But as soon as the power came on, there was a separation.

Some people went back to normal life right away. Plants in Brockville started to call and say, "Staff can report back to work." We got some irate calls about that, too, from people in the fringe areas: "What do they expect us to do, leave our homes?" The excitement of the power coming back was great for Brockville. But you got to remember, in all the surrounding areas there was nothing happening. As the days went by, people became antsy. It would be, "My neighbour's got power – how come I don't have power?" From Monday on, there was still helpfulness. But there was also anger.

I did not have the immediate answers. I would tell them that. I would assure them that if the reeve called, I would ask about their particular area. But in most instances, the reeve didn't know either. One lesson that I think has been learned from this is that the reeves really have to know their municipality, every nook and cranny of it. Because you have to be able to answer to your people.

On the Wednesday, at about ten o'clock, I got a call from a lady who was looking for a particular type of wick for a lantern. She lived in a trailer park out in North Augusta – the area that was, potentially, not going to get power for a month or six weeks. I think it turned out to be only three weeks. Anyway, she needed this wick and she couldn't leave her house. She announced it on the radio, phoned me back about half an hour later, and she'd had ten people out with wicks already.

This particular Wednesday, I finished at noon. And as I was leaving the station at twelve-thirty, this guy comes up to me. He's got a wick. I didn't have the heart to tell him that the lady had called back and that she had more than enough wicks. I thanked him and I told him, "You know what, I'm going to drive it out to her." Eileen and I hopped in the car – I hadn't been out to North Augusta to see all the damage – and we found our way to the trailer park. There was this lady on crutches – she definitely couldn't have gone anywhere – and she gave me the biggest hug you could imagine. By then she had about twenty-five wicks, enough wicks to last her for an eternity.

For his work in the ice storm, Bruce Wylie was named 1998 Broadcaster of the Year by the Ontario Broadcasters Association.

PHIL NORTON

Power outages are an accepted part of life for residents in the Châteauguay Valley, southwest of Montreal. And ice storms are nothing new either, especially to the highland homes in the Can-Am border region. Although I now reside in the urban environs of Châteauguay, I lived through and photographed many an ice storm while living twelve years in the apple country on Covey Hill.

Rural folk know well that a disaster can fall suddenly from the sky in the form of freezing rain and isolate them for many days. When fallen trees would block roads and bring down telephone and electric lines, my neighbours were quick to get to work with chainsaws to clear the path. Then we would gather around a farmhouse kitchen table with candles, playing cards and drinking a bit of gin, and wait for the Hydro crews to reconnect us to the outside world. Despite the inconveniences, there was always something special about those storms – the outdoor tranquility, the indoor camaraderie, the sharing of resources, and the common feeling of victory when all returned to normal.

So when freezing rain struck in January 1998, and some trees fell and the lights went out at my home in the city, why should I think it was going to be any different? As usual, I snapped a few photos of frozen maple branches and street crews sawing up and clearing tree debris, with no inkling that history was in the making. As the lights stayed out, and our house grew colder and reports of widespread devastation were coming in, it became obvious that I would have to get out to photograph this event. But as much as I wished to return to the rural area and my former Covey Hill neighbours (who faced a much graver prognosis from Hydro-Québec than we did), I set my own family's comfort and survival as a higher priority.

Our street lost power for eleven days. We were fortunate to find lodging a few blocks away with friends who had a gas stove. With our nine-month-old baby and our pet turtle in tow, my wife and I moved in with the Rowats and a few other refugees they had invited. Meanwhile, I made regular visits back to our freezing house to feed our cat, drain the pipes, clear fallen branches, and pack frozen meats in the ice outside. Getting out to photograph history maybe wasn't the last thing on my mind, but changing diapers by candlelight, cooking on the gas grill and chopping ice out of the driveway took precedence. My wife, who is a church minister, and usually the one giving help to others, admitted that the tables were now turned: we needed help.

With a weariness of body and spirit, I managed to push myself out the door in the early days of the ice storm to make a random photographic record. The pictures that resulted fail to convey the physical difficulty involved in making a simple shot. For instance, to get a photo of a parking lot of ice-covered cars, I had to negotiate a sloped surface of ice. Using my heavy camera bag as an anchor, I proceeded toward my subjects with cautious steps. For another shot, I slid down a frozen bank to get close and then realized that the only way out was up. With the soft heel of my rubber boots, I managed to break the ice enough with each step to get out.

Meanwhile, the freezing drizzle created havoc on the camera equipment. Lenses quickly became soaked, and required constant wiping before each shot. For a much published photo of the "Ice Chrysler," I pulled the camera from under my coat, clicked one frame, then zipped the camera back in and walked on. Under normal circumstances, when

I see a potentially good photo I fire off several frames at different angles and different exposures to be sure I've captured it.

Cold and moisture can also cause the electrical systems of modern cameras to fail. When this occurs, I use a manual shutter setting and an estimated exposure. Exposures in the rain were extremely long due to the dim light, and required a steady hand. Photographers also had to be careful as limbs and wires were crashing to the ground all around us.

Changing film was a challenge, too. It was nearly impossible to do in the rain, because the smallest drop of water on the film could cause it to stick inside the camera, against the back. But if the operation was performed in a warm car, then the cold lens or cold film could fog.

Without experience, needless to say, the logistics and technical demands of photography in bad weather could spoil any creative initiatives. Thus, the ice storm of 1998 required tremendous expertise of photojournalists, as well as exceptional willpower and stamina. But for all the hype over the photographers' heroic efforts, Dave Sidaway of the Montreal *Gazette* (who had more photos in *The Ice Storm* than any other photographer) told me, "People don't realize that this is the sort of thing we live for."

The staff shooters carry out their regular assignments each day without fanfare, but when history happens, they are prepared to leap into action and capture it with endurance and a creative eye. Being prepared to record history means, first, recognizing that history is actually happening. Because this disaster arrived insidiously, some photographers missed it completely. Even those whose work appears in *The Ice Storm* wish, in hindsight, that they had shot more. Like fishermen, we can all describe the big ones that got away – the prizewinning shots we could have had if only we'd had the time or the energy to park, shoot and ask people's names.

Among the photojournalists from various news media, ice storm anecdotes abound. Staffers at the Montreal newspaper *La Presse* recount one about their colleague who was assigned a photo to illustrate the danger of chopping ice from rooftops. The next day he went onto his own roof anyway and promptly slid off, breaking a bone.

As the stock-photo administrator for the *Gazette*, I saw firsthand how the storm caught the interest of the world. My department transmitted the pictures everywhere – literally – over the next several months. Magazine and textbook publishers, film producers, insurance companies, law firms and corporate annual reports wanted our disaster images.

But for photographers, it was the publication of *The Ice Storm* that became a source of pride and a symbol of our contribution to the community. We were out there in blizzard winds with the Hydro crews; we were with the crowds in the shelters and shared their feelings of discouragement; we captured it all on film, so that what we felt and saw is what will allow generations to collectively remember the Ice Storm of 1998.

In spite of looking after his family during the crisis, Phil Norton succeeded in taking many superb pictures. More than ten of them were published in The Ice Storm.

GHISLAINE ARCHAMBAULT

We sent out the first press release from the hospital on the evening of Tuesday, January 6. But at that time, we had no idea how serious the crisis would be, or how long it would last. In one of our buildings, the Hôtel-Dieu, an emergency generator had been in use since the power went out at nine that morning – but the power had come back at 4 P.M. Little did we know that it would go again the next day, and stay out for twenty-one days.

The hospital serves a population of 110,000, not just in the city of St-Hyacinthe but also in the smaller centres and rural areas around. Being part of the famous "triangle of darkness," it was one of the worst-hit regions in all of Quebec. The crisis stretched us to our limits, and beyond.

I moved out of my home and into the hospital – I slept in a little room up on the tenth floor. Most days I would get up at five in the morning, because the journalists would start phoning at six or six-thirty. Often I did many interviews a day, as well as writing the press releases and serving on the support committee for our staff. Most of the interviews, especially the ones for TV, I never got to see. We worked very closely with the local radio station – during the crisis, local radio became a crucial force.

At first we were asked to provide refuge to as many as 150 older people in the Hôtel-Dieu. But the need was so great that within a week the number was up to 400. The chapel in the Hôtel-Dieu is extremely beautiful – we turned it into a shelter. At the same time we were giving shelter to many of our own personnel and to ambulance drivers as well. And of course, we had to carry on with the medical work. The army provided us with camp beds, because we didn't have enough hospital beds for everyone to sleep on. We reopened wards that had been closed because of budget cuts in the previous years. Somehow we made it through.

For the older people, especially, it wasn't just a question of meeting their physical needs – it was also very important to help them maintain a sense of personal dignity. We bent the rules where necessary. I remember we gave shelter to one old lady who refused to leave her freezing-cold home unless she could bring her cat with her. So the cat came too.

We did everything we could to give people a feeling of calm and security. The hospital's cafeteria became a gathering place – we realized how important it was to be able to provide people with a good cup of coffee. We established a daycare centre, staffed by family members and hospital employees. We managed to create a hairdressing service and a system for getting cash, because none of the bank machines were functional. We had performers come in – clowns and magicians, a country-and-western singer, a Dixieland day, even a mariachi band.

What was so good about it, looking back, was the openness to new ideas and the openness to other people. Why can't we be like that all the time?

Every day would bring a new challenge, and you could never predict what it would be. We never stopped. We never had time to reflect, because the situation kept changing. One day it might be the influenza. Another day it might be the generators needing urgent maintenance, or the lack of orthopedists, or problems with the laundry system, or the ice chunks that fell from the eleventh floor and broke through the Plexiglas in the emergency ward.

When it was announced that we'd be without power until at least January 25, morale fell. You could feel it. Finally we had to say, "Don't think about the twenty-fifth of January. Just keep going." Then soon after that, the influenza epidemic began. And it lasted four or five days.

These performers visited the big hospital in St-Hyacinthe in an effort to raise spirits during the long weeks of darkness.

By Wednesday the twenty-first, we had more than 170 cases of influenza in the hospital, mostly among the older people. So we had to put the hospital on an emergency footing, mainly as a preventative measure. Visiting was kept to a minimum, and when visitors were in a patient's room they had to wear surgical masks. The army helped us vaccinate everyone against influenza as fast as possible.

That was the week when I put out a really unusual press release. Instead of beginning with the latest facts, it started like this:

"Yes, there's fatigue. Yes, most of us are still displaced from our homes. Yes, we're still working very hard. Yes, the children are still out of school. Yes, we're worried about our homes. Yes, there's ice all over the place and we can't even go for a good walk . . . *but we're getting over the flu and the overcrowding.* Yes, the food is excellent. Yes, we've been able to keep the premises clean. Yes, our support staff is exceptional. Yes, our teams of health-care workers and volunteers are showing tremendous kindness and doing tremendous work. Yes, our morale is fantastic."

During this whole time, I only took one day off from work. I packed my little suitcase and went home. That was when I really saw and understood what other people in St-Hyacinthe were going through. Before then, you see, I hadn't been out in the city – I'd been in the hospital the whole time! It was good to be home but it didn't feel right: my place was with the management team. I was there twenty-four hours a day. We ate, we slept a little, we were surrounded by our friends and colleagues – but mostly, we worked.

I saw very little of my husband during the crisis. He's a pharmacist in St-Hyacinthe, and he had to work long hours every second day. I have a picture of him, still wearing his white smock to work when his colleagues were dressed in winter coats. I called him "my Daniel Boone." He stayed at home. He went out in search of wood, he looked after the house and the fireplace. He was in survival mode.

We each respected what the other was doing and how the other was living. But I found that he was deeply affected by the crisis. For several weeks, we were on completely different tracks. I'm very effervescent and outgoing, I always have lots of adrenalin in my system, and in the crisis I was always busy with other people – whereas he became withdrawn. He was alone so much of the time in those weeks that he was thrown back on himself. Afterwards, he was so tired that he needed a tremendous amount of sleep. It was something we had to get through as a couple. But in April we went to Italy together for a holiday, and that was good.

In the middle of February, when everything was back to normal, the hospital management invited seven hundred people to the Hôtel Gouverneur in St-Hyacinthe for a super party. It was an emotional release for us, and well worth the cost. We had an orchestra and everyone danced – we even had a simulated blackout! We gave out souvenir brochures and ice storm medals. Through the crisis, we had developed a tremendous solidarity – the mayor said we were like a beacon of light to the community. The party helped this feeling carry on.

Ghislaine Archambault is in charge of communications for the Réseau-Santé Richelieu-Yamaska in St-Hyacinthe, Quebec.

MARCEL COULOMBE

I'm a hydro lineman for Detroit Edison. But I come from Montreal. I left in May 1966 and went to work in Chicago, then Indiana. I ended up in Detroit at Christmas of '67 and I've been working for Detroit Edison for more than thirty years.

We saw about the ice storm on TV and I talked to my family on the phone – they all live around Montreal. On the Saturday I talked to my brother-in-law and I said, "We'll never go there, it's six hundred miles away." That night a guy from the company called me and said, "D'you want to go to Montreal?" I thought he was joking.

We left about six on the Sunday morning. There was a convoy of about thirty-five trucks, maybe sixty people in all, driving up the 401. The first night, we all stayed in the Ottawa area. Then half the crews went directly to the South Shore and the other half of us stayed in the Ottawa Valley, working near Montebello on the Quebec side. We formed into ten crews, with three or four guys per crew. The group I was with were pretty much all American. But there were four or five other linemen originally from Montreal who came back up. A lot of us moved there in the '60s for work.

I'd never seen anything as bad as this ice storm, and I've worked in several tornadoes in the Midwest. I had seen the pictures, but I was still surprised – the pictures didn't tell the whole story. Usually you have several poles down, but you never see fifty miles of poles, all down. It was an experience!

We stayed in Ottawa for a week and then we moved on to St-Césaire, on the South Shore, where there was much more damage. One thing all the linemen said was, they couldn't believe how they were treated by the people. People were super nice. You'd pull up at the door and they'd be smiling.

At first I stayed at the Governors' Hotel in Ottawa. Some of the guys got to stay at the Château Montebello! But when we moved to St-Césaire, it was totally different. We stayed at a cross-country ski lodge near Bromont, thirty-five miles away from where we were working. They had power in the lodge, but there was no restaurant, no TV in the little rooms, nothing fancy at all. But hey, everybody was tired. We were there to work.

The army has a college at St-Césaire and they set up a food line. So we'd have our meals with the army. They had a big tank generator that powered the college. Hydro-Québec set up a headquarters there. There were hydro people from all over the place – I ran into people who were there from Vancouver Island!

I did get to see some of my family. A couple of my brothers and my brother-in-law drove down to St-Césaire, and we had lunch together at the college.

After we did our day's work, we had to go back to the college and line up to eat. Then we'd get on the bus and be taken to the ski lodge. Next morning the bus would be there at five-thirty to pick us up and take us off to the college for breakfast. We'd work twelve-hour days, but if you count all the time on the bus, it was more like sixteen hours.

One night we had a big snowstorm. Even the army didn't want to drive us back to the lodge – they had orders to stay off the road. But a school-bus driver took us over there. He was a hell of a nice man.

I stayed two weeks in all. Other people from Detroit Edison stayed longer, but I fell on the ice and injured my shoulder. We were pulling wire on the ground and I fell. My shoulder was pretty badly bruised – I was off for several weeks.

The first week we got to Canada, everybody was saying to me, "Why in the heck did you leave a beautiful country like this?" I said, "Well, for the money and this and that." We were in the Ottawa Valley, the temperature was only just below freezing, the sun was shining over the hills, and it was so pretty: picture-perfect.

But then we moved on to St-Césaire, where it was snowing every day, the temperature dropped below -20°C, and it was all flat land. After a few days there, the guys were saying, "No wonder you left this goddamn place!"

Marcel Coulombe lives in Wayne, Michigan.

MARILYN MOFFATT

As a registered nurse in a small eastern Ontario hospital, I found the prospect of three twelve-hour night shifts in early January very daunting; coupled with getting out and about in freezing rain, the prospect was downright depressing. The storm hit us in two waves, causing power disruptions of twenty-seven hours and then, twelve hours later, of fourteen days. The first wave seemed to be the usual – no big deal, just an extra little bump in life. Monday it began.

Tuesday, January, 6, on my way home from work, I was startled by a beautiful sight: the prettiest blue flash of light alongside the road. I now know why the colour is called "electric blue"; it is the most vivid blue imaginable. I also had visions of live wires falling across the road and hitting my car. Not unexpectedly, the power was out at home. Still, a few hours and Hydro would have it repaired, right? My husband was in the process of reporting the failure, the last time the phone would be used for several days. I was more concerned about Alex Dow, an elderly cousin who lives next door and whose only source of heat was electric.

The power, this time, was off until ten-thirty the next morning. Of course we didn't know that at the time. It would be the first time in thirty years that the power was off for longer than twelve hours. We were fortunate that we had two woodstoves and so could cook food and stay warm. I was prepared to leave early again so that I could shower at work, if that was necessary. It was necessary, of course.

I arrived at work – a twenty-minute drive away on a good day – to find a full complement of patients had been transferred from a nearby nursing home that was not equipped with standby power. These patients were all elderly and many were physically handicapped. The hospital was operating on generator power and would do so for several days. Having faced an eventful night I prepared to go home – only to be faced with a car completely encased in ice and – guess what – the ice scraper inside the frozen car. Try bashing off an inch of ice with a shoe!

I decided to check on my cousin Wednesday morning; that was a trek in itself. The way over from our house was slippery and branches impeded our way. Alex was still as feisty as ever, refusing to budge and wanting only to be left alone. The temperature in his house was not too bad, being around 10°C. I decided, however, to enlist the aid of his doctor in seeing what could be done to prevent a tragedy. As the phone lines were down, we drove to her office in the town of Russell. Dr. DeBanné decided that a house visit was required, and she was prepared to take action if the power was to be off much longer. This was no sooner decided than the power came back on. Alex was saved for another day.

With the power on, I took a long hot shower and was off to bed. Supper that Wednesday was cooked on the electric stove – the luxury! I went to work the last night in this stretch. The hospital was still working on emergency power and seemed able to meet our needs. All night one could hear the cracking and snapping of branches. At 5 A.M. there was a tremendous crack as the TV mast crashed down, breaking a skylight and filling the sunroom with ice. This room was obviously off limits now, but every other nook and cranny of the hospital was occupied by staff who slept over, both to ensure patient care and because their own homes were dark and cold.

The morning was cold, wet and dreary, and my mood was not lifted on the way home. Driving through the dark, deserted town of Vernon, I had the feeling of what it must be like after a nuclear disaster. It was beginning to dawn on me that this was perhaps more serious than a normal Ottawa Valley ice storm. When I arrived home, my husband told me the power had gone out at ten-thirty Wednesday evening. I was still concerned about my cousin – but after three night shifts, he could wait until I had some rest.

Up at noon, I heated some blankets on the woodstove and trekked over to my cousin, who was now more debilitated but as defiant as ever. The heat of the blankets, however, convinced him that perhaps it was better to be warm under someone else's roof than freeze to death in your own place. His decision created another problem: how to move an elderly, weakened person across three hundred feet of ice-encrusted, slippery laneway? The solution: get the next-door neighbour with the front-end loader to transport us! We must have looked comical: myself and my husband holding this frail body, the three of us sitting on a piece of plywood on the forklift of a tractor. It was cold and miserable, but the only safe way to transport Alex.

Friday dawned clear, sunny and mild. The rain had stopped and we would soon have hydro, wouldn't we? So what if we had three inches of ice on the wires. Alex had had a fitful night, falling off the couch and developing a severe cough that sounded like pneumonia. Our suggestion that perhaps he should go to the hospital was not in the least well received. Friday was occupied with collecting ice (there was lots around) to fill two outside freezers, and with melting snow so we could wash and make instant coffee, all the while trying to convince Alex that the best place for him would be in the hospital. In the late afternoon he finally decided that perhaps, after all, a visit to the hospital might just be the thing – but not until tomorrow. We were ready for bed shortly after nightfall.

Saturday morning was also sunny when I looked out the bathroom window and noticed something seemed to be missing. I finally figured out that it was the main power line. As a matter of fact, the power line along our road had collapsed. Later we would count about one hundred snapped-off poles within a kilometre of our gate. More important, there was a pole across our laneway, completely blocking access. There was simply no way for us to transport Alex to the hospital and no way for an ambulance, or any other vehicle, to come up to the house.

Our ever thoughtful neighbours, the Hendrikx family, came to our rescue. They came up just to see how we were, and discovering that Alex required hospitalization, went to seek help. Shortly after, there was a knock on the door and two large, strong and very polite soldiers asked if they could be of service. They certainly could! We cleaned off one of our cars, and the soldiers placed Alex in the back seat and covered him up. I sat in the back seat holding up his head as one of the soldiers drove down the lane. They lifted him over the downed wires and pole, and carried him into a waiting municipal vehicle to be taken to the hospital.

Marilyn Moffatt lives outside Kenmore, Ontario, and works at the Winchester and District Memorial Hospital. Alex Dow was released after a short stay; he still lives in his own home.

DAVID LEONARDO

This may seem a boast, but if the Montreal area should suffer an emergency from weather or war, readers can expect to see an expanded edition of the *St. Lambert Journal* (circulation 11,000). Before the ice storm, this would have been wishful thinking. Today, I know this little newspaper could fill big shoes. That's because when all other newspapers on Montreal's South Shore collapsed, the *Journal* continued to publish, just one day off schedule.

At the best of times, this bilingual community paper is a miracle. With a full-time staff of just three, we publish fifty times a year for St. Lambert and environs. This is about as small as it gets for weekly newspapers, with the publisher – myself – filling all roles. Many people, often without malice, wonder if this lone independent weekly will close. (They've been wondering for eighteen years.) So when an emergency like the ice storm occurs, the logic is that a little organization should collapse on the first breeze.

The *Journal*'s story is about dedication defying logic.

On a suffering scale, St. Lambert escaped the punishment meted out to St-Jean and Boucherville; the worst-hit districts in this city of 22,000 missed power for just six days. Still, St. Lambert took the first blows. Mayor Guy Boissy instantly saw the potential for greater damage and, on the afternoon of Tuesday, January 6, the city declared a state of emergency – the first Quebec municipality to seek help.

As city officials consulted their emergency plan, down the street at the *Journal*'s office nothing was happening. Some of the Wednesday edition was ready for the press, but with Tuesday as the final production day, many pages remained in unpowered computers. Two battery-operated laptop computers could have been used, but the laser printer lacked power.

From our second-storey office in a commercial block, I could see the street lights were on. This brought a memory of a solution I once used when the power was out on a Christmas-edition deadline. I sent a brave soul up the lamppost, who unplugged the Christmas wreath and then connected an extension cord that led back to the office. The computers and printer worked fine and the deadline was met. Later on, the city declined reimbursement for the stolen electricity, professing ignorance.

There was still a breaking story to cover. As the newspaper's only journalist, I switched roles to cover it. On day one of the storm, I knew the ice storm had potential to be an even bigger story. If the power transmission lines suffered an onslaught, all of the province could be knocked out.

On the first day I took many pictures and more notes than I needed for several stories. So many tree limbs had brought down power lines, the forecast was for three more days without power. Three shelters opened and the city prepared others. Well-to-do residents took cover in Montreal, as 90 percent of St. Lambert lost power.

On a personal level, working in the cold and freezing rain drained me. After work I looked forward to a hot supper. Fortunately, my wife Barbara and I found a restaurant with power, arriving at Kenny Wong's on Taschereau Boulevard well ahead of a seventy-five-person lineup that lasted all evening. We ate quickly so that others could get a seat. The dinner was an eerie experience that left us with a portent of what might come.

We declined a room at a motel with electricity. A "no pets" rule was still in force, and we wanted to be with our golden retriever, Tabloid. That night we returned to an unheated house. As I snuggled in a sleeping bag, I worried that my double pneumonia of a year before might return.

Surprisingly, there was power at the office on Wednesday, the second day of the storm. Our part-time translator, Paule Turgeon, arrived for work and I began writing and laying out the newspaper. With every phone call there was more news. Limitations of time, as well as a fragile power grid that could crash at any moment, made for the most stressful deadline I can remember. Looking at this twenty-page tabloid, I now notice typos and missing paragraphs; but it had the news. Some headlines: "What to bring to the emergency shelters." "Be careful, stay alert." "If the emergency continues." "Fire on des Landes St. causes $50,000 damage." "Notice from emergency measures coordinator."

At 6 P.M. the printer's courier picked up our files. An hour later, we lost power at the office. At home the power was still off, so we considered a shelter. A few shelters accepted pets on a leash, but sleeping with a hundred other bodies would be difficult. Some heat remained in the

*In the Champlain College shelter, evacuees were delighted
to read fresh copies of the* St. Lambert Journal.

office, and there we returned. Tabloid, who joins us at work every day, was perplexed as to why we were sleeping there.

Early Thursday morning, a ringing phone woke us up from the hard office floor where we had spent the night. The caller was the press foreman from St-Jean, who told me, "You are one lucky guy." As the night shift at the press witnessed a show of live flying wires in the sky, the plant was hit with a power outage. It struck as the *Journal* was on the press. Luckily the run was 75 percent complete.

Barbara, Tabloid and I caught up with distribution manager Brian O'Malley axing five-inch ice slabs off the roof of our truck. The van was loaded with newspapers and we decided on a limited delivery: newspaper stands at stores that were still open, some house delivery, and two shelters, including the large one at Champlain College.

We followed Brian on some of the route. A frightening moment came when the van passed under a sagging power line that swept the roof. The line, with its white camouflage of ice, was fortunately very dead. At the Champlain College shelter, I felt a professional thrill to see a crowd descend on the newspaper bundles for the latest news.

We returned to the office to conduct business as usual with a single working phone line. Later on, a search for gasoline led us to a hundred-car lineup on Taschereau. Remembering an out-of-the-way gas station, I found just three cars lined up in wait. We spent another cold night, this time at home.

On Friday morning power returned to our house, so I went to work alone. With the courts closed, my wife's legal practice had come to a stop. This was the worst day of the storm, as a major power failure pulled downtown Montreal into the crisis. With the core of the Montreal area paralyzed, despair deepened off the island. As bad as it had become on the South Shore, seeing the Montreal skyline lit up always gave some hope of refuge. Now this was taken away from us. By evening the situation seemed desperate.

Earlier that day I followed St. Lambert police to several calls and left a piece of my car in a snowbank. I also followed a pair of linemen brought in from Connecticut to help Hydro-Québec with the mounting repair work. The team was a curious mix: René Rioux (originally from Asbestos, Quebec) speaks little English, while David Jones (originally from Deseronto, Ontario) understands no French.

I went home that evening and the power was out again. That weekend we took shelter in Laval with my wife's parents, who miraculously had electricity. Never was a visit to the in-laws more enjoyable. In the comfort of a heated house, I leisurely wrote most of the next edition of the newspaper.

On our return to St. Lambert Monday morning, we found much of the South Shore was still without power. A view from a highway overpass made that clear. As well, a low-hanging cloud of chimney smoke indicated that fireplaces were still heavily in use.

As I passed the hooker motel on Taschereau, I noticed the parking lot was empty but lights were on. By accident or design, this was the only empty motel with power. I noted that it could also be the new headquarters for the *Journal*. Fortunately, power had returned to our house, and that's where we all worked from.

But problems still plagued us. The Chinese elm in the backyard had wrapped itself around our power line. How long before it came down?

Where to develop film? Which gas pumps were operating? Most important of all: where to print? With the St-Jean press knocked out, I turned to an old contact south of the border. That week, the newspaper was printed just outside Burlington, Vermont. (When the Canadian dollar was higher, I printed my newspaper there for a year.)

In the following weeks, the *Journal* was printed in Quebec City. Then the St-Jean press found a generator and the trying time for the newspaper came to an abrupt end.

Some advertisers refused to pay their invoices for what I believe was the best issue ever. Yet a heavy demand came for back issues to be sent around the world to disbelieving relatives and former residents. In the aftermath, City Hall gave the *Journal* a new stature. The newspaper figures prominently in St. Lambert's updated emergency-measures plan.

The ice storm stress made me rethink my life. Ron Seltzer, the ex-publisher of a Montreal weekly newspaper called the *Downtowner*, died from a heart attack while shovelling ice. I am still working to improve my health. Although I prefer to avoid another emergency, I continue to plan for what if.

David Leonardo is the publisher of the St. Lambert Journal.

RON HRYNIOWSKI

I'm a family doctor in Hudson, Quebec, which is a town of about six thousand people. We have a big family practice and we see all ages. Hudson has a relatively elderly population, and they were adversely affected during the ice storm; I think the storm affected the children least. Quite a few people just left: they went to hotels in downtown Montreal. But a lot of the elderly wouldn't leave.

Most of our patients were without power for thirteen or fourteen days, though I had patients from Ste-Marthe that had no power for up to twenty-eight days. A couple of them were farmers, young guys, and they were really badly affected. They were feeling a lot of financial stress and they were also struggling to get water to their animals. They would come in with extreme exhaustion – they had to keep hauling water from a creek to the barn – and there's no remedy we can give for that.

The clinic has a generator which we keep for emergencies. It's hooked up to run the emergency room, where we can put in stitches, and also to this office. When we lost power, we put the generator on, but we ran out of gas – there was no way to get gasoline for the first two days, and we had to close for a day. The firemen had gasoline, but they wouldn't give it to us: they said they needed it for their chainsaws.

But then we got donations of gasoline from patients, so we could reopen – it was just cold and dark. I was wearing a tuque as I worked. We have little space heaters that work off the generator, but it was still cold and awkward. It's hard to examine people if they can't take their clothes off! I exercise every day, and in the ice storm I wasn't able to exercise. So I got tired too.

In the beginning we had a lot of people who got abrasions on their eyes from chipping the ice off their cars. They would be hitting the windshields with their hammers, and the ice would fly up and get them in the eye. It would scratch the cornea. We saw at least a dozen of those cases. They'd have to wear a patch and get checked the next day. It's nasty.

We also saw a little bit of frostbite in the second week when it got really cold. Mostly teenagers who didn't wear their hats outside. And of course we saw some burns. A couple of kids got burned on their wood-stoves. We saw some cuts, from people using chainsaws and having accidents. But I don't think I put on more than one or two casts, which is about average. A lot of the people who are very mobile had left the community anyway, and these are the people who usually break bones. From the number of people in my clinic, I would figure about half the population had left.

And of course, we had the elderly with their carbon monoxide poisoning and their hypothermia. They didn't go out that much. They were stuck inside.

I think when the army guys showed up, the population really liked that. They felt reassured. Every morning we would go into the shelter, in the local community centre, and do medical rounds, just to make sure everyone was okay. Once the army was there, people seemed happier.

They were all elderly in the shelter. They were all from the senior citizens' apartment complex – you have to belong to the Legion to live there – and they were moved out into the community centre. Most of them were our patients anyway. One time a lot of people got food poisoning, and they were all having diarrhea and throwing up. That was towards the end. There was only one bathroom, so it was a real mess. It could have been salmonella, but we couldn't identify it because the labs were all closed. People blamed the chicken cacciatore.

We also had a couple of our borderline personality types, close to schizophrenic, who just couldn't cope. They started having hallucinations and could not function in an emergency shelter. So they were taken off to Valleyfield and hospitalized.

In the week after the power came back, it was relatively quiet here in the clinic. People were really tired and they just slept a great deal. But then it got busy a couple of weeks later. That February we had a flu epidemic.

What I noticed after the power came back was that among the elderly, the aging had accelerated somehow. People seemed like they were ten years older, and I mean almost all of them. I'm talking about very vibrant seventy-year-olds, who are more like eighty-year-olds now. A lot of people didn't feel they had to leave their homes. They felt they were comfortable – they even said they weren't cold! You get to a point when you don't realize how bad it is. You're numbed. Some of them, their thought processes were so cloudy they weren't aware of the crisis. I attribute it to the hypothermia and the carbon monoxide, because a lot of them were using candles to heat their homes. They were really stubborn and refused to leave. These people have aged dramatically.

Ron Hryniowski has been a family doctor in Hudson for the past twenty-two years.

7

THE HEARTBREAK AND THE JOY

nforgettable" is one of those terms, like "it goes without saying," that ought to be taken with a few grains of salt. Memories are shifty, malleable, not always reliable. I tend to disbelieve people who tell me they can remember every detail about the ice storm. Every detail? To forget is as natural as to breathe.

But — and this is a large "but" — there are certain moments in any life where memories fasten and take lasting shape. I'm speaking about moments of intense emotion and pressure: the birth of a child, a family death, a wedding. Even with the passage of time, the living memory of those events remains with us — not in every detail, of course, but with an intensity that is slow to fade. They become a part of who we are.

Each of us tends to associate these moments with a particular weather, place, or time of year. A March snowstorm will always remind me of the birth of my younger child; the week before Christmas will always be coloured by the remembrance of my father's death. A calendar is not just a standard collection of pictures and dates hanging on a wall; a calendar can be a deeply subjective item, full of secret pitfalls and pleasures.

The ice storm was memorable enough. What must it be like to suffer its implacable demands at the very time a loved one is dying? Or to get married, or give birth to a baby? The following stories — each of them written a year or more after the event, and each of them to do with Montreal — give us an idea.

GAIL HAMER-HOWELL

At 3 A.M. on January 6, I was awakened by the silence of the house and the coldness of the bedroom. I opened the patio doors and I could hear the cracking of the branches as they tumbled to the shimmering ground. It was an eerie, scary sound. Little did I know it was the beginning of the worst year of my life.

On December 23 the doctor had told us that my husband's lung cancer had spread to his liver, and there was nothing more they could do. George was getting weaker all the time, and he could just get out of bed to go to the bathroom. On January 5 I went to make arrangements for his funeral. Being a barbershop singer, he wanted specific pieces of music at his funeral. By this time we could talk about things like that.

After being awakened by the cold, I went upstairs to look outside. I could see flames in the tree across the street. The branches were touching the wires and causing the fire. I called 911 and the fire truck came, but they told me it was okay. They watched it for a while until it went out.

The house got colder and colder. By the afternoon, George's son Wayne called. He lives in the new section of Greenfield Park and he still had power. I got George bundled up and we went over. But just as we got there, Wayne's power went out too.

We stayed there for several days. All of us were in the living room, because the fireplace was the only thing keeping us warm. George slept on a couch or on a mattress on the floor. I slept on a mattress beside him. Our grandchildren went off to stay with friends in Montreal who had power. I think maybe they were having a hard time seeing their beloved grandfather in such a condition. Meanwhile another couple came to stay as well, and I remember one night Wayne's wife, Diane, made a dinner using fondue pots and a camp stove in the garage. We actually had a sit-down spaghetti dinner.

One day I went out for a walk. The streets were deserted and the devastation was like in one of those science-fiction movies. Finally I saw a flickering light on in a home where I knew the family. They were huddled in front of candles.

George was sleeping a lot, he was barely aware of what was going on, but he wanted to go home. He couldn't understand why we couldn't

Gail Hamer-Howell and her husband, George, shortly before his departure for the hospital where he would spend his final days.

go home. I kept trying to convince him that our house was colder than this one. I find it hard to accept that some of his last days were spent lying in front of his son's fireplace, trying to keep warm, instead of in his own comfortable bed that he loved so much.

During the night I'd have to take him to the bathroom, and that was cold too. At one point Wayne told me how much it meant to him, having his father there. He said he could now understand what I was going through, because when people just visit someone who is very sick, they don't see what goes on during the night. But he thought I should get George to a hospital. I said I would try the next day.

Finally someone lent us a kerosene heater. We had it in the kitchen but I was worried about the fumes, so I would open the window. It's amazing how fast the room would get cold and we'd have to stoke up the fireplace again. Wayne had to keep going to out to get more wood anywhere he could find it.

About a week after the storm began, Wayne had gone back to work and a young black soldier knocked at the door. He said, "I smelled kerosene." He was a cute little guy. I hugged him and I was crying on his shoulder. He tried to console me but I could see he felt awkward – he had probably never experienced anything like this in his young life. He called another soldier; they huddled together and then they called an ambulance. Pretty soon we had two firemen, two soldiers and three paramedics all tramping around, bringing in wood and telling me that we shouldn't use kerosene any more. I called the Jewish General Hospital in Montreal and they said, "Don't bring him in, it's a zoo in here." But one of the soldiers said, "You can't stay here!" Luckily the people at the Jewish General were able to get him admitted to Mount Sinai, because they called and said, "There's a place for you here."

George was able to walk to the garage with help, and Wayne drove us to the hospital. On our way we drove past our home and I saw George wistfully looking at it. I think he knew he would never see his home again.

As we were driving, my mind travelled to my parents, Tom and Ruby Hamer, who were going through the same thing in Lancaster, Ontario. My dad was on oxygen and had been put in the Cornwall General during the crisis. My mom, who was diabetic, refused to leave their basement apartment at my brother Grant's house. My brother and his family were sticking it out with my mom. Here I was, going to a warm, safe place with my husband, and unable to help or visit my parents. I felt like a refugee with all my bags.

When we arrived at Mount Sinai, it was like a hotel. It was so beautiful and so warm I started to cry. They put me up too. At first I slept in a room with three other men and my husband. After the fourth day they admitted us to a semi-private room with nobody else in it, and I could push my bed up next to his.

One night I found George lying in the fetal position, with his head at the bottom of the bed. I knew then that the end was near. He was starting to bloat up and I went looking for a doctor. I was surprised to see Dr. Vallejo, whom I knew from visiting George's brother in the Veterans' Hospital, and he was just as surprised to see me. He could not believe the change in George's condition since the summer. "Why aren't they giving him diuretics?" I asked. Dr. Vallejo explained that diuretics would have drained the wrong parts of his body. But then he said to me, "Mrs. Howell, I understand you want to take him home. Please reconsider. Remember, sometimes big things happen to make other things happen.

Maybe the ice storm happened to bring you here to this beautiful safe place. He's being taken care of. You're being taken care of."

That night I went to George and I said, "You know I promised that you'd die at home. But I'm afraid, and the house is still cold. Would you forgive me for not taking you back there?" He said, "Of course I do, Gail." That was like a weight lifted off my shoulders.

Meanwhile the power had come back on at our house. I was afraid to leave him but I went back home to see what shape the place was in. My brothers Tom and Brad had come in and drained the pipes. The house was still cold, the dishes were piled in the sink and the Christmas decorations were still up. They looked cheap and tinny. I looked out at the backyard and someone had sawed up all the big branches that had fallen over. I later found out it was Sean, the boyfriend of my niece Allison. One thing the storm brought out was a lot of Samaritans.

My husband was always a joker, and on the Sunday he perked up a little and cracked a couple of jokes. But I remembered my mother's words, "The light is always brighter before it burns out."

On Monday morning, January 19, I woke up at 4:30 A.M. because George was moaning. I gave him a pain pill to swallow, but I noticed after a time that it was still on his tongue. In a panic I squashed it and tried to get him to swallow it again. I knew then that I had better call the kids, Gail, Wayne and Jason, to come in right away. Then I held his face in my hands and said, "George, think of Lake Carmi! I'm rowing you around the lake and it's glistening, you're catching a bass. Do you see it now?" He looked at me through a haze and nodded with his eyes. I said to him, "I'll always love you. Go home now. Like we talked, send your spirit home or to someone." He nodded to me and I kissed him goodbye. A few minutes later, just before the kids came in, as I cradled him in my arms he gently passed away.

I found out later that his spirit did go, because Jason's wife, Nathalie, woke up and George was standing in front of her, beautiful like he used to look. She said, "I'm afraid!" He said, "Don't be afraid, I love you all and I have to go." Alone at our house our son-in-law Michel was in the shower and he thought he heard calling. He turned off the water and felt a presence in the house. I know George went home.

Finally I came home. But for another week and a half, I had his family here with me. Gail, Michel and their three kids had moved into our empty house. They live in Iberville and they had no power for twenty-eight days. The kids had taken down all the Christmas decorations as a favour to their grandma. So when I walked in, the house didn't feel so much like a place people had fled.

George's funeral was on Saturday, January 24, and there was a blizzard. Despite the terrible weather conditions, there were twenty-three barbershoppers at the funeral. They sang the Lord's Prayer. At George's wish we played "Just a Closer Walk with Thee" in New Orleans jazz style. Someone turned around to me and said they could just see George dancing up the aisle. When we arrived at the crematorium, the limousines were having a fight in the parking lot because of so much snow. Someone forgot to pick up the sandwiches, and by the time we got home with them, we had to pass the trays over people's heads, the house was so crowded. It was such a party! George would have loved it.

After the funeral I was able to visit my parents. Dad had come home from the hospital once their power had come on. He was in bad shape. I thought I was going to lose him the day after burying my husband. Miraculously, he pulled through. He eventually passed away in my arms at the Ottawa Civic on June 6, while my mom was in the Cornwall General. Her diabetes had gone out of whack and she was having congestive heart failure. Thank God I was with her when she died September 6, three months to the day after Dad. I know in my heart that my three loved ones are together and we will meet again.

Some of you, reading this, are maybe thinking this is just a story about someone's death. But a death is hard enough to go through, and adding the stress and hardship of that storm is something no one can understand unless they've been through it. Like the new growth of the bent and broken trees, life goes on, and I believe my three guardian angels have helped me get through. It's been over a year now since George passed away. As I look out the front window at the new buds on my maple tree and see how it survived that terrible storm, I realize I'm a survivor too. In George's joke collection I found a blue ribbon decal that reads, "I've survived damn near everything." I stuck it on my car.

Gail Hamer-Howell lives in Greenfield Park, on the South Shore of Montreal.

BERNADETTE TRELAWNY

My husband, Chris, and I first visited Montreal in February 1997, to investigate a possible job opportunity for him. I knew that Montreal winters could be cold and snowy, but I had never heard of the weather expression "freezing rain" until January 1998.

The visit in February was a success. Chris moved to Montreal from our home in England in May 1997, and I joined him in September, by which time I was five months pregnant. Our first baby was due to make an appearance on December 28, 1997. We had left friends and family behind, and knew nobody in Canada other than Chris's new colleagues at the International Civil Aviation Organization. We spent the fall settling in and decided to make our home in the N.D.G. district.

Christmas and New Year's came and went, and no sign of the baby. I shovelled show on Christmas Day to help the process along, to no avail. On Monday, January 5, my obstetrician, Dr. Vyta Senikas, confirmed that I had been booked into the Royal Victoria Hospital the following day to be induced. The hospital was due to call me to confirm the arrangement. On Tuesday morning Chris went to work and I stayed at home to get myself prepared.

The electricity had gone off at about 2 A.M., but as it had happened a few times before for short stretches, I wasn't concerned. By lunchtime the power was still not back. We had only one telephone, powered by electricity, so I couldn't make or receive calls and I didn't know if the hospital had been trying to get through. I decided to walk to the end of my road and use a public telephone to call the Royal Vic. As I walked along the road, branches were falling off the trees and a big one just missed me. I decided that this was a very unwise thing for a nine-months-pregnant woman to be doing, so I turned back and went home.

By the time I arrived the power had come back on, and I was able to call the hospital. They confirmed that they were expecting me at 6 P.M. The hospital instructed me to take a long hot bath and eat a nice hot meal. I began to make a shepherd's pie. Meanwhile the power was going on and off. I ate the shepherd's pie half-cooked and my nice relaxing soak in the bath was by flashlight.

Chris, having returned from work, loaded up the car and drove to the hospital very slowly. We didn't arrive until 6:45 P.M. The night-shift doctors and nurses were arriving late because of the weather, so Chris and I ended up playing Trivial Pursuit – the Canadian version, of course. At 10 P.M. things got underway. The following day, at around 1 P.M., Dr. Senikas entered the room with a gleeful call of "The coach is here!" At 2:26 P.M. on Wednesday, January 7, Harriet Laura Trelawny arrived, weighing seven pounds four ounces.

Harriet was a very healthy baby and I was doing fine, so we were due to transfer to the maternity unit. First, however, the nurse insisted that I eat something. When I removed the cover from the plate, a shepherd's pie lay underneath!

The women's pavilion at the Royal Vic is located just under Mount Royal, and the first night all we could hear were the branches breaking off trees and falling to the ground. At this point we began to get a feeling that this wasn't a normal Montreal winter.

Harriet was a very placid baby who wanted to sleep, eat and be cuddled. She was very forgiving when Mummy and Daddy were attempting to change nappies and swaddle her for the first time, just like we had been taught in class. We were learning to bathe Harriet, developing the feeding and sleeping schedule, and looking forward to going home.

But on the Friday morning, the day that we were due to leave hospital, our neighbour Marie-Christine Guiot came to visit us to tell us the bad news. Most of N.D.G. was without power, and a large oak tree at the front of our house had split in two and taken the electric cable with it. We would need the services of an electrician to get reconnected and this was going to take some time.

Suddenly panic set in. We have no family in Canada, we have a two-day-old baby, we are supposed to leave hospital at lunchtime – where can we go?

Several of Chris's colleagues offered assistance, but they were losing power, too. We approached Anna Balenzano, the assistant head nurse, and she came to our rescue. Anna arranged for us to stay at the Royal Vic for at least the next couple of days. Beds in the maternity unit were needed, however, and so we were transferred to a non-baby ward in another building.

That night the Royal Victoria Hospital was plunged into darkness. Its only electricity was being operated by emergency backup. We had a

Harriet Trelawny, four days old, in the arms of her father, Chris.

portable radio and we began listening to CBC Radio to find out the latest. It seemed that things were going from bad to worse. More power was going off, people needed to boil water and were unable to buy food, and a few people were dying of hypothermia and carbon monoxide poisoning. What was happening to Montreal?

The following days were very tense. We wondered what was going to happen: would we be able to stay at the hospital, when would power be restored, and how and what would we eat? We were new parents, changing nappies in the dark, and we were very anxious that Harriet not cry at night and wake the whole ward up. To get food we had to visit the staff canteen, which was running by candlelight. Somehow it managed to supply hot food. Chris and I would take it in turns to go and eat, wondering if supplies would get too short and they would need to limit the food to staff only.

It was difficult to get news to our families in the U.K., who had been leaving messages by the hour on our home voice-mail. We hadn't even been able to tell them the sex of our baby.

The extended stay meant that Chris needed to return home to get extra clothes and baby items. It took him over three hours to chip the ice off his car, and he was only able to get it out of its original parking spot with the assistance of another motorist.

We felt very lucky to have been able to stay at the Royal Vic. We tried to get into the famous baby routine as best we could under the circumstances. Being at the hospital meant that we could have Harriet weighed every day, and we had plenty of assistance from the Maternity Co-operative Care Unit, especially nurse Betty Brodeur. We were not supposed to walk around the hospital with Harriet in our arms, so we wheeled her around the hospital in her crib.

News of our extended stay was getting around the hospital, and we were approached and asked if we would do an interview for CBC Radio. We thought it would be a nice way to say a public "thank you" to the hospital, and we agreed. After the interview was aired, the hospital and CBC Radio were inundated with calls from people offering us assistance. Then CBC-TV approached and asked if we would do an interview for them. Wondering what we had got ourselves into, we nervously agreed. So Harriet was on the local CBC-TV news show, *Newswatch*, at less than two weeks old. We finally left the hospital on Saturday, January 17, full power having been restored at home.

This was an experience that we will never forget, and one that we do not wish to repeat. We were completely overwhelmed by the response of the people of Montreal to our situation.

I am delighted to say that Harriet is doing really well.

Bernadette Trelawny is now a student at Concordia University in Montreal.

LYNN GARFINKLE

We aren't totally crazy people to schedule a wedding in January in Montreal. There were reasons. My sister Lisa was living in India and it was the best time for her to come in. And Kenny and I wanted to get married on a Saturday, so that people could stay and party as late as they wanted. But in the Jewish religion, you cannot get married on the

Sabbath, so in order to marry on a Saturday, it must be in the winter months when the sun sets early. Regardless, the date was set: January 10. We had to hand-deliver many of the invitations because of a postal strike.

As the wedding approached, the weather got worse. Five days before the wedding, I got a call from the dressmaker: her power was off and she was not sure how she was going to finish the dress. My heart skipped a beat. But my eldest sister, Cory, called her and arranged for us to drive up so that I could try the dress on by candlelight. Friends kept calling to say they were not sure they would be able to make it into town, as airports were closing. My mother tried to hide her tears but we were getting a little nervous. Not to mention that our parents' houses both lost power, as did the Shaar Hashomayim synagogue where we were going to get married and the Westin Hotel where our pictures were to be taken. This was getting scary!

For some reason, our apartment never lost power, unlike all the buildings beside us. Someone was looking out for us. Our rehearsal was to take place at the synagogue Thursday night, with a party at my parents' house after. The synagogue somehow got power for three hours just at the time we needed it. The night before our wedding, Kenny and I had to sleep in our apartment. We thought we would be a little traditional by having me stay with my parents before getting married, but we ended up having friends stay with us and our families stay with friends. As we went to bed in a bit of panic, Kenny turned to me and said, "Lynn, all that really matters is that we get to spend the rest of our lives together – whether by candlelight or generator, that's all that counts." I knew then that tomorrow was going to be perfect.

I woke up in the morning and headed out with my dad to get ready. Kenny, trying to respect my desire to not speak the day of the wedding, kept his eyes shut and talked to me through our friends. When I walked outside, the rain had finally stopped and I noticed Kenny's car was gone. It had been towed, and he spent his first waking hours searching for it and laughing at our luck. After chasing down the tow truck, Kenny was directed to his car, which had been towed two blocks away with no fine, only a note stating that they had to move the car for cleaning purposes, sorry. I couldn't get my hair done where I had planned, as they had no power, so the hairdresser came to us instead. After that, I headed over to the makeup place. Little did we know that CTV would be there, too, to film the lucky "ice storm bride." At least all those who could not come in for the wedding got to see me on our big day.

Well, I was as pretty as I was going to be, and Kenny was on his way to the hotel for pictures, so off we went. As my father and I pulled into the hotel downtown, we were forced to dodge falling ice from the roof and had to park illegally, as there were no spots. I literally carried my dress in over my head. Both Kenny and I were in shock at what was happening in the hotel. It seemed as if it was the only building in the area with power, and everyone and their pets were walking into the hotel/shelter. Picture this: ladders being carried up the stairs to fix the shattered glass, generators being placed everywhere, dogs running around and kids playing on the floor with their toys. Still, we kept our smiles on, even with the big black circles under our eyes. If we'd made it this far, we could do it for another twenty-four hours.

When we saw each other for the first time, Kenny in his tux and me in my bridal gown, we were both filled with awe and forgot all the craziness we had been going through. The photo shoot went off without a hitch. Okay, maybe one: one of the bridesmaids and an usher ran in after a five-hour drive from Ottawa, just as we were ready to start the bridal-party photos. At least they made it on time, even if they had to brave sleet and snow. Nothing was going to stop this wedding.

Now we had to head over to the synagogue in Westmount for the actual ceremony. Behind the scenes, generators were being rented, gas stoves were being prepared and the band was bringing in acoustic instruments, just in case. We were slightly late and ended up walking in through a room full of guests; they ignored us appropriately. We were not at all shocked to find that there were a few more hurdles to jump. The rabbi was over an hour late and the flowers had not yet arrived – but we had power. This was due primarily to the fact that Hydro-Québec had prioritized the synagogue so it could act as a shelter to neighbouring residents.

The wedding did begin, and was magnificent, and almost everyone made it into town. We both remember walking down the aisle and seeing faces that we had thought were not going to be there. The party went on until 4 A.M., as everyone wanted to dance and had nowhere else with power to go. We did not stop smiling for one second. It was such an emotional night, where friendships shone and our two families felt even closer. As we were about to leave, we decided to donate the food to the shelter in the hope that they would have as great a night as we did.

In the morning, as we checked out of the hotel, it lost power. So did the synagogue. At least they had good timing. We went off for our honeymoon in the sun even though the airport was to be closed. But guess who was on our side? The airport was open for a few hours at just the right time. And we got bumped up to first class out of pity.

This is the kind of story we will tell our children. Nothing can really faze us now. We have been married for over one year, and are living happily ever after.

Lynn Garfinkle is regional director for the B'nai Brith youth organization. She and her husband, Kenny Etinson, live in Montreal.

CONNIE TURNBULL

My father suffered a massive heart attack on New Year's Eve, 1997, and died instantly.

His funeral was planned for 10 A.M. on January 5, at a church in the west end of Montreal. My dad came from a large family, now scattered all over Quebec and Ontario, and they and many others wanted to pay their final respects. He had studied law at McGill, but worked throughout his life in various charitable and social-service agencies – he'd been blind since he was eleven, and wanted to use his training to help others who might be facing the same prejudices and disadvantages he had encountered.

The funeral was very well attended, but freezing rain had been falling through the night, and the roads had started to become impassable. Those who had come from out of the city left directly after the service in the hope they would get at least part of their way home in daylight, and many of the local, often elderly, mourners were worried about their safety on the roads and sidewalks.

My sister lives in the eastern downtown area of Montreal, my mother in the west end close to the church, and I live off the island, about fifty kilometres away. On the morning of the funeral, my husband and I had known we had to leave ourselves plenty of time to get in to the city, but our trip took almost two hours. The main highway was completely clogged, and we had worried that we would miss the official limo to the funeral parlour. We eventually got off the highway and tried to find our way through back streets, but still the going was very slow. Fortunately the whole city was running a little behind schedule, and we did arrive in time.

After the funeral and minimized wake – much to my father's despair, I'm sure! – my husband and I limped home to find that our power had gone off. We live in a semi-rural area – part original farming land, but now expanding to include bedroom communities of baby boomers transplanted from the city – and we draw our water from a well. Of course, when the electricity is off, the pump from the well is disabled too, so we had no water either.

We suffer many power outages in this region, so we immediately went into "camping mode" – we pulled out kerosene lamps and candles, fired up our basement woodstove and living-room fireplace insert, closed down blinds on the windows to contain the heat, and tried to open both fridge and freezer as little as possible. The next morning, though, we were still off, and the battery radio told us we were not at all alone. My husband had recently become a victim of corporate downsizing, so he was able to maintain the house while I dragged off to work – thank goodness, or we might have faced far more serious problems.

We buried the contents of our freezer deep in the snow, and moved perishables to a cooler on the back porch. My office in St-Laurent, which borders on Montreal, never lost electricity – we are right around the corner from a fire station – and each morning I would go in early, take a sponge bath in the kitchen, and make *hot* coffee. I would bring an eighteen-litre bottle of water home from work every evening, so we could at least flush the toilets and brush our teeth – and still have enough left over for a medicinal scotch.

Some parts of the city kept their lines up longer than others, and initially my mother was unaffected. Eventually, though, she lost her electricity (including heat) and went to stay with my sister. Kathie still had periodic power, and her friends around the corner seemed to be on a different grid altogether; there was usually a warm house within fairly close call.

But my mother was a worry to both Kathie and me. She is blind, like my father, but both my parents have always been fiercely independent. My mother is very proud of her own private space and detests being branded as handicapped. She certainly wanted no concessions made just because she couldn't see. Nevertheless, we all knew that she couldn't remain on her own with the city shutting down around her, and we tried to organize ourselves so that she would never really be alone.

She came to stay with us, sleeping in flannel sheets in St-Lazare over the first weekend, tuning in on our battery radio for news and updates. On the Monday, one week to the day since the beginning of the storm, I brought my mother into work with me, and she settled in our little boardroom with her knitting and a Braille book. Although she was away from familiar surroundings, my office was at least warm, and the continuous supply of coffee and water was a treat. That evening my sister came to take her back downtown. I believe she stayed with Kathie one more night, and then power was restored to her condo. Our power at home in St-Lazare stayed off until the following Sunday: thirteen days and eight hours in total. I can still remember the elation I felt when I heard my house begin to hum and buzz as the various machines started to run again.

My mother is extraordinarily stoical, and showed very little grief throughout this ordeal. We were all so preoccupied by day-to-day survival that our loss was put on hold until we had time to grieve. The distraction of the storm and aftermath served as a buffer: by the time it was over, we had learned to adjust to my father's sudden death.

Connie Turnbull is an office manager who lives in St-Lazare, Quebec.

URSULA MUELLER-JUDSON

My baby was due on January 15, 1998. When the freezing rain began, about ten days before, I stayed indoors to avoid a fall. I felt nervous and trapped. When all of Montreal lost its power on Friday, January 9, I became more and more frightened. I started to worry about how to get to the hospital. I live in Westmount, and as the streets got iced over, it became clear that a car would not be able to make it up to the Royal Victoria Hospital. Reports of long waits for ambulances, and of over-crowded and understaffed hospitals, increased my trepidation.

On Saturday I started having contractions. I felt quite certain that this baby would be born very soon, since my son had been born one and a half weeks before his due date. However, this delivery would prove to be different. The contractions had subsided by Sunday night, although my mental state was deteriorating.

I was getting up frequently at night to drink water. To my horror, after a night of drinking litres of water, I found a note that Westmount Public Security had slipped through the mail slot, warning residents not to drink the water. After a series of frantic calls to the community health clinic and the hospitals, I finally reached an obstetrician and found out that my baby was not in any danger.

I did not have to go to a shelter because I was able to stay at a neigh-bour's house that had both a fireplace and a gas stove. Later I was upgraded to another neighbour's condominium, which still had power. We had hot water in our house and spent the nights at home. My four-year-old was aware of the confusion around him and sensed my nerv-ousness, but he was quite thrilled to sleep in one bed with his grandmother, who lives upstairs from us.

Finally, on Monday night, power was restored in our neighbourhood. Although there were still many problems throughout the city, it appeared that things were improving, and my attitude became much more positive.

Cecilia was born on Sunday, January 18. I remember seeing the poor damaged trees on the slope of the mountain from my window at the hospital, and feeling relieved that I had a healthy baby in my arms and a warm house to bring her home to.

Unfortunately, Cecilia was jaundiced and needed to remain under bright lights. The hospital was still running partly on generators due to the damage the ice storm had caused. One night, the power had to be shut off in our building for six hours. Only essential equipment needed for newborns could be run by the generator, and Cecilia's lights required too much power. She was therefore moved to the Neo-natal Intensive Care Unit, which is located many dimly lit, winding tunnels and hallways away from the Postpartum Unit. So there she was, an eight-pound, one-ounce newborn among the tiny premature babies in the NICU.

When Cecilia was finally discharged on January 23, a severe snow-storm made it impossible for my husband to drive up the hill to the hospital. The snowfall on top of the ice that had still not been removed made it impossible for city crews to clear the downtown streets as usual. My husband left the car on Sherbrooke Street and walked up to the hospital to tell me that we had to stay another night. He returned at seven-thirty the next morning and brought us home to an ecstatic four-year-old who thought life was finally back to normal.

Ursula Mueller-Judson teaches English and modern languages at a Montreal-area college. Cecilia is doing fine.

DIANE BLANDER

The ice storm was extra memorable for the reason that my mother died at the Montreal General Hospital at the height of the storm. Living in Ottawa made it a challenge for me to get to the hospital and back, emo-tionally and physically. Finally I decided to leave my car parked in the hospital parking lot for several days while I stayed with my sister, who lived fairly near the hospital. My father was staying there, too.

It was interesting spending time at the hospital, where many visitors had decided to stay in waiting rooms as they had no power at home anyway. The staff and volunteers were especially considerate to families of the sick and dying, realizing the extra pressure that everyone was under. My mother died under caring hands.

I yearned to go home to Ottawa to be in familiar surroundings, and an hour after her death, I set out. But I discovered my car was coated with a couple of inches of solid ice. It took well over an hour of chop-ping and heating the car to make it driveable in rather awful weather conditions. The physical work of chopping was actually a good outlet for me.

Driving was still slow everywhere, but I did manage to get to Hudson, where I was forced off the highway by a roadblock. I thought it would be an opportune time to check on my parents' home, which had been out of power. I did this, but found the house chilled in more than one way, and unbearable. The village was almost deserted, but I decided to check on an elderly friend of theirs. I was so happy to find Joan and her two precious dogs to share the night with by her fireplace. I think that she, too, was pleased to have company descend on her at this time. We slept a few hours and I was treated to bread and butter, and soup warmed on a small camping device. I urged her to leave as soon as possible, and said I would check back on her.

The next morning I decided to try the highway once more, and made it to the Vars exit, where I was forced off the highway once more by a patrol car. The officer was unable to offer any suggestions for an alternate route, saying that conditions were continually changing on all roads because of falling trees. I just decided to let my instincts lead me, and asked for help whenever I came across someone. The only worrying feeling was that the homes looked so deserted. Having a cellular phone with me did give me some feeling of security along the way, when the reception was good. After what seemed an eternity, I found a way into Ottawa with the help of some knowledge I had acquired exploring the area in my job as a real-estate agent.

My strong urge to return home was fuelled also by the need for a shower and my own bed to curl up in, even though it was still afternoon. My conception of time was gone, as I felt so exhausted from lack of sleep in the past week. Once I was home I knew that I could now collapse.

Returning to Montreal for the funeral was less traumatic. I felt that everything around me was also grieving. Somehow, this was a comfort.

Diane Blander is a real-estate agent living in Ottawa.

BARRY BELOFF

Getting married for the first time at an advanced age – the upside of fifty – I wanted everything to be perfect. No one had figured on the ice storm.

But I'm getting ahead of myself. Let me tell you how my long-delayed march to the altar actually began. In January 1997, when I was living and working in Toronto, I came home for my father's funeral. While I was in Montreal, I was introduced to Ora Lvov, a young woman from Russia via Israel. We went out together, and in time, although I was commuting to and from Florida on business and we were a generation apart in age, we fell in love.

At midnight on my birthday, November 24, as we gazed out from the lookout atop Westmount, over the winter wonderland created by an early-season snowfall and the lights of Montreal, I asked Ora to be my wife, and she accepted. We agreed to marry in sixty days, more or less, knowing full well what a challenge that time frame would present. After checking with our immediate families and closest friends, we set a firm date of Sunday, January 18, 1998, and I began to look forward to my happiest Chanukah-Christmas-time ever.

Except . . .

We didn't know so many suppliers of the goods and services we'd need would be closed over the holiday period – and even longer, because January is the off-season for weddings in Montreal. We hadn't realized that so many friends would be away, and that finding their out-of-town addresses would be so time-consuming. And we certainly didn't anticipate the gigantic ice storm that hit on January 5.

The downtown hotel where we were then living was Wedding Central. It eventually lost power for one twenty-four-hour stretch, with frequent, shorter interruptions before and after. But for the first couple of days, we didn't think there was a problem. We were in denial, too busy to worry about anything else. Besides, what were two days of freezing rain? Montreal could handle that.

But telephone interruptions kept us from contacting our suppliers. Responses to our 375 invitations, already delayed by the holiday period, slowed to a trickle when the ice storm and its aftermath bogged down the postal service. We finally realized the full seriousness of the situation when we saw our storm as the lead item on the CNN world news, hour after hour, day after day. And when the power was off, we had to walk twenty floors up and down to our temporary home in the hotel.

There were dozens and dozens of phone calls and faxes from guests wondering if the wedding was still on. We debated long and hard, and decided to go ahead. We were in love, we wanted to be married – and we would be, even if the rabbi was the only person who showed up.

A mere ice storm couldn't erase the newly-wed smiles of
Barry and Ora Beloff. (Photo: Asbed)

Only later did we learn of the Hebrew custom that one cannot change the date of a wedding after it has been announced publicly.

Meanwhile the Shaar Hashomayim synagogue, where the ceremony was to be held, had become a shelter for many local residents forced from their homes by the lack of electricity. After much thought, we decided they would be "unofficial" guests. Who could ask them to leave? But they were able to go home a couple of days before the wedding.

Finally the day arrived. And the guests came, 260 of them – from abroad, from throughout the United States, from across Canada. I saw them with joy in my heart as I walked down the aisle. I thought of how fortunate we were to be so happy while others were still suffering the effects of the storm. I delighted in the strong voices of the four world-famous cantors, longtime family friends, each from a different city, who had promised they would be there when (or if) I married. And I thought how precious our memories would be.

But even though it had been about a week since the storm ended, I noticed an undercurrent of uncertainty, even worry, throughout the day. As little groups of people chatted at the cocktail party before the ceremony, you could overhear snatches of conversation – "unknown damage to the roof" and "no report on the summer cottage" and "not much reassurance from my insurance man" and "no guarantee of a flight home."

At the dinner after the ceremony, several old friends offered toasts and best wishes, and a more relaxed feeling seemed to spread through the room. Then a writer I'd known for a long time spoke. He told the guests that when we'd worked together in several different offices I'd had in Montreal and Toronto, one thing was the same. Whenever people gathered at the water cooler or the coffee machine, the conversation always got around to my being the perennial bachelor, and the same question always was asked: "When do you think Barry will get married?" My friend always had the same answer: "Barry will get married when all hell freezes over."

Then he paused. What started as a tentative chuckle or two in the audience just grew and grew until people were holding their sides and wiping their eyes. That broke the ice, if you'll pardon the expression, letting the good times roll.

After the good times had run their course, about 3 A.M., Ora and I went back to the Westmount lookout where this chapter of my life had started fifty-five days earlier. It was, as before, a clear night, but this time it was ice, still coating the tree branches and power lines, that caught the twinkling of the city's lights and provided the beauty.

I mentioned earlier that I had wanted everything about this wedding to be perfect. But, thinking it over, perfection can be boring. We'll be able to tell our children about all this, about the time their parents married. Overcoming the problems of "the storm of the century" gave a special beginning to our life together.

And, after all this, the millennium certainly doesn't scare us.

Barry Beloff is a public-relations consultant and businessman living in Montreal again. Much later in 1998, Ora Beloff gave birth to a daughter, Samantha Lily.

EVA PUSKAS-BALOGH

Just four months before the ice storm began, I moved my parents from Toronto to live with me in Pierrefonds, on the West Island of Montreal. My dear mother – only seventy-three, diabetic, with heart and blood-pressure problems – had been diagnosed with terminal cancer. She'd been told, bluntly, that she had only a few months to live. The chemotherapy didn't help, the cancer attacked all her internal organs. We did not tell my father this, as he is frail, has suffered several strokes and is also diabetic. Mum didn't want him to know just yet. It was the first time in their lives he was not told the truth.

One day in Toronto I discussed with Mum – just the two of us, in the quiet of the night – her dying. She asked me not to admit her to a hospital. She wanted to die at home, surrounded by love and family. Her only deep concern was, what's going to happen to Dad after she was gone? I promised the same care for him. Neither of them would have to face death alone in a hospital corridor. I wouldn't put him into an old-age home, either. With all these promises, my parents became my responsibility. I gave up my regular activities and took an active part in the process, moment by moment, of Mum's dying. After all, she gave me life and had brought me up.

The shock of her illness made me angry at the world and at her doctors, and every night I quarrelled bitterly with God. For my parents' sake I did not permit myself to show any fear, as I had to be the strong one. Those few months were a gift for us. But I wished for more time, wished to be able to do more. Mum deserved more from life. I absolutely adored her.

We had installed Mum's hospital bed in the living room just days before the storm. The CLSC – the community health centre – had supplied it along with home nursing care. Also, the Victorian Order of Nurses visited her daily as Mum's condition deteriorated. I needed help with her feeding and personal hygiene. She was tired, unable to stay up, and we had to increase her painkiller dosages. I administered her daily injections, drugs by the hour, and spoon-fed her. I had a grumpy, sick father and a gravely ill mother to look after. Now, without power, I was distraught with worry. The small kerosene heater was hardly sufficient to keep them warm.

*Rescued from a frozen garden, these pet ducks spent weeks living in
Eva Puskas-Balogh's bathtub.*

During the days, somehow we managed. But the candles and the
kerosene fuel were slowly being used up. "What am I going to do?" I
asked myself as the drugs got dangerously low.

The food supply held out for a few more days. I hauled stuff from the
refrigerator to the balcony. On top of the kerosene heater, I could boil
water, warm up soup and make some cream of wheat. But from the first
day on, Dad complained bitterly about the temperature. The hot-water
bottle was constantly under his covers to warm his feet. I had to keep
him in bed, with several layers of blankets, duvets and covers. Mum never
said anything about her pain, but was concerned about how to keep Dad
warm. She had a lifetime of experience not to burden anybody.

The rabbit, Cilly, and the dog, Ajax, kept close to the tiny heat source.
In the evening the finches, lovebirds, canaries, doves, budgies and other
birds hovered in the living-dining room, perched up on the chandeliers,
bookshelves and light fixtures, as the solarium cooled off at dusk. Out
in the garden, the ducks called in distress, awaiting drinking water. I had
to shake off the feeling of despair and bring them their drink. They
complained bitterly as ice pellets strained their feathers. Under my arm,
one duck at a time, we made it back to the solarium. This used to be my
paradise: some sixty different kinds of birds and about three hundred

plants, including tropical flowers. They were in full bloom just days ago. Now they were stiff with frost. The grapevines in the yard lay demolished, crushed by the awning. I brought the ducks into the house with me – at night in the solarium, they would have perished.

In front of the house, my car was frozen to the ground. It was covered in an armour of ice. Piles of broken branches made the walkway treacherous, and with an axe I chopped a path through several feet of deep ice. I made a six-inch-wide channel to walk, just enough for one foot behind the other. But the salt and sand supply had gone, and it was impossible to step on the stairways. I had no idea how the nurse came by. Here she was, crawling on all fours, up to the door, to see Mum. Her visit was my only living connection to the outside world. The radio announced, she said, that kerosene and some generators would be available in the town of Hudson. Somebody must go there for me, when the roads were safe.

I was supposed to drive to Cornwall, one hour away, to pick up the drugs for my parents, as their prescription had been transferred there from Toronto. Mum's and Dad's provincial medicare involved a lot of paperwork that wasn't even done yet, but her illness rapidly progressed. Different health and pharmaceutical laws are mind-boggling, as the provinces don't accept reciprocity. For us, the Toronto physician had to confer with the oncologist in Montreal in order to get a prescription filled in Cornwall. Thank heavens the phone lines still worked. Knowing of our awful situation, relatives and friends from all around the world called us.

Well, we had to have supplies somehow! My friend John closed his chiropractic office, as his patients all cancelled. He had only a small Coleman lantern and all his fuel had been consumed. The cold chased him out from his house. For hours he chiselled off the ice from his car. Happily, he arrived to stay, bringing some canned goods.

Kind and concerned policemen, two of them, called on us daily. They visited also during the nights with their flashlights and banged on the door. Each time they spoke with Mother, and tried to convince her to be moved with Dad to a shelter. Mum asked the policemen to come close to her bed. With a small voice she told them about some of the conditions she had endured in her lifetime: in the war, in the revolution, in the refugee camps. So close to her death, she explained, she would not spend any time in a shelter. She was used to blackouts, cold and hunger. They were easier than dying.

The authorities realized that Mother wouldn't change her mind. I promised to guard the heater closely, air the house regularly and make every effort to prevent a fire. Generally we kept composed under the pressure. Father didn't want to leave Mum and go alone to a shelter. With the blood-thinner medicines he'd been taking since his strokes, he just could not get warm, not even in the summer. But Mother managed to convince him to go to relatives in Toronto on the first available flight, as he could not cope with the cold any longer. I assured him it was for only a few days. Using John's car I drove him to the airport early one morning, and off he went.

The following day we ventured to Hudson and purchased kerosene and candles, but all the generators were sold. People fought and grabbed at the twelve-litre containers from the delivery truck like crazed animals. The drive was a nightmare in this crystal land. The devastation took our breath away. I cried for everybody, for everything.

Helen and Rudy, who live in Dorval, offered us a warm, home-cooked meal, as they had had their power restored. They offered us a bath, too, with piping hot water. We badly needed it, but I put it off, every day waiting for our power to come back on. It would be several more days yet, said the man on the radio. Finally we carried Mother to the car and made her comfortable in the back seat. She was so frail and light, but was in high spirits to visit, for the last time, old friends. At Helen's place I put Mum into the tub, washed her hair and gave her a bath. We managed to laugh at the situation as I dried her off and dressed her in clean clothes. She even felt hungry. Next into the bathroom went John, and finally myself. I never appreciated warm water more than that day. It was a heavenly feeling to be clean again. How we take everything for granted!

Next day John volunteered to drive to Cornwall to pick up Mum's medicine. It took him several hours to reach Cornwall, and then he called from the drugstore to say there was not enough morphine. He had to drive to another, larger drugstore. Yes, the ice in Cornwall was just as bad as on the West Island, he said. He arrived back late in the evening, with some fuel for the car and Mum's medicine. What a relief.

Across the street, my neighbour Maria suddenly had lights in her living room. She called to tell us that her son had managed to buy a generator, and she invited us over, for a bath, to warm up. Mum's spirits picked up again. She would go, she said, if we carried her across the street. Mother collected all her strength and willpower, and we again had a welcoming bath and a couple of hours of heat. "Life is beautiful," John said, smelling of soap. I will forever be grateful to my friends for offering their help and hospitality.

The next morning, Helen and Rudy were banging at the door. Rudy looked beat. Then he told us that he had driven out to Île-Perrot, to his son's place. There, under the ice behind their shed, was an old, rusty woodstove. With his son, he pickaxed for hours to free it. He bought some pipes for a chimney and borrowed some wood from his son. They put it all on a truck, and here he was, wanting to carry it into the living room. Quickly the house became a flurry of activity. In the middle of the dining room, as the table was moved out, Rudy carried in some concrete blocks. With those on the white broadloom, he made a fireproof foundation. John, Rudy and Mark from next door tried to move the colossus up the icy stairs. The cold, slippery woodstove must have weighed a ton. They used some ropes, and after a few hours, it was inside.

Three puffing, tired, heroic men pushed and dragged it into the dining room. The rusty woodstove was lifted onto the platform. Several policemen visited and shook their heads in disbelief – they'd never seen anything like this in their lives. In the fading daylight, Helen cut wood with a handsaw on the balcony. Rudy removed the dining-room window, cut a large sheet of aluminum from the garage, and made a hole for the pipe to go outside. He climbed up a stepladder in the yard and fixed the chimney all the way to the roof. It was getting dark when we lit a match and started a fire in the old stove. Sizzling, it melted buckets of water, which we immediately collected. In a half hour the house started to warm up. Laughter sounded in the living room. We made Mother sit with us around the heat. The dog, rabbit, birds and ducks all surrounded the woodstove as it steamed like a locomotive. I put some potatoes on top, and we had the most delicious baked potatoes for supper. It was a feast fit for a king.

As long as I live, I won't be able to repay those dear friends for their act of kindness. They did all this for my mother. After they left, in the warmed-up living room, Mum talked spiritedly late into the night. John and I were around her; we enjoyed the closeness. Mum's worries were now that I should go to bed and take some rest, as I had been on my feet for ten days with hardly any sleep. I realized Mum kept a mental account of each and every day.

Now we had heat, it was easy for the nurses to wash Mother, change her bedding and give her warm food. Dad called several times every day, asking for a progress report. When we told him about the wood-stove, he wanted to come home.

Mother's high spirits in those few days made it a joy to be with her. Suddenly I hoped that she would get better – I wanted her to live! One afternoon she sat up, asking to look out to the street. I pulled the drapes aside for her to see. With a weakened voice she described to me her inner world, where I could not follow her any longer:

"You see, my darling, there is crystal lace on the windows. Each one magnificent, each one a different design. I have looked at them for the last ten days and I learned from this crystal lace. Now, from the heat, they have disappeared, and as they melted they took on different shapes, renewing themselves into stars. So is life, changing, renewing. I am not afraid to go. I have made peace with it. When you see those frost crystals on the windows, think about life. Don't cry. Think about me, and as a beautiful new crystal, you carry on."

Mum never spoke again. The priest came and she received her last sacrament. The next day the power came back, and so did Father. Mother died shortly afterwards at home, as I held her hand.

Eva Puskas-Balogh is a poet, writer and journalist for Hungarian newspapers. She is the founding president of the Hungarian Literary Association of Montreal.

8

ENJOYING THE STORM

he very title of this chapter may raise your hackles, may appear to you a joke or an insult. "The storm was a nightmare," you might feel like saying. "People died. Homes were ruined. How could anybody in their right mind enjoy it?"

But many did exactly that. I confess, it took me a long time to realize it. The point was forcibly brought home to me in the fall of 1998, when I spent a week doing publicity for McClelland & Stewart's book of photographs, The Ice Storm. One morning I was on an open-line radio show in eastern Ontario, explaining the difficulties of the crisis to listeners who needed none of my explanations, when a woman phoned in and said, "The ice storm was wonderful, I can't tell you how much I enjoyed it."

"You what, ma'am?"

"We had a woodstove," she said, "and for more than a week, we provided dinner for all the neighbours who didn't. The laughter we had! It was such a good time that in January, when the first anniversary rolls around, we're going to invite those people back again to celebrate."

She rang off and another woman came on the line. "Don't talk to me about the ice storm," this caller began. "I don't want to hear anything or read anything or think any more about it. My husband and I were without power for seventeen days – we couldn't even flush the toilet! I just want to forget."

It was a good lesson in the individuality of memory. Both women were right to recall the storm in the way they did, for both were being true to their own experience. It would be worse than futile to try and persuade them otherwise. As the months and years pass, we naturally begin to forget details of a crisis, leaving the crucial instants and emotions highlighted. But what is crucial to you may be *utterly trivial to me, and vice versa. No one has the right to say what anyone else who lived through the storm ought to remember.*

This chapter presents the stories of those who found the storm a pleasure, an inspiration, a chance to see the world afresh – or an opportunity to be brilliantly ingenious.

SHELLY CAMPBELL

We went eight days without electricity and I had the time of my life.

My aunt and uncle and their daughter stayed at our house during the storm. We have a woodstove and gravity-fed water, so for us it wasn't really tough to endure. All our food was buried in the snowbanks around our house, but each night we could have a hot meal.

Each day me and my aunt would go down to her house to make sure the pipes weren't frozen. She borrowed the neighbour's generator to keep them thawed. After finishing at their house, we would go around to the elderly in the community and see if they needed anything – food, water, more blankets, or just someone to talk with. I met a lot of people I hadn't met before and found they were very interesting.

After a day out, when we got back home, my dad would go down to the barn to make sure the water was thawed for the cattle. If it wasn't, we would light a candle and place it underneath the water pipe to warm it up.

My favourite time was the evening. My mom would light the two oil lanterns and some other candles, placing them around the house to brighten things up. Then everyone would start playing games and talking together. In my spare time, which I had a lot of, I even managed to crochet a rabbit pattern that had been lying around the house from years before.

My family, just like the community around, really grew close. I'm glad I got to experience what the ice storm was.

Shelly Campbell lives in Harrington, Quebec, and attends Laurentian Regional High School in Lachute. She was thirteen years old at the time of the storm.

DALE SIMMONS

That first day when the power on our street went out, our neighbours, one of only three houses left with electricity, had the foresight to start a large pot of stew cooking on the stove for dinner. They invited four other families in from the bitter cold, and the count climbed to twenty-six — eleven children, ten adults, three hamsters, one cat and one cockatiel (a colourful, crested parrot more at home in its native Australia). Special accommodations had to be arranged for our animal friends to ensure that the cat was kept away from the rest of the menagerie.

Put eleven children, ranging in age from two-and-a-half to eleven, together and you'd expect havoc to reign. Surprisingly, there were very few fights. Perhaps they sensed the urgency of the situation around them and the importance of pulling together and getting along. We had trouble believing there were really that many people under one roof. We worked as a team coordinating meals, with contributions arriving from each household as we emptied our fridges and freezers. Along with our first dinner of comforting stew, we enjoyed pre-outage freshly baked French bread from one family, and wine from another's cellar. In fact we ate wonderful meals, around a crowded table, the food tasting all the better because of the camaraderie and sense of sharing.

As nightfall came and with dinner out of the way, the children settled themselves downstairs. Once, when all was quiet, too quiet, I went down to investigate, and there they all were, snuggled together under blankets, taking up every available inch of the couches and recliner, attentively watching a video that somehow, miraculously, all had agreed on.

The adults, sprawled all over the living room, gathered in a circle to play the word game Catchphrase, having procured the necessary triple-A batteries for the timer. What ensued was a rollicking evening filled with much laughter, good-natured teasing and some fierce competition. Most of us hadn't played such games for years and were amazed at how much fun we had. The children, drawn upstairs by our unrestrained whoops, watched their parents' unusual behaviour with expressions of bewilderment playing across their faces. A neighbour from across the street stopped by with a kettle to get some water boiled for a late-night pot of tea. As the water heated, she joined in the game. It was with great reluctance that, after a few rounds, she carried the steaming kettle back to her waiting family.

Warmed and in high spirits, we went off to our respective homes to sleep for the night. In the morning, back at our neighbours', we compared notes over a communal breakfast, all agreeing that it had been a cozy night thanks to heaps of blankets.

On our second electricity-free day, one of the other three neighbours with power did a house-to-house check on the rest of the street, bringing flasks of coffee and offers of help. Checking in with us to report on the neighbourhood, we shared information on who had left and who were choosing to remain in their homes. We felt a sense of responsibility to watch over the abandoned houses and to keep tabs on the remaining residents. We were greatly impressed with one neighbour's pioneering spirit. Alone with only her dog for company, she was boiling water for tea, and cooking not-so-frozen dinners on a shovel in her fireplace.

Bluish-green flashes lit up the sky and heralded the return of our power after thirty-four hours. During the time without electricity, we had found much more than just a warm place to while away the days; we had felt the greater warmth of generous and caring neighbours.

Dale Simmons is an Ottawa gardener who prefers digging dirt to shovelling snow.

GEORGE JOHNSTON

The ice storm. We hear it as we wake and turn over during the night, and there it is, still making its presence felt on the trees, poles and power and telephone lines when we rouse ourselves, early, for breakfast and a bath. Bath indeed! We manage it, but it is hardly better than a cool lukewarm.

The electric furnace, our only source of heat, has been off since we retired. Good thing that we cook with gas! Our stove makes hot cereal, toast and tea for us, and for Sally, our neighbour, whose stove is electric.

What now? Luckily we have a small battery radio from years back, and it can still just make itself audible. News, all comparatively local, and advice. Drain the plumbing! Do not open the freezer!

Then our doctor, Jeannie Rosenberg, phones. She and her husband, Hugh Sutherland, would be glad to put us up, they would come and fetch us. Hugh has a sheep farm on the outskirts of town. They have a big woodburning stove in the kitchen that heats their whole house.

Then Sinpoh Han, our rector, and his wife, Christine, propose taking us in. But Jamie Quinn, our son-in-law, has already come to scoop us up and drive us to their place, six miles southwest in the country. He and our Nora have an organic market garden there. They have three young, Seamus, seventeen, Katy, fifteen, and Jonathan, twelve, all on hand, along with Jonathan's friend Matthew King.

Five and a half days of festival for us and the young. A splendid array of jigsaw puzzles, some very grand, alternate with games of cribbage. Much music. Besides piano practising there are duets, Katy with Ellie Moss, her friend from the second farm east. There is much visiting back and forth with neighbours. For Jeanne and me it is a reminiscence of regular country life in the early 1920s.

There is little enough leisure for Jamie and Nora. They fetch in water from one of their irrigation ditches, twice a day, and pour it into the bathtub upstairs. This just takes care of light personal washing and not-unduly-frequent toilet flushing. Jamie fetches drinking water from the nearest neighbour's well, half a mile away. Their own drinking water is normally fetched up from a deep well near the house, by electric pump.

Damn! says Jamie. I have been meaning to put a hand-pump in the cellar. Wait till this lot is over. Now and again we walk out to glimpse an amazing world. Branches are down everywhere. Beneath the trees the icy ground is thick with them. Some trees are leaning badly, and many birches are right over, their tops frozen into the ice. Power and telephone poles are down, and wires lie beside the roads, and on them. Hydro trucks have been coming in increasing numbers from upper New York State, to lend a hand.

After two days the weather clears marvellously, and our walks are now in bright sunshine. What scene has ever been so strange and beautiful as the ice-coated trees have made, with many of their fallen branches on the glistening ground beneath? There is a glory about it that we could not have imagined, and are not likely to see again.

Our holiday is brief. After a few days the power is back on in our townhouse, so Jamie drives us home. We are sorry to leave, but our separate lives, theirs especially, can now take up again.

George Johnston, who was eighty-four years old during the ice storm, is one of Canada's most respected poets. His collected poems, Endeared by Dark, *were published in 1990. He lives in Huntingdon, Quebec.*

GHISLAINE SALVAIL

"A city paralyzed in crystal": that was the front-page headline of *Le Devoir* on January 7, 1998, referring to the metropolis. But Montreal was not the only crystallized city: St-Hyacinthe also glittered. At dawn, the scene was both beautiful and terrifying. The frosted trees lay broken under the weight of garlands of ice, diamonds too heavy for them to wear. Streets that were strewn with branches and shining like mirrors would go untouched by traffic. Electric wires trailed across the frozen ground, still imprisoned by ice. What a desolate landscape had been created in the course of that crazy night, as branches shattered with a noise that hurt the ears to hear!

In the towns and villages of the ice triangle – a shape defined by the cities of St-Hyacinthe, St-Jean and Granby – row upon row of Hydro-Québec pylons had collapsed. Their metal bodies lay recumbent in the fields like the skeletons of great animals struck down by lightning.

We were living through a catastrophe. The region's economy would suffer lasting damage. Each home was isolated, each person cut off from the outside world. On radio programs, the anguish was palpable.

Faced with the gravity of the ordeal, fifteen religious communities came together to raise money: more than seventy-two thousand dollars in total. The Sisters of St. Joseph – the order, based in St-Hyacinthe, to which I belong – were chosen to manage this money and to use it to help people in need, as well as small businesses in danger of closure or bankruptcy. Other social and ecclesiastical bodies donated their money, their time and their premises; churches, schools, convents and community centres were all opened up. Generators and firewood arrived from all over. We are not alone – we have brothers and sisters who care about other people surviving in the dark and the cold. Solidarity forever!

Doors opened, tables were laid. Neighbours who, until yesterday, ignored each other came together around a stove, a fireplace, a furnace. Lasting friendships were formed. Reserve supplies were combined. Kitchen shelves and freezers emptied so that meals could be shared. In short, we carried out small actions that warmed and nourished – both literally and figuratively speaking. Whoever said we were living in a time when individualism ruled, and when "every man for himself" was the order of the day? The ice storm showed that prejudice to be a lie.

Out of forty-four thousand people living in the region, about twenty-seven thousand were able to resist the cold and stay home, thanks to the care of their families and neighbours. Each lodging contained families that bore a strange resemblance to those of yesteryear – it was again an everyday event to find thirteen people at the dinner table. Solitude was replaced by solidarity.

What was there to do during those long candlelit evenings? Conversations would last into the small hours of the night. Old memories would spring to mind. While the soup heated up on the woodstove, there was time to rock babies and entertain children. Some people tell us they sang the old songs of Father Charles-Emile Gadbois that were once so dear to the hearts of people in this area.

And as sisters, we were able to share our good fortune with our employees. All of them were invited to take refuge with us, thanks to our powerful generator. It didn't disappoint – it burned nine thousand litres of diesel fuel to maintain our heat and light. About eighty lay people were able to benefit from this.

In the course of intimate conversations, people who remain very private during work hours behaved quite differently. Many of them told us about their needs, both spiritual and material. Exchanges of prayers were a comfort, an encouragement. What we did, other parishes and religious communities did too. Even though we were the prisoners of weather, we were on a work of mission.

Ghislaine Salvail, a member of the Sisters of St. Joseph, lives in St-Hyacinthe and writes regularly for Catholic magazines in Quebec. She also does pastoral resource work with families in the diocese of St-Hyacinthe.

DALE MORLAND

My wife Susan and I live in an old brick house near the Experimental Farm in Ottawa. Ice storms are not exactly rare in the Ottawa area. In the thirteen years I have lived in this town, I have never had to buy wood for the fireplace; I can count on a good supply from fallen branches, due to the ice storms which happen almost every winter. The major one in 1998 was simply particularly severe, and I now have enough wood for years.

Power failures are rare in the middle of Ottawa, but they do happen. In the rural areas, you can expect them.

Years ago I noted these facts and thought about what could be done in my place if we lost power. I noted we had a fireplace for basic heat, camping equipment for essential cooking, city water which is highly unlikely to fail, and natural-gas water heating, also highly reliable. The only item that might have been a problem was whole-house heating, as the furnace requires electricity to operate.

It didn't take too much investigation for me to realize that there are only two items in the furnace needing electricity: the gas valve and the fan motor. The gas valve is a very small power consumer, and uses 24 volts AC (alternating current) in normal operation. But the fan has a fairly large motor using normal house-line voltage. It seemed obvious to me that this would be a good application for pedal power. We needed only to set up a bicycle arrangement to drive the fan, and some kind of electrical scheme to turn on the gas valve. I had intended to run an experiment sometime to check out this idea, but like a lot of other projects (I have a long list), it never got further than accumulating bicycle parts. Raising three boys, renovating a house, leading Cubs, Scouts and Venturers, rock-climbing, vacationing, house maintenance, music-making and so on – activities that compose my life – took greater priority. So my idea stayed no more than a thought.

Then the '98 ice storm happened.

At first we thought it might be a short outage. We live near a major hospital, and the power is very reliable. With many alternate routings, there was a good chance that power would be restored fairly quickly.

On the first evening, we prepared dinner on our Coleman stove (outside, of course, to avoid the fumes). We had running water, both cold and hot, unlike at the cottage, where it is only cold. We had heated our living room very comfortably with the fireplace; our candles and kerosene lamps were burning, giving a pleasant glow to the scene; Susan was reading; my youngest son, Cameron, was playing his mandolin; I was playing my accordion; we were singing and having a good time, when the lights came on and spoiled it all. Cameron went back to his homework and we proceeded with our normal activities. We thought that might be the end of it.

The next day we had another failure. At dinner I mentioned the bicycle idea, and everyone was enthused, especially Cameron and a friend staying at our place, Bob Hillhouse. So now I had to actualize this concept. We dug the bicycle parts out of the garage, along with some odd scraps of wood and plywood, plumber's strapping and screws, and we concocted an arrangement to allow us to stabilize the bicycle and pedal it in place. I happened to have some surgical tubing on hand, as it is useful for clamping large pieces of wood together for glueing, and the tubing served as a belt between the bicycle wheel and the pulley on the furnace fan. That part was pretty straightforward, and we were completely confident we could make it work.

The part that required experimentation on the spot was the bit about getting the gas to flow so we would have flame. Now, I am an electrical engineer, and arrived at such a state by being interested in electrical things for as long as I can remember. Some time during the years of playing around with electrical devices of various kinds, I had determined that relays which normally run on AC can also run on DC (direct current), but at a much lower voltage. Thus I felt that since the gas valve normally uses 24 VAC, it might very well work from 12 VDC. We happened to have a small gel-cell battery of 12 volts which my son had been using in his robots, so we didn't have to lug in the battery from the van. With a couple of clip leads attached to the battery, we disconnected the wires normally powering the valve, touched the leads to the terminals on the valve, and lo, "We have ignition!" (My exact words.) Exhilaration prevailed. Cheers all around.

So, we assembled the apparatus, turned on the gas and proceeded to pedal. We did not have an ideal arrangement for this. The bicycle had been installed upside-down, to make mounting on the plywood sheet easier, but that meant we had to sit on the washing machine, giving a somewhat awkward angle for the legs. But it worked okay. About an hour's pedalling took the house temperature up from 15°C to 20°C, and the individual body temperatures much higher, as it was fairly strenuous. If you have ever tried out the bicycle generator demonstrations at science centres or technical museums, you know the effort needed to get even a small lightbulb glowing. So, even though the fan motor is a fractional horsepower motor, we still couldn't equal it. But it was good enough. All the males in the house took turns to even out the workload.

With that in place, we were able to endure our short time without power very easily. We were out only two days. It would have been tiring to have a longer outage, but our set-up would have worked. The surgical-tubing belt probably would have had to be replaced.

One thing should be mentioned here. There is a real potential danger in turning on the gas valve directly. This bypasses all safety features for automatic shut-off in case of overheating. We always had at least two people on the spot when we were operating, one to pedal and the other to monitor the temperature of the furnace (it appears on a thermostat dial of the safety switch in the plenum). It would have been possible to connect this safety switch in the circuit, but I felt that direct monitoring was okay. If the gas valve was left on unattended, the furnace would melt. I do not recommend that anyone try all this unless they can draw on appropriate experience.

Dale Morland must be one of Ottawa's most resourceful electrical engineers.

KRISTEN RITCHIE

We woke to a wonderland of ice, where the horizon of land and sky connected in a continuous blue that complemented the greyness of the ice. We crept our way into the village and at once recognized the strength of this silent storm. Hydro lines were down; clocks and radios, too. We were now an island in the truest sense. I welcomed the opportunity.

A twenty-minute ferry ride from Kingston, Wolfe Island is a kind of community that I hadn't been a part of since I was a kid – an open, peaceful, rural landscape. A place where you know your neighbours by the kind of truck they drive; where Sunday visiting still exists; and

The message that Kristen Ritchie and her Wolfe Island friends
used the ice storm to convey. (Photo: Virginia Clark)

where, in the village, there will surely be someone to greet. And so when our basement flooded, we didn't have to look far for help.

We had taken in a houseful of folks – with two woodstoves, beds to spare, a cold room to store our food, and endless candles to lighten the darkness, we had ourselves an extended New Year's party. While some of us chose to explore the icy landscape, keeping in mind to step over fallen lines and stay clear of crackling oak trees, the rest of us took turns cooking up a meal or, with a book in tow, giving in to the silence and finding a warm, comfortable spot to read. After all, Mother Earth was clearly in control, and nobody was going to try and defy her. And when we grew weary of the stillness, we communed at the fire hall, where you were sure to meet a crowd.

It was here that the strength of the island was revealed through tireless volunteer effort. Many of us took turns cooking meals for the Hydro workers and the islanders, even driving food to people who were stuck indoors because of fallen poles. Indeed it was a unique experience and I enjoyed all of it.

During a time when there was much debate between preserving the ferry or building a bridge to the mainland, a change that would inevitably shift the essence of the island, the ice storm revealed the island's self-sufficiency. And when we were in need of supplies, the ferry proved faithful, never missing a beat.

It became apparent that we were the focus of media attention when Prime Minister Chrétien's chopper landed near our yard. Why we received so much exposure wasn't clear, but I decided to use the opportunity. My heart pounded with fierce determination to find the words to express my feelings about this gentle, pastoral paradise of mine. So simple.

Kristen Ritchie is a Kingston writer.

DENIS POIRIER

I am a civil servant who works in Hull, and after the ice storm began, the federal government closed my office for a week – those buildings drain a lot of power from the Hydro-Québec system. Instead of just sitting around, I decided to help out. My wife works in the head office of the Red Cross, and we arranged for my in-laws to look after our son. He was only four at the time, and we didn't see him too much. But my in-laws understood that some people really needed help. I ended up putting in a lot of ten-hour days for the Red Cross, doing a lot of driving especially. But it was fun!

I have a four-wheel-drive van, and one evening I had to drive out to the shelter in Plantagenet, on the old Highway 17 that goes along the Ottawa River. I drive that road often and I know it well. That night I went and picked up a whole load of blankets that The Bay had donated. It took me a couple of hours to get to Plantagenet, because the road was so icy. I was about the only vehicle on the road. It was weird, driving and not seeing any lights from streets or houses – just total darkness. I was amazed at how total the blackout was. Once I reached the shelter, which was in a school, I found it had a real good atmosphere. It was nice to see all the families gathered there. Everyone helped unload the van, and they said, "Come in and have a coffee!" They were well set up with a generator from the fire department.

I think the storm was often traumatizing for parents, but the kids had a pretty good time. Another day I went to the shelter in Clarence Creek, and I saw all the kids were in one corner. They had a few military people in the shelter, and the soldiers had all the kids doing sit-ups and push-ups. They were keeping the kids amused.

One evening the Red Cross got a call from a shelter looking for baby formula. It had to be soy, because the baby was allergic to milk, and there was none available in the area. I had to deliver food for four hundred people to a nearby shelter in Alexandria, so they asked me to purchase and deliver the needed formula. I went to a pharmacy – I had my Red Cross hat and arm band on – and I explained to the woman behind the counter what I needed. She not only gave me the formula, she also said, "Do you need diapers?" I said, "Well, we can use whatever you'll donate." So she gave me some packages of diapers too.

While I was out doing deliveries in the country one night, I came across a truck parked by the side of the road, in the middle of nowhere. I stopped to see what was going on, and it turned out the guy was watching a Bell generator. It was hooked up to some boxes so that they could boost the power in the phone lines. He had to stay, or else the generator would have been stolen. But he had his TV on in the truck and he was watching the Senators game. He was happy.

The first few days, I didn't charge for anything. Then someone said, "Look, we can pay for your gas." So I charged for the gas – but nothing else. I just wanted to volunteer and be involved in the whole operation. I just wanted to do my part. I did get a few free lunches – it was amazing how many companies donated food to feed the staff and volunteers who were working such long days.

One evening it was ten-thirty or eleven and I was pretty tired. I was just about to pick up my wife – she had been answering calls in the office all day – and go home. But then a senior citizen phoned and needed some food. He couldn't get out of his house, he was on an oxygen cylinder. So I took him some food and *then* I picked up my wife.

I also worked at the Red Cross warehouse for a couple of days. I was unloading trucks by hand, since I was not allowed to drive the forklift. All kinds of donated supplies were pouring in from Tim Hortons, WalMart, Zellers and many other companies. While I was taking inventory, I was interviewed by CTV News. My relatives saw me on TV but I missed it – I was too busy!

There were some problems at the beginning with the military, the regional municipality, and the Red Cross not working as a team. It would have been more efficient if they had all got together to organize a central depot where supplies could be sent in, and from there distributed to the various shelters. As it was, we had to pick up supplies from three different places. After nine days, the military finally came to pick up and distribute all the food and supplies from the Red Cross.

Then my job was done. My volunteer days were over. What a great experience!

Denis Poirier works in the Department of Legal Services, Human Resources Development, in Hull, Quebec.

BILL DODGE

I remember waking up in the middle of the night, a young child, unaware of the FLQ and the historic tensions that were bursting out into the open in Montreal in the 1960s, to the sound of breaking glass. The noise that had startled me from my sleep turned out to be the result of two bombs exploding within seconds of each other. The first bomb had blown the whole front entrance out of the brick house directly across the street from where we lived. The second bomb had damaged a house around the corner on Westmount Avenue. Fortunately, no one was injured by these blasts, but I still remember the sound of the windows in our house vibrating from the shock waves. Instead of shattering all at once, they broke in an eerie sequence.

Recalling this experience from childhood, I'm reminded of the difference between the many jarring sounds that break through the white noise of our lives, only to recede again, and those sounds that have an almost archetypal force to them. Whether they spring from the natural world or from human conflicts, there are certain sounds the body never forgets.

Vermont's "ice storm of the century" began for me with a crack of wood that jolted me out of bed. The sudden snapping of a fifty-foot black locust tree in our neighbour's backyard had all the force of a gunshot. It was followed by a terrible rending noise as the heavy ice-laden tree fell to the ground, narrowly missing our neighbour's roof. The impact shook our whole house. As I stood at the window listening to the tension-filled trees, their branch tips bent almost to the ground, I

One of the many casualties of the storm along the
older streets of Burlington, Vermont.

was in awe of this huge creaking armour of ice that nature had created.

The ice storm damaged nearly one million acres of forest in Vermont and cut off electricity to more than thirty-five thousand people. The damage was concentrated mainly in the low-lying northern region along Lake Champlain. Vermont's governor, Howard Dean, responded to the crisis with the largest disaster mobilization of the National Guard since flooding overwhelmed the state in 1973. Grand Isle County was Vermont's hardest-hit area, but the governor also declared states of emergency in three other counties. He even issued a special public appeal on behalf of the cows on Grand Isle. They were in danger of dying because farmers couldn't ventilate their barns.

Huddled in sleeping bags around the gas fireplace that was our only source of heat for two days, we listened to the bones of the wind rattling over our Burlington house. We were among the lucky ones who didn't have to sleep in an emergency shelter. Although the half-dozen oak trees in front of our seventy-year-old slate-roofed house were dropping their ice-laden branches one by one, the worst damage we suffered was a leak over our attic bedroom. Once their initial fears subsided, our two children experienced a special re-enchantment with a world that had turned suddenly into a giant ice sculpture. This magic soon rubbed off on their parents and sent us all outdoors to explore the streets in our neighbourhood.

At the Mater Christi School, a block away from our house, one of the oldest pine trees in the state had been claimed by the storm. Our children had been climbing in its branches the previous summer when they were still students of the Sisters of Mercy and were complaining regularly about the Sisters' academic regime. On the same street as the school, many mid-sized maple trees had been split right down the middle of their trunks to the ground, their main branches pulled apart like wishbones. The spruces and fir trees looked like so many collapsed umbrellas. Utility poles were leaning precariously towards the ground.

Early estimates suggested that half of Burlington's trees were damaged by the storm, but the true effects are still not known. Wet weather in the summer of '98 helped many sugar maples to recover, but the susceptibility of some damaged trees to disease and insects means that it will take years before the final outcome of the ice storm is apparent. If there is a silver lining to be found in all this destruction, it has to be in the actions of countless citizens who came to the rescue of both young and old Vermonters affected by the storm. This spirit of generosity was also demonstrated by the mayor of Burlington, Peter Clavelle, who organized the delivery of firewood and dry logs to Iberville, a city in the St-Jean-sur-Richelieu area, where Quebeckers were forced to endure almost a month without power.

Many utility workers from Vermont, Maine and other U.S. states also crossed the border to help Hydro-Québec repair its severely damaged infrastructure. This happened despite an expensive power contract between Vermont and Hydro-Québec which was signed in 1991 and is now pushing Vermont's power companies to the edge of bankruptcy. A key component of this contract (there are still another twenty years remaining on it) was the promised reliability of Hydro-Québec's power. That sales pitch may need reworking in light of the almost three-month disruption in power transmission to Vermont that followed the ice storm's supposed act of God.

After living in several Canadian provinces, Bill Dodge and his wife, Bene, now run the Silver Maple Gallery in Burlington, Vermont.

GERRY ROY

Some twenty-five years ago, on a Sunday afternoon outing with the children, we saw at a flea market a small, rusty, cast-iron box stove resting on the ground, without legs. It looked rather helpless, forlorn and unappealing. For some reason, its legs had been placed inside it. It had been cast in 1898 in a small Quebec village in a now-defunct foundry. We bought it to serve as part of the decor and as a conversation piece in a semi-finished basement room which had been built as part of a house extension a few years before. We took it to a sand-blasting shop where they did a splendid job of cleaning it. It came back a gleaming grey. Since any self-respecting stove must be black, we polished it with stove polish to a smooth, velvety finish. For realism, and for usefulness, the installation was completed by connecting the stove to a chimney flue opening.

Well, during the ice storm crisis, that stove was a lifesaver. In St-Bruno, my wife, Lise, and I were without power for fifteen days and the stove provided us with heat, cooking capability and peace of mind.

Our neighbours, both seniors like ourselves, happened to be sick when the storm struck. Not bedridden, but really not well. We therefore invited them to move in with us for the duration, thinking that our power supply would be restored within a few days. They accepted. The stove in the basement, just below the family room, provided adequate heat to the upper room. So for five days, our guests slept on the couch in the family room while my wife and I slept in our bedroom, which was getting colder every day. However, with extra blankets and wearing jogging suits, we managed quite well. When we slipped out of bed in the morning, needless to say, we rushed to the heated room.

The first five days, we ate a hot dinner in the family room, on a round table just right for four people. An oil lamp in the middle of the table gave atmosphere. Cooking dinner on a small stove in the basement and carting everything up and down stairs requires some planning. As the planning of meals was refined, fewer trips were made, but many were required nonetheless. As sample dinner menus, we had lamb stewed in mushroom sauce with vegetables, sirloin steak with homemade mushroom sauce, Chinese hotpot, pasta with meat sauce, all complemented with wine. One day we even had an entrée of snails in a bubbling hot and beautifully seasoned butter sauce. During the entire crisis we did not once eat canned food.

By the fifth day, our bedroom was getting too cold, about 8°C. In the semi-finished room where the stove was located, we built a platform with a large wooden bed frame that belongs to one of our daughters and had been "temporarily" stored in our basement, along with some of her other belongings, for seven or eight years. We carried twin mattresses downstairs and placed them on the bed frame. To avoid the colder air near the floor, the bed frame was elevated onto four big wood pallets that were – and are – slated for splitting into firewood. So on the fifth day, we slept in the basement. Because we had equipped it with a standby pump about twenty years ago, our sump did not overflow and the basement stayed dry.

With the limited wood supply, the oncoming cold snap, and their own state of health, our neighbours decided they would be better off at the shelter in the local high school. Lise and I then moved all our activities down into the basement and left the upstairs unused, except for a bathroom. Every second day, I visited our neighbours at the shelter, and while there I took a hot shower. As darkness set in by late afternoon, and with only two oil lamps for lighting, which are insufficient for reading, we had little choice but to have early dinners and retire very early. On two or three occasions we played cards after dinner, but our interest in the games was short lived.

Although not by design, we had settled around the stove. All our activities centred on it. We relied on it for heat and for our meals. It had become our lifeline, as the kitchen stove had been to our great-grandparents, to whom, however, it was normal and not a hardship. But then, they were unaware of electric lights, central heating, electric ovens, radio and television. . . . The same storm a century ago would surely have been an inconvenience but likely not a crisis. Our basement room had become our kitchen, our dining room, our living room and our bedroom. It had become a one-room house. Oftentimes during our stay near the stove, seeing the casting date on it, 1898, I reflected on the foundry workers who had cast it. Little did they know of the heroic role their creation would be playing a hundred years hence. Our stove had by now truly passed the test of time.

Dishes in the kitchen cupboards were getting much too cold, and at first were heated in a makeshift fashion. When we moved downstairs, we built a wide shelf, suspended from the ceiling joists with sturdy wire, directly above the stove. On it we placed all the dishes we normally used, and, being directly above the stove, they were kept nicely warm. A woodstove requires a good supply of air – and so did we. In our basement room, there are three windows that are fortunately large enough to provide reasonable light in the daytime. The one closest to the stove was used for ventilation. Its vent slots, being kept open at all times, provided an adequate air supply. However, a cold air flow came down on whoever was sitting in the chair on that side of the stove. To avoid the cold draft, we fashioned a baffle with piece of plywood to divert the air upwards – another improvement to our comfort.

The constant change of air plus the heat increased the dryness in the heated room. To correct the situation, moisture had to be added constantly. So, we kept a large pot full of water on the stove except at cooking time. This had a double purpose: it provided humidity in the air as well as hot water for washing dishes and for our sponge baths. As the joists for the floor above are still exposed, we drove about a dozen nails into them and hung up clothes to dry on clothes hangers. Drying clothes was quite fast and, in the process, it too provided some of the much needed moisture to the air. Only the essentials were washed regularly, again using the hot water from the large pot on the stove.

One would think that spending most of our time in a single room meant that we had little to do. True, the housekeeping was simple, but practically everything had to be done during the eight hours of daylight, except the preparation of our evening meal. There was a little laundry every day, dishwashing, a bit of cleaning, chopping firewood and carting it from the wood pile, frequent stoking of the stove, errands to fetch groceries, odds and ends to make our stay in the basement a little more bearable, and of course our sponge baths. I also did a bit of yard work at home and at a neighbour's place, cutting branches and propping up the telephone line. Somehow, these tasks filled our days. We did take one or two hours every day to read the Montreal papers, one English, one French.

By the twelfth day, we felt that we had had enough, but being well aware that others were in far worse situations, we were willing to go on. Actually, we had not much choice. It was then that we decided to step out a bit beyond going out for errands. My wife spent three days helping out at the local shelter and coming home at night – a different atmosphere from the basement routine! On the fifteenth day, I had two appointments in Montreal, where power had been restored almost entirely. My wife reached me at one of them to happily announce that we had power at home. I suddenly had the feeling that something was draining out from my body, possibly tension or fatigue, or both. Whatever it was, it was followed by a long sigh of relief. Midway into my second appointment, an eye checkup, a power failure forced its cancellation.

Lise and I get along pretty well, but we have always maintained a certain independence from one another. We are not at a loss when one of us is away; sometimes we vacation separately. We have joint activities and we have separate activities. We have common friends and we also have separate friends. I play three sports and my wife devours books. I don't know how to define our relationship, but it works. Although we are together most of the time, our house is spacious enough so we can avoid being in each other's way. Until the ice storm, we had never lived in such close quarters, practically twenty-four hours a day, for such an extended period. But even though the situation was anything but easy, our nerves somehow did not get frayed. In retrospect, we would think that the crisis was a sort of test of our relationship. If so, we surely deserve a pass mark – a good one!

Gerry Roy is a retired consulting engineer and an ardent do-it-yourselfer in St-Bruno, Quebec. He has worked on major infrastructure projects as well as his own basement.

CHRISTINE McILREAVY

I live in a large townhouse complex, with sidewalks intertwining through the houses and garden areas that look so attractive in the summer. During the ice storm, the scene outside was breathtaking in beauty: trees coated in ice, every imaginable thing coated in its own casing of ice. But the buildup on our sidewalks was making it impossible to walk, so no deliveries of any kind had been attempted. Most of the residents had left home to stay with friends who had light, or in hotels that had power.

I was sharing my days with my friend Lorna. Each afternoon we would settle down on the couch with our hot-water bottles and nice warm blankets (one red and one blue), tucked well in so as not to lose one tiny bit of heat. This day, we had put our books down and drifted off into a comfortable sleep. A sudden noise disturbed this peaceful scene . . . the doorbell?

Impossible! No one could walk on the treacherous eight inches of ice. Trying to gain some sort of dignity, I answered the door as wild thoughts flew through my mind.

There, to my surprise, was a delivery man trying to balance the most wonderful arrangement of flowers. Bright yellows, red and blues stood out against the stark surroundings of ice, and all protected in transparent wrapping, with a matching bow. The look of amazement on my face was apparent as the delivery man reassured me the flowers were for me.

As I closed the door, still in shock and holding the floral arrangement, I came in sight of my friend, who had just awakened from her nap. To be sure, she thought she was in heaven! Can you imagine the laughter as we carefully placed the flowers in our freezing room, instantly transformed into a special place?

This wonderful surprise was sent from friends in Wichita, Kansas. They had been watching our problems unfold on television. It certainly brightened our day and gave us a memory we shall never forget: flowers in the midst of the ice storm of the century.

Christine McIlreavy is a retired nurse living in St. Lambert, Quebec.

9

DAMAGE CONTROL

eteorologists aside, we don't remember the ice storm because of the weather. The weather was a catalyst, a provocation. What mattered most were the experiences it spawned, the feelings it provoked.

On the first day or two, it turned careworn adults into artists, amazed by the evidence of their own eyes, seeing the fractured world anew. Thousands of people took their cameras in hand and gingerly stepped outside, determined to preserve this glittering evidence of a world where the rules, as well as the trees, were broken. Many of those pictures would prove disappointing, because the sun hardly shone for five or six days and the sky in a lot of amateur photographs – my own included – is a dreary, louring grey. But also, I suspect, the experience of the storm was too overwhelming to be easily captured on film. Noises of breakage were coming from all directions; everywhere you looked, there was proof of pressure, transformation, collapse; it wasn't easy to find the right frame in which to capture all this change.

Days passed. Over time, anything – even a crystallized car or garden – starts to seem familiar. In any case, not everybody during the ice storm had the privilege to stop and look, just look, with the childlike sense of wonder the storm deserved. For most of us, the wonder faded as the fatigue grew. Besides, the freezing rain had consequences: flooded basements that were anything but picturesque, broken bones that would take longer than an electricity network to heal, lost income that could never be retrieved. For many people the storm turned into a battle, a whole series of battles, to limit the harm. Some things could be saved, others restored; but the harm was sometimes permanent.

This chapter describes how individuals in three provinces and many walks of life fought to save or heal themselves and what they loved. In a few cases, the *fight was not so much material as psychological: to keep a relationship alive; to keep faith in oneself and one's community under conditions of enormous stress. Hearts, no less than basements, are prone to damage.*

ROSE DeSHAW

I think my first mistake was being born in Alaska, the home of frigidity. Which meant that I started my life off cold and never got warmed up. Forgive me if it sometimes seems that God sent a massive ice storm simply to get me out of the book business. I went to bed January 8 over my Kingston shop with cats, dog, husband – and below, some 35,000 old books nestled alphabetically all snug on their shelves. Next morning, no heat, no water, and whether I knew it or not, no shop.

My second mistake was building shelves – in the shop – that blocked the pipes that delivered our hot-water heat from a boiler in the basement. Over a period of twenty years, as we got more books, I built more shelves till The Idea Factory was a single-file labyrinth some ten feet high that wove around and through the entire downstairs. Nobody ever said anything about asking a plumber before we built.

There were boxes of books on the floor as the shelves spilled over and boxes on top of those. There were stacks of poetry jostling geography and blocking the nineteenth-century novels that leaned up against the Greek and Latin classics. True, more than three people in the shop at a time was overcrowding, but the books were what was important. We used to joke that they bred in the dark. Perhaps they did.

The boiler hadn't ever quit before. With all the insulation the books provided, it hadn't ever gotten really cold in the shop or in our apartment upstairs. So when we woke up freezing in the dark along with everyone else, we figured we'd sit tight. The dog was bigger than a pot-bellied stove and just as warm. With him and the cats in bed, we weren't entirely without heat. So we hung out in bed, listened to the radio telling us to stay home and took showers at the YWCA. Next door, a fifty-year-old maple fell on our neighbour's brand new van and crushed the roof. Live power lines pulled loose and lay in the streets, sparking.

Our pipes and boiler froze up solid even though we got plumbers to come in twice and stumble around in the dark to determine just how much trouble we were in.

I would never hold up under torture. It took less than a week before I cracked. We were sitting at McDonald's four blocks from home. There was light and heat and people going about their business. And we were supposed to return to what I started calling "Our Book Freezer." In the block around our premises was darkness, a tangle of fallen trees, dangling wires and ice. These two halves of our world seemed unjoinable.

We evacuated. Cats to the vet. Hound with us to move into the one-bedroom apartment of a young student who had a middle-aged mastiff and a Great Dane puppy. He was also hosting a couple with a Doberman and had another student with a husky over for dinner. A tight, furry fit.

The student moved in with his parents, taking one of the dogs. After fighting over the single bed with the mastiff for a week, we moved in with the other student, who had also been hosting ice storm victims. Both dog owners were young enough to be our children.

It was three weeks into the storm by then. The power was back on. Including ours, except the places where the fuses had short-circuited, due to leaks. But we had no heat, no plumbing, and we weren't about to get any as long as the pipes remained hidden by the masses of books.

The local paper put us and our books on the front page, in colour. And our credit union called and offered us their staff room upstairs beside the executive offices. Two vacant, unfurnished office rooms with toilet, fridge and sink. Free rent. We relocated for the third time and collected the cats. Now it was time for the books.

A sincere little troop of Boy Scouts offered to haul the books off, individually, to storage. I couldn't imagine how long that would have taken – if we had had anywhere to put them. The corner of a church basement was offered. Another basement was suggested, one that didn't *always* flood in the spring. Somebody thought they could find a truck. But I knew we were talking hundreds of truckloads. Not only did we have to get the books out, but the shelves too. Our insurance broker in Toronto, a personal friend, wouldn't return our calls. Our insurance company said there was a clause whereby they didn't have to pay us anything.

It was obvious we needed money, even with the offers of help and the free rent. We sat our aging selves down and tried to imagine doing the sorting, trucking, storing, unbuilding process in the cold. And after repairs, its reverse. Given our physical condition and need for income to fix things, only one solution presented itself. Sell out.

The local paper ran another front-page story. We trickled back into the shop icebox to look at the books. I had always seen a great many of the titles as a trust. If I didn't have them available till they came back into vogue again, who would? There was the set of red-covered classics on the blood, given me by an elderly nurse who had rescued them from a hospital-library dumping. All my Kennedy stuff, John F., Robert, Jackie, Joe, Rose, and their marriages and divorces and the ripples caused by their lives. American popular culture. Nineteenth-century minor women novelists, waiting to be rediscovered. Who cared but me?

But if we didn't clear out, we would have to remain at the credit union, and sooner or later they were bound to notice we were still there. About then the Siamese got out and raced around the executive offices, over the mahogany desks, with the hound close behind. As we lay on our futon on the floor, we could hear the *ca-ching* of the cash registers downstairs and the ringing of the business phones. The CEO's wife made us a lasagna with her own hands, and he sent an enormous food basket, but it wasn't home. Home was cold and freezing, the Idea Factory from hell.

We started to sort after writing a very difficult advertisement for a sale in two weeks' time. After an hour, our brains began to freeze up. We managed to clear some trails through the premises, to put up signs about wholesale prices and to find books under other books we hadn't seen in years. The neighbour with the crushed van had run an extension cord to the insurance company behind him and plugged in two heaters. He loaned us one. It sat beside the phone, which never stopped ringing. If anyone invited us over for coffee, we'd go into their bathroom and take a bath.

The day before the sale, it was obvious we weren't going to make it. There were still umpteen Shakespeares sitting on John Cheever and John Donne and John Bunyan, and all of Commonwealth literature balanced on a small furnace the plumbers had thought we could use and had left behind when we couldn't. The house wiring wouldn't support a generator. *Life* from the 1940s was being trampled underfoot, together with some copies of the British forerunner of *Reader's Digest* from the early 1800s.

There was a knock on the front door, probably the 285th since we'd started sorting. There stood a friend with a broom and a take-charge attitude. "Okay, let's move these and stack these and take these down and store these," she said. A sort of mouth-to-mouth resuscitation, not only for us but for the shop. By evening, I thought maybe we could do it, if we let only three or four people in at a time.

In the morning it looked as though everyone in our town of 150,000 was lined up in the yard. CBC Radio came in first. "How do you feel about losing the business you spent a lifetime building up?" (Pretty well like a death in the family.) Then came the hordes. Multitudes. Wall-to-wall book lovers. I cowered up front by the heater and made change from one pocket to another. My husband squeezed into the rest of the shop and helped solve logistics problems of how to get at the books we were supposedly selling. Hilaire Belloc, C.S. Lewis and P.L. Travers went out the door along with handbooks on gold mining and old physics texts in German.

It took a while to get everyone out when we had to close. More were still coming. We'd go back to the credit union, roll and deposit all the change, crawl upstairs and fall asleep on the floor with our still-skittish animals curled close beside us. In the morning there would be another lineup.

People brought hot soup, muffins, coffee, bags and twenty years of memories. Stories of the books they'd bought from us and what had happened as a result of reading them, the progress of their ideas and the people they'd met while browsing, squeezed between the shelves. Pictures were taken, inside and out. Periodically we'd stop and rush over to use the neighbour's bathroom across the street.

Crates and boxes and bags of books went out the door, and yet when you looked around you could hardly see where they'd been. It was like the Red Sea rushing back behind Moses. We packed and sold and still they filled in the spaces where their brother books had been. And then it was the last day of the sale, and we closed the doors and looked around at rooms that were still entirely full of books. The principal of a new school that wanted our shelves came over with an editor friend and spent the day dismantling boards with crowbars. I heard them plough through Newtonian physics, Keynesian economics and the poetic influence of Dylan Thomas.

Two local booksellers took books for credit, for trade, for love, in little bags, bit by bit. In the meantime I went to the supermarket two blocks away and someone said, "Isn't it wonderful that the ice storm is over?" and I growled at them. Outside, the box-boy said his uncle, who was the drummer for a band called Blind Fury, also installed furnaces in his spare time, and would we like him to come take a look?

With all the devastation in town, getting a plumber was like winning the lottery, especially a plumber who was awake. Besides, the Blind Fury name seemed like an omen. The uncle-plumber-drummer also dabbled in electrical work, knew bits and pieces of all the other trades, and where to get anything in town at the right price. A scraggle-bearded angel. The mounds of books began to diminish. A bookseller's three sons were trucking them to another shop called Books in the Woods, which was out of town: down, up and around on an unpaved dirt road near a small lake surrounded by aspen, beech, fir, oak, maple and masses of sumach.

Seeing the books depart was like watching something living go away. Kittens or puppies, maybe. Would they be treated well? Would they go where they would be useful? Would I ever see them again?

By then we'd been living away from home for two months. To most folks the ice storm was fast becoming a memory, but nobody mentioned that to me after my first growl. We'd spent every cent from the sale, maxed out our line of credit and our credit card, lost our stock and our business – and then one day a carpenter-plumber-singer friend of the uncle-plumber-drummer said we could probably move back in if we wanted. "It doesn't leak much," was the way he put it.

What it was, was empty. The whole downstairs. No books, no shelves, no business. I could recite which titles had sat where in the empty air.

A government commission on the ice storm came through town. Everyone on the panel recognized me with an unnecessarily guilty start. They'd talk about being without power a whole day, two whole days, then look at me apologetically, much to the out-of-town moderator's bewilderment.

Then I began to talk about the bomb that was the ice storm that had gone off in my life, blotting out the past and obscuring the future. Bomb? Nobody's dead. Neither of us have completely broken down into our component parts. Even the cats and hound survived our changes of address.

"Ice Storm 10, Home Team 0," I tell someone later, in a bookshop.

"What're you doing in here?" the clerk says. "I thought you were out of the business?"

"So if I'd had a clothing shop you'd expect me to go around naked?"

I thought maybe writing it all down would make it be over for me. Nope. Didn't work.

Rose DeShaw is a writer living in Kingston.

SALAM AL-MOUSAWI

Date: Tuesday, January 13, 1998.
Time: 11:45 A.M.
Place: LaSalle, Quebec.

That day, we had electricity. I was hosting relatives since they did not have electricity. We were ten people: my wife, my two kids, my mother-in-law, my two brothers-in-law, my sister-in-law, her two kids and myself. We were eight in the living room, following the news on TV. The home is a rented upper five-and-a-half in a duplex.

My wife, my two kids and myself were sitting on the floor against the wall. My mother-in-law and my brother-in-law were sitting on the sofa; one of my sister-in-law's kids (fifteen days old!) was in a swinger and the other, Ali (two-and-a-half years old), was in a safe-stepper. Suddenly, the ceiling collapsed right in the middle of the room, and a lot of water poured right on top of Ali, just next to the TV!

The part of the ceiling that crashed was about three square metres in size. The ice on the building roof had melted, and the water leaked through many openings in the roof and accumulated on the inner ceiling. Luckily, it did not touch any of us, since we were against the walls – except for the frigid water that hit Ali. The previous night, five adults had been sleeping right underneath the part that collapsed.

We managed to calm down everybody and a warm shower gave relief to Ali, who was in shock for minutes. Nobody was injured, thank God. We have a carpet steamer that we used to vacuum all the water. It took us until the night to mop up most of it.

Two days after the collapse, the ceiling in my bedroom started leaking water. I informed the landlord, who opened a hole to let the water come out and reduce the pressure. The next morning, I could see the sky from my bedroom through that small opening! At this time my relatives went back to their home, and my wife and I and our two daughters (then aged one-and-a-half and two-and-a-half) were sleeping in my bedroom, fearing it would collapse on our heads at any moment.

It took three days for the landlord to cover the opening in the living room with a plastic-bag type of cover. After about three weeks, he rebuilt it. I still feel unsafe about the way it was done.

Salam al-Mousawi is a Canadian citizen originally from Iraq. He works as a software developer for Future Electronics.

GAIL GOLDSTEIN

On January 9, we were at my mother's apartment in the Montreal suburb of Côte St-Luc. The power had gone out at our house the day before, and it went out in her eighth-floor apartment that afternoon. My husband had a portable gas camping stove, which he was trying to light in order to make some hot water for coffee. He was in the process of doing so when the whole thing blew up in his face.

He didn't want my mother's apartment to burn down, so he attempted to pick up the flaming stove and throw it in the sink. Unfortunately, he dropped it and had to pick it up again.

The second time, he managed to get it in the sink. In the meantime, the smoke detectors and the fire alarm in the building went off, causing quite a commotion. Neighbours rushed out into the lobby to see what

Jack Goldstein is normally clean-shaven,
but with the burns to his face and hands, he couldn't shave for weeks.

had happened, and the superintendent hurried upstairs to see where the
fire was. My eleven-year-old son panicked and ran down the stairs in
the apartment building, but when he saw that no one was following
him, he came back upstairs crying.

After everybody calmed down, I looked at my husband's hands,
which were hard to see in the dark. He said they were all right – he
wasn't complaining of too much pain, just that it was "burning" – but
I called the district health centre, the CLSC, down the street in
Cavendish Mall and told them what had happened. He didn't want to
go, but they told me to bring him in there immediately. He drove the
car. Thank goodness the driving wasn't too bad and we didn't have to
go too far.

They looked at him right away and told him he had second-degree
burns on both hands and part of his face. He was lucky to be alive! They
cleaned his hands and face with some sort of antiseptic, put on antibiotic cream, and then bandaged up his hands so that it looked like he

was wearing two big white oven mitts! He was quite a sight. I had to drive home.

The next month or so proved an ordeal, as he couldn't do anything for himself. I had to bathe him, dress him, feed him and bring him to the CLSC almost every day to change the bandages. I have to say that the nurses and doctors were marvellous – I have only good things to say about them. My husband took about a week off and worked from home – he was the manager of a telephone company. After that, I had to drive him to work. He was in pretty good spirits, considering. But because of the ice storm, my kids were home from school. By the end of January, I was exhausted.

Gail Goldstein is a mother and homemaker in Côte St-Luc, Quebec.

LAURA-LEE NEIL

For two weeks I was imprisoned in my home, had no TV and was deprived of all contact with my friends. We had to stay with a friend of my father's. The electricity would come on only for a few brief moments, then we would be showered in darkness again. We had to keep all our food outside in the snow because the fridge broke down, and every night we would argue about who slept where. We were completely overcrowded, but I guess that's better than being alone in the weather. As the saying goes, "Misery loves company."

Of course there were some good sides to it. We would always be outside playing on the new fresh carpet of snow left for us every morning. And we did miss a considerable amount of school. The road across the street was completely covered in ice, so all of us would just run and slide on it. We didn't have to worry about cars because no one dared to even try to drive. I took a couple of pictures of the view – it felt almost like we were in a new world, isolated from busy roads and snowblowers and a cacophony of street voices.

One day my father went home to check our house. He was greeted by a stench so disgusting, he went to the basement to find the sewage system had broken down. My father called the landlord, but the landlord was cheap – instead of hiring a repairman, he thought he could fix it on his own. He started messing with the knobs and from the tank came loads of grossness. It hit his face and blew him off his feet. For a week or two after that, we had to keep plastic sheeting on the air vents. The landlord never tried again to fix the sewage system on his own.

Laura-Lee Neil lives in Morin Heights, Quebec, and attends Laurentian Regional High School in Lachute. She was thirteen years old at the time of the storm.

LOIS and BRUCE CRAIGMYLE

Bruce: On the Sunday we took down the signs for the gallery, which had been open till Christmas, and on the Monday we ordered oil for the furnace. It looked like an average freezing rain. The snow was a bit crusty, like normal for freezing rain. The oilman came on the Tuesday and we started to realize how bad it was. He tried navigating his truck into the driveway and we were cautioning him to watch his step because the path was starting to get pretty slippery. Barely an hour after he left, a large branch came crashing down from the poplar tree and landed on the driveway right where his oil truck would have been parked. So that was a hint that things were getting a little strange.

By Wednesday evening the power started going off here in Howick, and we put batteries in the radio and started listening to CBC to figure out if it was more than just our local area. By Thursday the phone line was down – I went out and gathered up what was left of the line, and coiled it at the foot of the telephone pole, so the snowploughs wouldn't get tangled in it. We started feeling it was a pretty severe spell of weather, but we still didn't know how widespread it was.

By now branches were starting to fall pretty regularly, and we put some plywood on the front window. But then a branch came through the sun-porch window. The batteries in my little cordless drill were still holding up, so we covered up that window, but I was running out of plywood. Then on Friday, the spruce trees started shedding their ice and branches – a symphony of *boom, boom,* almost like mortar going off – and chunks of ice the size of footballs would hit the ground. By that time we had our friend and neighbour Joanne here with her two children, and they were camped out in the front room, where the fireplace is.

Lois: They were living in an apartment down the road, and with the power out, they had no heat. When their plants started to die, they got a little scared. The Friday night was most frightening – we put the whole family in here to keep them together, and Bruce and I tried to sleep in the gallery by the big Freeflow stove. But we couldn't sleep at all. I sat on the chair, Bruce was on the hired hand's bed, and the whole house started to shake.

Bruce: And it usually takes a pretty big truck rolling down the street for you to feel the slightest tremor. It was just so spooky. You couldn't really sleep because you never knew when something was going to come crashing through the windows. It was bizarre.

Lois: Through the fits of Friday night, trying to sleep, I had this dream. The last thing I saw before going off to sleep was the house across the street, the brick one, and it was just a sheet of ice. In the dream we woke up and we were able to get out of the house, but it was a hundred years in the future. And there was nothing out here – nothing. Everything was either like a snowstorm or else it was sand.

Bruce: Our neighbour lives maybe a block and a half away, and we walked back part of the way on Colville Street, the next street over, where there's quite a few large, old trees. But it's not the main road, so it wasn't as well-cleared by the snow-removing equipment. And it looked like a road out of the ice-house scene in *Doctor Zhivago*. Everything was frozen over, gnarled, twisted, and lines were down everywhere. Within a few days we started seeing military vehicles rolling through the village and we knew it was heavy-duty.

Lois: A couple of our friends were able to make it into Montreal, and they'd stop in to say, "Do you need anything?" They picked up my blood-pressure pills. But they wouldn't come near us without hard hats on. We've got the oldest trees in the village, and the tallest ones, and you took your life in your hands to go out.

A few years ago we had the chimney redone and we put extra tiles, the cement ones with the hole in the middle, down each side of the fireplace. And on the Sunday night, we baked a salmon in there. I had it in the freezer, and you had to eat what was in there. It was a fair size, about two feet along. We stuffed it and rolled it in foil and stuck it down one of the holes in the chimney tile. It took two hours to bake, and normally a salmon would do in forty minutes. And we tried to bake potatoes – now we weren't very successful with those. We had to slice them because they weren't baked through. But the salmon was superb.

Our friends stayed with us for about a week. We have the dogs in the house at night, and in the morning Charlie, the eleven-year-old, would get up and put the dogs out and feed the birds in the yard. Tim, he was seventeen, had the fire going. The mother, Joanne, had the coffee going. And I would come out of the gallery, sit down and have hot toast and coffee. I just felt like a queen!

But everything had to be done before dark. Joanne and I would start dinner at noon. We tried to make candles, because we were running out, and we got over-enthusiastic – we were trying to pour hot wax into plastic containers, and everything went running through, all over the rug. But that wasn't really a disaster, that was fun for Charlie. He said, "This is so much fun, I do chores, I go out and gather wood with Bruce – I don't ever want to watch television again!" We told ghost stories and things. The minute the power came back on, we were sitting on the couch and I said, "Charlie, you said you never wanted to watch TV again." He said, "I never said that!"

Bruce: I think we went seven full days without electricity. It was so foreboding – we didn't have a sunny day for a week or more, and the days seemed even shorter. When the power did come back, it was only a half-relief, because you couldn't really get around. Both our cars were frozen into the driveway. Lois's car had the roof dented in from branches hitting it. We couldn't leave the village – we were sort of stranded. I had to use a pickaxe to break the shards of ice, and it took a good month to free part of the driveway. You'd run into branches that were frozen and twisted within layers of ice. The whole front yard was a write-off for at least a month.

Joanne was able to get out with her car, but she couldn't park in the driveway – she had to park in the churchyard behind us. It was nerve-racking for her, because they were saying on the radio, "Unless it's an emergency, don't go to work." But she was working for an insurance company in Ormstown and her boss called everyone in. It was a really difficult drive, with no electricity and the streetlights being knocked out. She said, "Could I leave an hour early, at four o'clock?" He said, "Yeah, but I'll dock your pay."

There was a shelter set up in the old school down the road, and after a while tempers started foaming up. Howick was sort of like the end of the universe. They had ordered maybe a hundred surplus beds, and as the days went by they were wanting to know where the beds were. Finally they heard there was a mix-up in the order and the beds had ended up in Warwick, Quebec. I guess "Warwick" sounds a bit like "Howick." But no one really knows where Warwick is – it's probably even smaller than Howick – deep in the heart of the Townships, maybe. And they never got their beds at the shelter.

Lois: We were outside one day and we saw this strange vehicle. It looked like a telephone repair truck. And they stopped and were looking for three houses down the street. I said, "You wouldn't be a telephone man, would you?" They said they were, and from New Brunswick. So we hauled them in to put the line up. They had to climb to the top of the roof here, the peak. So Bruce was directing traffic out on the road, because they had to bring the line from across the street, and I was holding the ladder while the guy was up on the roof putting the telephone line back. They weren't supposed to fix our house at all, but they did – it took them two hours.

Bruce: We slowly started getting back to normal then. We have a little workshop on the property and we started doing repairs for the house – it was built before the 1830s, even before there was a town here. And then, at the end of March, the water started rising.

We're maybe three or four hundred feet away from the English River – it's usually enough of a flood zone to handle all the water. By the Friday night the water was getting irksome – you could tell it wasn't

The English River near its peak in Howick, Quebec, during the March flood of 1998. It was, as Bruce Craigmyle says, "like Part Two of the ice storm."

going down. On the Saturday we were manning the pumps, and that night the workshop was overwhelmed with water. I had to start pulling everything upstairs. The roads were closed and Howick was once again isolated. This time we didn't see the military vehicles, but we saw the all-terrain police vehicles, the ones that are part boat.

Lois: The main floor of the house stayed dry, but it took a lot of praying. On Sunday night the water was just lapping up against the electrical panel. The house had twenty-six inches left, and she was rising one inch an hour. It was midnight when she started to go down. That saved us. I have paintings all over this floor, and if it had been flooded we would have been finished.

Bruce: It was like Part Two of the ice storm. The weather was balmy, like May two months early, and we had a good dose of snow a week before everything started melting, but the reason the flood was so severe is that all the fields were just slicked over with ice – sealed shut with ice.

That compounded everything, because the tributaries filled up instantly and the water cascaded everywhere. There was nothing Nature could do to absorb that much water.

Lois: And during the flood, I had another dream. My husband died ten years ago and Bruce made a coffin for him, with carved dolphins on it. Jim is buried down in the churchyard, near the bridge. In the dream the coffin comes up the river and my husband lifts the lid – I saw the carving of the dolphins very clearly – jumps out of the coffin and starts bailing the water. When Jim got the coffin bailed out, he gave me a tip of his hat, jumped back in the coffin and rode down the river again. I knew then that he's quite happy where he is. He was telling me in the dream not to worry.

Lois Craigmyle and her son Bruce run Galerie Craigmyle in the village of Howick, Quebec.

MICHEL LEGAULT

January 1998 will remain engraved forever on my memory, and here's why. During the freezing rain I went outside to break the ice, but imagine my surprise when I slipped and crashed into the ice violently with my head. My wife, arriving just at that moment, helped me get up and led me back into the house. I was dazed and I kept falling asleep. Seeing the gravity of the situation, my wife phoned 911, and a few minutes later, an ambulance arrived with sirens flashing to take me to the Charles LeMoyne Hospital in Longueuil. During the journey, I started to stammer. I was afraid, but mostly because of the speed of the swaying ambulance.

When I got to Charles LeMoyne, I was questioned often. "What is your name?" "What is the name of your mother?" "What is your date of birth?" Maybe they thought I was nuts. Not taking any chances, they wanted to test me with a scanner, but the hospital didn't have enough electricity for the machine to function. I would have to be transferred to the Pierre Boucher Hospital in Boucherville.

But how to get me there? Ambulances were in short supply, so the authorities called on the army. Which is how I came to be taken to Boucherville in an army ambulance decorated with a red cross. I was accompanied by a soldier as well as by an IV with a drip bag hanging from it. The streets of Longueuil were impassable. I was holding onto my drip bag with both hands, and smelling a strong odour of gasoline coming from the ambulance. They had already anesthetized me once and my headache was terrible.

At Pierre Boucher I was tested with the scanner, but they couldn't detect anything unusual. So I was taken back to Charles LeMoyne in the same ambulance, with the same headache. I spent the night there. Next morning the hospital generator went wrong, and the intensive-care patients were transferred to Pierre Boucher by helicopter. It felt like wartime.

I went back home with my wife, but there were more surprises waiting for me. The house had lost power, and after two days the water began to filter through our bedroom window and drip onto the floor. Taking my courage in both hands, I decided to ask my neighbour for help in breaking the ice in the gutters up above. Not the right move, because I slipped once more and fell, you guessed it, on my head.

This time I didn't go to hospital, but for the next month I was a little deaf. Now I can laugh at these adventures, but in January 1998 I didn't find them funny at all.

Michel Legault works at a post office in Montreal. He lives on the South Shore.

LOUISE HALPERIN

I was already very sick with bronchitis when the ice storm arrived. I toughed it out alone in my Montreal apartment for two days and two nights, and by the third day, January 7, when it was clear that the electricity wasn't coming on any time soon, I started calling up friends to see if I could move to someone else's house for what I figured would be a day or two.

The electricity was out at our home for about a week and a half. But that wasn't the end of it. The building I used to live in is a high-rise, about thirty-five years old, with over a hundred units. It has a lot of corroded pipes which, all year round, burst. In the past eight years, when my father and I were living there, we had four floods. The worst one was last year, just after the ice storm. We were on the second floor and we had extensive flooding, cracked ceilings and cracked walls. The after-effect of all this flooding is that the building is full of mould. I did not have asthma when I moved there twenty-four years ago. Now I have asthma, and I'm more susceptible to bronchitis.

One family was kind enough to take me in, but after five weeks I thought, "I've imposed on their hospitality long enough, and I need my own space." So I thanked them profusely, found an apartment-hotel downtown, and moved there. I was displaced from my home for a total of three months.

Normally I live with my father but he was in Florida during all this time. I was glad about that, because he's in his eighties and not in excellent health. But it meant I had to deal with everything by myself, including the insurance. In the long run, we were lucky with our insurance company. I heard stories from other people whose insurance companies gave them a hard time.

I tried to look on the bright side, see it as an adventure and not get too depressed – but I *was* depressed. What I went through was harrowing. In order to be responsible about things, I was schlepping from where I was staying, two or three times a week, to check on the state of the apartment. Every time I went, I got more and more dismayed, because things kept getting worse.

The ceilings in my father's bedroom, the living room and the vestibule had a lot of damage to the paint and plaster. There was paint peeling away. The parquet floors were damaged by water, and the tiles were buckling all over the place. There was a disgusting smell of wetness and mould. When the repairmen finally started working on our apartment, they had to break through the walls to get to the pipes. They were iron pipes, badly corroded, that had not been replaced in thirty to thirty-five years. We could well imagine that they might burst again at any time. Conditions got so bad that, by order of Montreal city officials, the building was closed from January 12 to 22; tenants, many of them elderly, had to be evacuated.

I remember visiting our apartment one day, and looking at the plants which had been deprived of warmth for long enough that most of them had died. I had to carry plant after plant down the hall to the garbage room in tears. Ironically, the cacti did not die, being used to a desert environment and extremes of temperature.

One of the things that was particularly hard on me was the sense of isolation. I was busy on the phone a good two or three hours a day, talking with friends just to stay in touch with people. It was hard to get around, because of the ice and my continuing bronchitis. I couldn't easily visit other people and they couldn't easily visit me. What hurt me was that very few people took the trouble to call me and ask if I was alive and well. I'm sure of this, because my call-answer service allows me to call in for messages.

Every time I went back to the apartment, I was alone. That was very hard. But I was getting stupid comments from people. I guess they were trying to be helpful, but it wasn't helpful. They'd say, "Oh, your insurance will pay for this!" Well, nothing had been paid for yet. But one friend, hearing me tell my tale of woe, said something extremely succinct and insightful. She said, "It sounds like you're suffering from shock and grief." I went, "Exactly!" No one else got that. I was grateful that she did.

I was taking weekly Hebrew language classes at a local synagogue. One day, before the class started, we were all sitting and chatting. One of the other students said, "We're having such a good time since the ice storm!" She lives in a private house in Westmount. "The neighbours are helping each other, we're in and out of each other's houses, the kids are enjoying it . . ." I wanted to strangle her! That was not my experience at all, and she was not seeing that. Call me a grinch or a grouch – but it was not helpful. I didn't go back to the class for a few months. I didn't want to have to deal with it.

It took a while to convince the landlord to get repairs done. There was a cute little Catch-22 that I heard from the landlord one time when I was complaining about repairs not having been done after he'd said they would be – "You weren't living here, so we first repaired the apartments of people who were living here." I couldn't live there! It was not fit to live in! He was trying to save money. He was not living there, he didn't see the damage. "Why should I pay for the repairs?" he said.

"This happened as an act of God!" Another person I would have liked to strangle.

One of my friends kindly gave me a big, green, bushy plant to lift my spirits. But it wasn't till well into March that I got over my bronchitis. I moved back to the apartment April 3, and we moved out August 18. I couldn't wait to get out of there! It was a beautiful building when we moved in, but it had become a dump.

As January 1999 was approaching, I became very apprehensive. Logically I knew that we were not necessarily going to have another ice storm, but emotionally it was an anniversary of a very traumatic event. So I did something a tad creative. I planned ahead, invited some friends to come over, and said, "If you like, why don't you bring a candle, and we'll just sit around a table and hang out together." And that's what we did. We had tea and cookies, and we didn't even talk about the ice storm. It was really helpful to me to get over that first anniversary.

Louise Halperin now lives in a different apartment building in Westmount, Quebec. Since she moved, her asthma is much improved and she never strangled anyone after all.

GARY FREEMAN

One morning I was cutting some firewood for my home, which was without power in the country two miles north of Avonmore. A friend of mine had torn down an addition, so I had a bunch of old wood. My chainsaw caught on a board under my boot, a piece of wood flew up, and this hidden nail ripped through my jeans and gouged my calf.

My first thought was, "Oh no, not again!" I've had a variety of cuts over the years. But this cut was about three inches long and very deep. It was bleeding pretty bad. I went back into the house and I tried bandaging it with gauze, but it wouldn't stay closed.

Now I'm an impatient person – I don't have much use for hospitals. I figured it was a twenty-minute drive to the hospital, and then a two-hour wait. Besides, if someone else had done it, it would probably have hurt. So I decided to stitch myself up instead.

I told my wife to get a needle and thread and some peroxide. This wasn't her cup of tea, because she doesn't like the sight of blood. But when I was pushing the needle through, it was hurting my thumb more than my leg, believe it or not. I was using a straight needle with a dull point and I had to pinch up the skin to get the needle in.

My fifteen-year-old son was there when this was happening. He and my wife both thought I was crazy. I didn't put a bandage on the wound – I figure it's better if the air gets at it – and I never went to have it looked at by a doctor, either. It seemed to be healing pretty good on its own. My kids started calling me "Dr. Quack."

But it did open up a few days later. I have this habit of staying too late talking to my customers, so the wife thought that instead of waiting around for me, she'd take the van, go home, and come back and get me later. Well, I thought she'd played a joke on me, so I started walking from Millington to Avonmore. During that walk, the cut opened itself. It was a real cold night – so cold I was walking with my hands down my pants. Fortunately she came and found me. A few days later I was able to take the stitches out.

The *Standard Freeholder* in Cornwall got hold of this story about the stitches, and from there it went on the CP wire, the *Ottawa Citizen*, Florida, Mexico, all over the place. At the end of the *Jerry Springer Show*, they used to have a blonde who would come on and talk about all the crazy things people do. One night I heard my kids saying, "Hey, Dad, they mentioned you on TV!"

I didn't mind. I thought it was kind of neat.

Gary Freeman owns a store in Cornwall, Ontario, that prints logos on sports jerseys.

MARIE ROBERTS

January 8 was our second evening without power during the ice storm. Candles and flashlights illuminated our Kingston home, and our woodstove provided warmth and was an adequate substitute for the microwave. Things were going fine. Then my Dad discovered something downstairs.

He shared his discovery by yelling something unintelligible, rushing upstairs and demanding that we stop our activities immediately. Then he and Mum searched for buckets, and my two younger brothers and I all trooped downstairs to see firsthand the flooding of our basement. Normally our sump pump takes care of the water seepage. Unfortunately for us, the pump requires electricity to operate, and the obvious consequence hadn't occurred to anyone. The result was that water had been quietly seeping up and creeping over the cement floor for fourteen hours. Luckily the unfinished part of our basement is a few inches lower than the carpeted and wooded floor. Nevertheless, in several hours, we could have done something for our neighbours: opened either a wading pool or an ice rink.

Two hours after we began bailing to save our basement, verses to "Down by the Bay" were no better than they were when we began singing half an hour earlier. Do watermelons grow near "the bay"? They *are* mostly water. We moved on to "There Was a Great Big Moose," which is a "sing the lyrics after me" camp song. Mum tried to follow, but usually changed the rhythm and the tune. I wasn't surprised – she comes up with funny variations of names of places, people, and movies all the time, because she can't seem to remember them. We sang "The Itsy Bitsy Spider," who I finally realized is *inside* the spout, otherwise how could he get "swept out"? It's only when you start bailing out your basement that the meaning of lyrics like these becomes clear. "Alice the Camel" was sung too. It would be amazing if we could change our bodies as easily as Alice does: with a song, a camel with nine humps becomes a horse!

For the first three hours of bailing, we set up a relay system of bucket-carrying, not unlike that of the Sorcerer's Apprentice and his broom brigade – we even had a broom participating. However, our system was less frenzied, didn't involve magic, and I think the apprentice's brooms were filling the cavern with water rather than emptying it. Our broom, guided by my dad, had the important job of sweeping water into the sump hole in the corner of the basement. The rest of us carried the buckets of water upstairs and dumped them in the bathtub.

After our initial three hours, we set up a system to pour water into the washing machine out-take, which you can reach while standing beside the sump hole. What was a five-person job became a one-person job, allowing us to set up shifts during the night. Despite our improved system, bailing the sump hole was a damp and dimly lit experience. This was appropriate, considering the *Funk and Wagnall's* definition of "sump": a cesspool or other reservoir for drainage. I often wondered whether it was a good idea to rub my eyes with hands continually getting splashed with cesspool water.

Bailing was the focal point of our ice storm experience. We still found time to observe our neighbours' activities, though, and while curiosity about other people is natural, we were taking unusual interest in other people's business. One neighbour was outside with his camera, and three of us flocked to the window to watch him photograph ice and tree branches. Then the people across the street brought some bags out to their car. "They're leaving," I reported, and my dad came to the window to see for himself. After two and a half days without power, our shift work ended, and we stopped monitoring our neighbours' activities. Life was back to normal.

Since then, I have rarely thought about being up at 2 A.M. in our dark and damp basement. Sometimes, though, an ice-storm-damaged tree catches my eye, and I remember bailing bucket after bucket of cold water, all the while being thankful that we didn't have something more difficult to face.

Marie Roberts is an outdoor enthusiast who has spent much of her time working outdoors with children since graduating from university.

ANNE ANDERSON

The numbers on my alarm clock are flashing again. To me it is just another of the many power failures I have experienced since I moved to Quebec. Mont St-Bruno has a lot of trees and they tend to fall on the wires. I get out of bed and wander to the window. Everything is covered in ice. The air in my apartment is chilly and I am anxious to get into a warm car. It won't last but a few hours, I say to myself.

Driving around fallen trees on the road is interesting, but I decide to turn around. The roads are icy and dangerous. It is still freezing rain.

This is kind of exciting – the whole country is talking about our crisis. I've never been in any kind of crisis before. I'm going out to take pictures. It is romantic and scary.

I moved here seven years ago with my husband. Since then we had a child, and now we are separated and I am living with my daughter, Roxanne, in an apartment. I am alone here. I have no family, but a few friends at work and in clubs I belong to.

I can't keep my daughter with me, because they say the power won't be back on for weeks. They say the pylons that I used to live near, before my separation, are all down. The schools are closed and there are no daycare centres with power. Roxanne goes to stay with her father. He has a fireplace. She will be safe there.

I drive my car slowly to my friend Michel's house. I've only known him for two months, but if it weren't for him I would be totally alone here. If it weren't for the kindness of his family, I would have no place to go. I have no electricity, a lump in my breast, my car keeps breaking down and I am a single mother. How many families do you know that would welcome me into their home and treat me as one of their own? His family did just that.

My office has power, so I go to work in the day. But after two nights, Michel's family lose power too. Now I must go back to the apartment. Michel offers to come and stay with me. The roads are empty, the town dark, the parking lot empty. There is one small candle burning in the corner-store window. That is all we find open in the town of St-Bruno. We arrive in the dark, at a deserted building. There are forty apartments, but only one couple and the concierge are there. A tree is bent over and blocking the entrance. We squeeze through the small opening, trying not to send this huge branch crashing down upon us. It is hard to see, and there is a long hallway, totally black. I am scared to be there alone. We stick together.

The apartment has gotten colder over the last two days. We light candles and put on as many clothes as we can. I'm glad now that my mother insisted I take home the eight comforters she was prepared to get rid of. She said someday I would need them. Today is that day.

My friendship with Michel is fairly new. We have been dating, but I hardly know the real him yet, and he has never seen the real me. Here

I am with my winter coat and a tuque on. I look ridiculous. It is so cold we take all of the empty pop bottles we can find in the recycling bin and fill them with whatever is left in the hot-water tank. Then we put them under the blankets with us.

We take one look at each other and laugh. We are both so unattractive right now, and so new to each other, yet he is glad to help me through this and I am glad he is here. I tease him that we look like *La Petite Vie*, a favourite sitcom here in Quebec, featuring a couple wearing plain, old clothes and tacky hats.

In the darkness we can hear ice crashing as it falls from the trees. It has been ice-raining for five days now. Today we heard that there could be looting. The area has been empty for too long. Then we hear a huge crash. It sounds like someone is breaking into the apartment. I am scared. I know there is nobody to help us, and the phone doesn't work without power. Michel gets up with the flashlight to investigate. I can't imagine how afraid I would be if he had not come with me – how sad and afraid. It was just another tree crashing down.

In the morning we place rows of tea candles on the table and I put my pie-cooling racks over them. We make toast on our makeshift grill.

The next day the water has been shut off by the concierge, and luckily for me he has put antifreeze in my washing machine too. We have to use pails of snow to flush the toilet, and we store it in the tub to melt, but it barely does. It is too cold in the apartment to melt much of anything, and I am starting to think the snow in the tub is making us colder.

Every morning I crack huge sheets of ice from my car, between one and two inches thick. I go to work, where it is warm, and find out how everyone else is coping. My office is open for the families of employees and an area is set up for the children, but it is too cold in my apartment for a five-year-old to sleep, so I still can't have Roxanne with me.

I get gas on the South Shore at the only station open for miles. In the long lineup of cars, I can see men with gas cans cutting in to the front of the line. Some of the motorists who have been waiting an hour are angry. Fights break out and the police are called. They put extra lineup monitors on duty.

Nights in the apartment are getting too cold. The heat has seeped completely out of the building and there is no more hot water left to fill my pop bottles. I wake up with my face and eyes frozen and sore. I have a headache every day and every night. I think of the homeless with a new empathy, and wonder how they survive months of exposure to the cold outdoors.

By the fourth night in the apartment, I can no longer stay. I am feeling sick, like a head cold is coming on. Michel has the opportunity to stay with his brother's family, but he decides to come with me to the local high school, now a shelter. He doesn't abandon me.

At the school we see people sleeping in open areas and classrooms. The hallways are monitored by soldiers. There are foam beds and baggage everywhere. The elderly are there, some obviously alone. I see a widow I know. She is reading in a corner. I imagine how she feels, her children so far away. I imagine how the very old feel. There are small children there. Families are there with crying babies and children running. We take an inch-thick foam sheet and make a bed on the floor of one classroom. The floor is cold, but not nearly as cold as the apartment.

The next morning my car won't start. I haven't seen my little Roxanne in nearly two weeks and she cries whenever I call. She misses her mom, and I miss her too. I need to spend time with her. Michel helps me get the car started, but the local garages have no power. I must take it to a town forty minutes away. It breaks down three more times during the three weeks of the crisis. Each time Michel comes to bail me out.

I haven't had decent sleep in two weeks and I can't find a cash machine on the South Shore that works. I get a touch of food poisoning. I can't find an open restaurant. Michel and I drive for an hour northeast to find one. We are tired of this and need to cheer up. I am dirty and my head aches.

The next day it is sunny, so I go for a drive to the Domaine-des-Hauts-Bois, my old neighbourhood. It is called that because of the enormously tall trees there. I can't find one tree that hasn't been affected. The ice is melting and some roads are flooded. I have to take detours to get around. My car rides like a big boat in all the slush.

I go to the highway to see the pylons. Their massive shoulders are crouched down, like the paintings in church of Jesus falling with the cross. On the way back to the school I see Hydro trucks lining the highway. I see trucks from Connecticut and New Brunswick, and the world is suddenly so small again. I wonder if anyone will let their cities know how grateful we are.

I return to the high school and bring the only thing I can to help, peanut butter. It makes me laugh to think I am repaying their kindness with peanut butter.

A co-worker and his family offer me a place to stay. I am grateful, but Michel's brother now has no power and he has nowhere to go. I will not abandon him.

We are starting to argue about the stupidest little things. We nearly give up on sticking this thing out together. It is hard to be away from Roxanne, but I realize I have found a true friend and we grow. We depend on each other. We comfort each other. We pull through.

Michel's family get their power back. So does most of Montreal. Out of 150 people at the office, I am the only one who is still without power, but the manager is compassionate and the company understanding. My ex is bringing Roxanne to meet me at the high school today. We need this time together.

Michel and I decide that afternoon to go and stay with his family again. The next morning we find out that the shelter we just left was evacuated at 2 A.M. because of a bomb threat. I think of all the old faces that were still there, and them having to go out into the bitter cold in the middle of the night. I don't understand how someone could be so cruel. I wonder when this will be over. I am sick with a cold and so tired I feel like a truck ran over me a few times. I walk with my head on backwards, I'm sure.

Three weeks after that first morning when the numbers on my alarm clock started flashing, the power is returned to the apartment and I am home again. The fallen trees and ice are being cleared away. The trees will heal. They will show their magnificent beauty again. Our homes are warm again. My daughter is back. The lump in my breast is found to be benign. I know what it is to have and be a true friend. We heal. I am grateful.

There is a song I sing. It is called "Hard Times, Come Again No More."

Anne Anderson came to the Montreal area as a military wife in 1991 and now works as a graphic artist.

EGON LEU

On Saturday, January 24, the ice storm was gone, but our roof was covered with more than fifteen centimetres of ice and on top of that, during the week, we got another twenty centimetres of fresh snow. As I looked over the situation, I decided to go on the roof and try to remove at least some of the snow. My decision met with disapproval from everybody in my family.

Despite the objections, I decided I knew better, and started to install the ladder in order to ascend the roof. My shoes were fitted with clips to avoid slipping on the ice, but unfortunately the clips were installed at the wrong place – between the sole and the heel, instead of around the sole of the boot. For that mistake, I paid dearly.

Standing on the ladder, I started to remove the snow to be able to step onto the roof. I progressed nicely and moved slowly upwards, getting rid of the snow. My wife came to watch me and to remind me every so often to be careful. Then, all of a sudden, disaster struck. My clips did not bite the ice any more and I started to slide slowly downwards. Realizing the situation, I started to turn around, hoping to get hold of my ladder, but unfortunately it was out of my reach! I was sliding slowly towards the end of the roof and I turned myself away from it, readying myself to jump into a snowdrift below.

Yelling at my wife to get out of the way, I prepared myself mentally as well as physically and – here I come! – jumped down nearly five metres into the snowdrift. I survived the fall and got up with the help of my wife, wringing for air, as the fall left me completely breathless. The reason: underneath the snowdrift we had at least fifteen centimetres of solid ice, and when my body hit the ground it did not break the ice. Instead, my six-foot-three frame folded like an accordion.

With the support of my wife, I walked away unstable and dazed – and the next thing I remember is lying in the snow face down. My wife shook me and yelled and struggled to get me out of the snow. I had fainted and lain in the snow for several minutes. Feeling drowsy, I slowly got to my feet and with my wife's help proceeded towards the door and the living room, where I lay down to regain control of my bearings and recuperate.

My back pain was endurable, but my whole body was aching, including my head. After some aspirins and a few hours of sleep, I felt rather well, except that my back was sore and did not feel good at all. However, with all my stubbornness, the suggestions to go and see a doctor were thrown to the wind. I spent two uncomfortable nights until, in the late afternoon of Monday, I finally let my wife make an appointment in the clinic for the following day. I hate being sick and I hate seeing doctors, but my pain had mellowed me.

Still in pain, I presented myself at the clinic. The first thing the doctor said after I told him my story was, "You are a very lucky guy – you could have been paralyzed. This happened to one of my patients, only thirty-three years old, who will spend the rest of his life in a wheelchair." Next step was the X-ray department. When I brought them back to my doctor, he looked at them and told me with a stern face, "Go at once to the hospital Emergency."

I had a fracture of the fourth lower vertebrae. It is rather a serious injury. In the hospital they fitted me with a steel corset, which I had to wear for over three uncomfortable months. But everything healed well, and the following winter I was able to go cross-country and alpine skiing without any problems!

Egon Leu lives in Boucherville, on the South Shore of Montreal.

ANNE COMPTON

Whatever else it was – dark, cold and inconvenient – the Ice Storm of '98 was a period of weirdness, or at least so it seems in retrospect. On the calendar of normalcy, five days were bracketed off. Hanging up the calendars on January 1, why didn't we see that coming? To those of us given to reminiscing, the storm-enforced strangeness seems now mostly comic, but the eerie blue light of that iced-up world did not fade without marking changes.

A feminist, proud of my self-sufficiency, I learned about my dependency on plumbers, electricians and the crew of NB Power – all men. I've never had so many "gentlemen callers." Possessor of three degrees and a c.v. of publications, I discovered that water and wires, not words, are what's important in such circumstances. Should I forget these lessons, there are daily reminders: my leather briefcase has permanent stains from candle drippings; there are tea stains on the rug from nights I stumbled, teacup in hand, through the unlit house. And, of course, on my tree-lined property, there are the gaps where six maples once stood, trees so damaged that they had to be cut down.

On three sides, trees mark the boundaries of my property, a hillside lot. The day the storm began here – a Thursday – my teenaged son and I ate a candlelight supper cooked on the woodstove. The power had failed at 4 P.M. It was day one, although, of course, we had no way of knowing that at the time. While doing the washing up (with melted snow), I turned from the sink to see a tree flaming just beyond the dining-room window. The unlikelihood of a tree bursting into flame in winter – of fire in ice – does not make for rational behaviour. "You stand here and watch the tree burn," I yelled to my son, pushing him into the dining room, "and I'll phone NB Power." They assured me that they would soon be along, and they were – five days later.

The flames subsided, but throughout the night sparks from those live, broken electrical wires arced into the sky and spilled in the direction of my roof and my neighbour's. In a parody of a hundred summer evenings, I sat for hours on the verandah on a white wicker rocker, too worried for sleep. Rain fell, froze, and transformed the world.

From time to time, in the darkness, transformers up and down the street crackled, flamed and went dead. Further phone calls to NB Power were pointless. On one occasion I tried to cross my iced-over garden to warn my neighbour about the plumes of sparks, but the shock that you get on an icefield under a rain of electrically charged sparks warned me off and inside. Tree limbs continued to crash to the ground, and for the rest of the night I kept my eyes fixed on the ceiling of my bedroom, waiting for a gap to open in the roof. Anything might happen. I suppose I slept.

Daylight revealed a wreckage of trees. In the garden and on the drive-way, heaps of helter-skelter limbs. "Desolation Row," one of the plumbers said upon arrival. He set down his toolbox and got his camera from the van. Months later, he brought me those photos. There's an unearthly blue light in spite of the falling drizzle. The mounds of broken tree limbs look like funeral pyres.

The plumbers drained the water. With no power and the possibility of falling temperatures, it was the only way to avoid broken pipes. By candlelight and by flashlight, they showed me how to restore the water should the power come back on. Given how busy they were, there was no guarantee they could get back to my house. I wrote down the list of "Ten Steps" and taped it to the useless refrigerator, next to the useless stove.

The end of the five-day period, like its beginning, was remarkable. In between lay the tedium of coping – carrying water and wood, cooking over a wood fire, keeping warm. I never left the house for long. My son came and went; he was needed other places, as part of a cleanup crew. I was alone with the two cats; I used them like muffs. After the plumbers left, I got my car from the parking lot of the posh golf club where I had parked it the day before. It was the only nearby lot of a sufficient size to ensure that branches could not fall upon a car parked at its dead centre.

That day and for the next three days, I cruised the neighbourhood looking for NB Power crews. I must confess I tried to bribe them. Their laughter cheered me up. Neighbours who had not lost their electricity gained infinite importance in their ownership of bathtubs and showers. "Hello. Can I have a bath?" Bathrooms, I decided, tell you an awful lot about people. I tried to remember if Karl Marx had linked plumbing to the class struggle. Why, I wondered, luxuriating in those cozy, functioning bathrooms, did some people lose power and not others? Did the fortunate ones have a mark above their door? My Presbyterian-raised friend, also a victim of the outage, said we were predestined – on the wrong side.

On the fifth day, when I came out of my house carrying bath gear and the briefcase covered with globs of purple wax, I rejoiced to find the NB Power crew in my yard. As I considered the best way to negotiate the icefield that used to be my garden and driveway, one of the repairmen came towards me. With a quiet chivalry, he offered me his arm and walked me down to my car, now parked at the bottom of my driveway. "You've got a scorched tree," he told me, in a voice that sounded congratulatory. I was oddly pleased. It meant, however odd these past few days, at least I had not hallucinated.

That evening when I got home from work, I cautiously tried the kitchen light. "Yes." And then a burner of the stove. "Hell" – the light wobbled unsteadily, on and off. "Not enough volts," I decided. On the car radio, I had heard about this problem. Cruising time again. I knew by now you got nothing by a phone call. About five streets away, I found an electrician just getting into his van. "Come to my house," I said. I was getting better at this. He came. His handheld gadget indicated that there were 230 volts coming into the house. "Don't leave," I said, and made him stand by while I ticked off the "Ten Steps for Restoring Water." Then I let him leave. These days I sometimes think of myself as a feminist plumber, but mostly I think nostalgically of my seventeen gentlemen callers in the blue days of January 1998.

Anne Compton lives outside Saint John. She teaches English at the Saint John campus of the University of New Brunswick.

NADINE BAILEY

On Thursday, January 8, about 2 P.M., as I was in the middle of a good action video, the lights went off in Alexandria. I was taking it easy because I had not had much sleep Wednesday night, listening to the rain falling on the tin roof of the apartment and the tree branches cracking all night. I had lain awake wondering if a huge branch would come through the roof. The seniors' centre was just down the street, so when the lights went off I headed there. At least it had a better roof.

It was dangerous walking, because branches were still crashing down, sometimes with transformers and loose wires. The centre welcomed me with hot soup and sandwiches. It was filling up quickly, because the storm was getting worse. To cheer things up, some people started a sing-along. They sang "Happy Birthday" for a teenager's eighteenth. I decided to stay overnight and got a lift back home, where I only had time to grab a few things for the night.

The centre now held a good number of young mothers and children.

The afternoon passed into evening, and the mothers were quieting their children down for the night. But late in the evening, word came that the young families would have to be moved, to make room for the seniors.

People crowded into the hallways until a room was opened downstairs near the Legion. Liquor was still being served, because a disaster had not yet been declared. It was almost 10 P.M. when a school bus, which had been bringing seniors to the centre, drove us to the local high school. I felt like a refugee in my own country. The weather had changed from freezing rain to ice pellets to snow and high winds. Branches were now flying through the air. A transformer near the centre exploded, shining a bright light through the blizzard.

The volunteer firemen were in charge at the school. They had just unlocked the school door when we arrived. I suddenly saw snow burning. Someone had tossed a cigarette butt down where the firemen had spilled kerosene while filling lanterns. The school was under renovation, and bare lightbulbs flickered precariously from extension cords strung through open beams in the ceiling. It was cold and very dark here, in contrast to the centre. I spread my blanket on the cold gym floor.

The storm was getting worse. The police tried to maintain hourly checks at the school. But as the crisis worsened, most of the firemen were called away, and air cadets – much younger than most of the adults present – told us they were in charge "under emergency procedures." Over time, the firemen were called away completely, and the police checks extended into seemingly longer time lapses and shorter visits. The cadets reported no problems. Community stores were being emptied of blankets and supplies as more and more people were directed to the school.

In the gym, a dangling lightbulb flickered all night. As families arrived, the cadets, in their heavy boots and uniforms, led them in and shone a flashlight on available spaces. Some mothers were having a hard time with young children. A family took up a space beside me. It was well past 11 P.M. The young boy beside me kept crying. I thought it strange, because he was about ten years old and hiding under his sleeping bag. I saw his father strike him repeatedly. I reported to the only volunteer fireman on duty that a man was constantly beating his young son while his pregnant wife and two smaller children sat beside him. I was told the provincial police would be informed. During the night, the family left the shelter.

A rumour got out that some classrooms were heated, and three of us moved into one of them. About 5:30 A.M. Friday, I woke to find a young man sitting near my friend, shining a flashlight in her face to wake her. It was a cadet, who said he had orders to "get everyone up for breakfast." By the way he was talking to her, I thought they were friends. But she didn't know him. That was our first night at the shelter.

On Friday afternoon, the storm had died down but it was still raining. I managed to get back to the apartment to change clothes and pick up a few things. Some families had gas-heated hot water, and I accepted the offer of a hot shower in a freezing house. I had to walk back to the shelter, and I remember feeling homeless, carrying blankets, toiletries, and snacks in a garbage bag, walking up Main Street and arriving wet and cold to have a stranger give me a pair of warm socks.

More people were now at the shelter and many had brought in food. The kitchen was being organized, and volunteers cooked and prepared all the meals. Local stores were more than generous in donations.

But as the firemen and police got busier with the crisis, we were left virtually on our own with the cadets. Local youths wanted to see what was going on at the high school. They had found a place to stay elsewhere and were just hanging around. Late Saturday evening, it became quite boisterous. When complaints were made to a female cadet, she informed us that the group of teenagers "refused to take orders from a woman."

At 12:45 A.M., I asked the female cadet sitting outside the gym door to stop the loud noise the teenagers were making in the hall. I also asked that the light in the gym be turned off and the door closed. Another cadet appeared and blocked my return to the gym. With his face inches from mine, he yelled at me that I was "distraught" and "out of control." I insisted they allow me to phone the police, but I was told to return to the gym. I quietly left the gym at a far exit and searched down a darkened school corridor for a public phone. I found one and got through to the Alexandria police just as the cadets shone a flashlight in my face. I urged the police to come, but the cadets took the phone from me and told the police they were sending a distraught person to the hospital and there was no need to respond to the call.

The young cadets, in military mode, put me up against the wall and restrained me. They then led me to a room and posted a guard outside the door. Another cadet remained in the room with me until a police officer arrived who told him to leave. I was so shaken I could barely speak. I tried to insist that some security other than the cadets be put in charge, and I complained that cadets were ordering adults around, instead of assisting them.

When the officer and I left the room, we found the army arriving at the front door of the school. At the same time, the officer was overwhelmed by other people wanting to file complaints regarding various incidents and disturbances. Some of my friends, noticing that I was missing from the gym, had started to look for me. During this chaos, an ambulance arrived for a "distraught person," which many seemed to be. The cadets and volunteers began unloading army cots. The police promised to increase security at the school, and by Sunday afternoon, after follow-up visits during which the police collected more complaints, some of the cadets were removed.

Sunday, I went home to dig my car out. It was frozen in the ground and I kept turning the engine on to warm up. The apartment was freezing cold. Friends came and gave me a hand, also offering a lift to Montreal, but I decided to stay behind to keep an eye on the apartment, because of break-ins in the area. I went back to the school shelter. Conditions had not improved, however, and the ice storm victims were becoming tired. One of the people in charge said that if problems persisted, we would have to stay in the gym "under house arrest."

The parents blew up. They had had enough even before coming to the shelter, trying to cope with the storm, preparing meals in the cold, and living without heat. Most of the mothers broke into tears. They asked for volunteers to come play with the children and give the mothers a break. Others demanded a security guard at the school at all times. Many wanted crisis counselling. It seems that Social Services were unaware at this point that any families were at the school. Late Sunday night, when a friend came to the shelter, I cried, "Get me the hell out of here!"

I went to stay in Cornwall and spent nearly a week there without my wallet. What was the point, anyway? No bank machines had been working in Alexandria. The events of the last two days had left me badly shaken, and on Tuesday I sought medical help. I had to go and eat at the Agape Centre. Army helicopters were constantly taking off from a nearby armoury. At least the sun was shining.

On Tuesday, January 13, an article would be printed in the Cornwall *Standard Freeholder* under the heading, "Volunteer faces sex assault charges." It read, "An Alexandria-area youth was charged with sexual assault while volunteering at a shelter in Alexandria on the weekend. . . . The seventeen-year-old youth, dressed in an Air Cadet uniform, told two women he could conduct body searches, police alleged." The following day, the *Glengarry News* quoted the mayor as saying, "He agreed that there were some difficulties with security at the Glengarry District High School Shelter but said these had been rectified. . . . He conceded there was an incident but termed it a 'minor misdemeanour' which had been dealt with by North Glengarry Police."

A friend drove me back to Alexandria on Friday, January 16. It was still too cold to return to my apartment, so I returned to the seniors' centre. Many donations had come in, and I was given a pair of new flannel pyjamas. I spent the night upstairs with the seniors. Some of them threw up all night. The St. John Ambulance personnel were kept busy cleaning. By morning, they were exhausted. I tried not to disturb a man sleeping upright at a desk while I reached behind him for my coat.

Early Monday morning, January 19, I returned to my apartment. Everything was frozen inside. I walked around with my coat and boots on, touching frozen clothes, furniture, my bed. I saw how shampoo coagulates, how houseplants freeze indoors, and how a crystal vase shatters when water freezes in it. I left the apartment door open, because it was warmer outside. The pipes had burst and my kitchen ceiling was falling down. My landlord was in no hurry to make repairs, because my lease would expire at the end of the month. That great action video was still stuck in a frozen VCR. Mice had eaten holes in my wool rug. Water damage was everywhere. I had to sit on a frozen sofa, for I had picked up the flu. I had stayed at different shelters for the past week and a half. What began as a pioneering adventure had become a nightmare.

Nadine Bailey is the pseudonym of a community volunteer who still lives in eastern Ontario.

IO

LIFE AMONG ANIMALS

*A*fter toughing out the storm for a few days at home in a suburb of Montreal full of breaking maples and birches, my family and I decided to look for refuge. Fortunately my mother scarcely lost power during the whole crisis, even though her home, in the heart of N.D.G., happened to be in one of the worst-hit areas of the whole city. Never have the virtues of underground wiring been so clear. My wife and I packed our two kids, ourselves and several suitcases into the car, and set out along the empty highways to my mother's low-rise apartment building. But we weren't the only members of the family in need of warmth. We also had to load up the car with a litter tray, rodent cages, cat bowls, cat food, rodent food, rodent water bottles, cat pills and cat litter: necessary supplies for a trio of hamsters and an old, deaf, much loved cat on thyroid medication.

I was worried about how my children would react to their new, relatively cramped quarters; I was worried about how my mother would react to this sudden invasion of her home. But I think, in retrospect, I lavished an inordinate amount of worry on the fourteen-year-old cat. Would he freak out, stop eating, try to escape, become incontinent? (No, no, no, and mostly no.) In fact, Fergus would receive even more attention than usual during those five or six days away from home. Caring for Fergus became a means for all the humans in the family to focus and channel our own anxieties. The cat rose to the occasion. The hamsters did fine, too.

We weren't unique. As the stories in this chapter indicate, a large number of people spent a lot of their time thinking about animals. The animals were, in the case of my family and many others, not just the objects of care but the givers of *comfort. It was a strange time for them, too. I wonder now if, on a symbolic level, the tending of animals was what allowed us humans to express our care and love for a natural world that was so deeply bruised by the assault of ice.*

And the animals – from chimpanzees to goldfish – proved to be surprisingly resilient.

GLORIA GROW

I look after fifteen chimpanzees. They'd been retired from biomedical research at the Laboratory for Experimental Surgery In Primates (LEMSIP) of New York University, and my partner, Richard Allan, and I built a sanctuary for them on the South Shore of Montreal. We have a farm with 108 acres of land. The first group of chimpanzees arrived in September '97, another group in October, and the last three in November – so at the time of the storm, the most recent additions had been here only for a couple of months. A lot of people had told us it was crazy to have a sanctuary for chimpanzees in Quebec. The ice storm made us think, "Maybe they're right."

The chimpanzees live in a building with a heated floor, and it stayed warm for the first couple of days after the power went out. Then it got cold. The chimpanzees normally have warm feet, but now they had icy little toes. We started using propane heaters. I was staying in there till midnight with them, and it was hard on my throat and eyes. Initially the chimpanzees seemed to be handling it quite well – there was plenty of food, at least in the beginning – but by the fourth or fifth day, they reacted to the darkness and the boredom. They were just getting used to our routine, and now it had changed. The darkness brought back some really bad behaviours. They would rock back and forth all the time; they would bite and pull their own hair; they would do some anal probing and smearing. They were also sleeping together, which normally they wouldn't do.

They were bored because they had no visitors. People who did try to visit, or to bring us supplies, were turning away because of the power lines that had fallen down over the roads. The chimps had gotten used to our volunteers, and they really missed them. Often I'd be the only person they would see in an entire day.

By the time we started really looking for generators, there were no generators to be found. One day the vet from LEMSIP, Dr. Mahoney, called: he'd heard about the ice storm on the news, and he wanted to see how we were doing. He was really opposed to our using the propane heaters. He managed to find a generator at the lab in New York, and Pat Ring, who works for us, went to pick it up. But it took him two days to get there, because the border was closed and no one could drive on Highway 87. When he finally arrived in the early morning, he turned straight around with the generator and came back up. The generator wasn't strong enough to power the whole building. But it allowed us to have lights and run the kettle and a pellet stove, so we could at least get some heat to the top.

One of the supporters of the Jane Goodall Institute is a businessman named Alan Maislin, and around this time one of his friends, Jimmy Hewitt of Hewitt Caterpillars, also got us a generator. But both these generators were run on gas, and no one was selling gasoline! Or only in very small amounts. After a couple of weeks, through the son of one of our volunteers, Mount Royal Walsh – a big welding company in the port of Montreal – got us a big generator. It ran on diesel fuel and cost an insane amount to run: about two hundred dollars a day. But when it was running, we did get power back in the whole of the chimpanzee building.

We also had to worry about food. Our fruit market, Fruits et Légumes Taschereau in St-Hubert, wasn't supplying us any more. Richard went to one of the only grocery stores that was open, and tried to buy cases of bananas. But they said they'd only sell him one case. Finally a volunteer for the Jane Goodall Institute found a grocery store in Lachine, on the island of Montreal, that agreed to give us some supplies.

We couldn't do any laundry, either. There was no water supply, and we had to give the chimps bottled water to drink. One good thing is that it was now so cold that the building didn't smell so bad. But it was still pretty gross.

Richard is a veterinarian. He runs a clinic in Greenfield Park and he went there each day. But that was very stressful, because not all his employees could get to work and people kept bringing their dogs and cats in for boarding. It's a good thing he has a cell phone, because our phone lines were down, too. Each night he would bring big bottles of water back from the clinic so that we could rinse the floor of the chimpanzees' building.

At least the chimps didn't get sick, apart from some runny noses. One reason might be that at one point all they were getting to eat was kiwis – the fruit market eventually did supply us with cases of ripe kiwis – and they're very high in vitamin C. We were also worried because eight of the chimps are immuno-suppressed – at LEMSIP, they were injected with HIV. It's not been proven that they'll get AIDS, but they do have a lot of health problems. The other seven were used for testing a hepatitis vaccine, and they're healthy.

It wasn't just the chimpanzees we had to worry about. We have over one hundred ducks, geese and swans, and they can all stay out during the winter because of the pumps we use for the ponds. But without any power to run the pumps, the water froze over. The birds would get so heavy they couldn't even walk – we'd have to bring them in and chip the ice off their feathers. Richard would go out with a long steel pick and break the ice. Sometimes he had to virtually pull the birds out.

During the storm my sister, her husband, and their little girl had a chimney fire. They had no home so they moved in with their four dogs and ten cats for three months. That was stressful, too. And besides the chimpanzee house, we have four other barns. We have more than thirty goats, thirty pot-bellied pigs, five llamas and four horses. Then as well as the ducks, geese and swans, there are also the ostriches, emus and rheas. In the house, we have eight dogs and four cats of our own. Altogether there must be more than four hundred animals on the farm. Pat had to keep going from one barn to another, taking the propane heater with him so that the other animals could have some heat and water. The power was out for eighteen days at our house and about twenty-one days at the chimp house. We were lucky, though, because the Hydro guys came in to visit the chimps. In this whole area we were last on their list, and probably wouldn't have had power for another week, but they felt compassion for the animals and made an extra trip to reconnect us.

I think the storm was even harder for Richard than it was for me – in fact, I don't think he's over it yet. He also had all the problems of his practice to deal with: money was going out, and hardly anything was coming in. And he had a hard time dealing with the destruction on our farm. So many trees fell on the plastic fencing, for example. We went out and found the llamas standing and looking over the fallen fence – they could easily have walked away, except that the fields were so icy they couldn't get across them. So all the animals had to come into the barns. The fallen trees are still a worry and a fire hazard in our woods.

Even when we started acting more normally, the chimps were still really stressed. Of course they'd been through that kind of stress, and worse, in the laboratory. I think they'd fare much worse if it happened to them now. But we learned some things about them during the ice storm. That's where their tea-drinking started: once we got a generator, we were able to get them hot tea with lemon and honey. We still do that – it's a ritual. One of our chimpanzees, Tom, will only drink Tetley's tea. We ran out once and tried to offer him some herbal stuff. He was really offended.

Gloria Grow and Richard Allan run the Fauna Foundation in Carignan, Quebec.

JAMES CUSSEN

"This should just be for a few hours," I said to my girlfriend, "like your average power failure." Janine and I live in Pierrefonds, out in the western part of the island of Montreal, and the freezing rain covered all buildings, power lines, trees, sidewalks and streets. By the second day we realized this might be more serious than we thought, as not only were we still without electricity, but the ice was still falling and there were stores and gas stations closing all over the place.

So there we were in the dark, and since we had goldfish, we had to be careful. They can live in cold water, but the water had really gotten colder in the last few hours. Our hot water had run out earlier in the day, so I put a blanket around the aquarium to keep it warm. When we woke up the next morning, we noticed the alarm clock was blinking. "James, we have power!" said Janine as she ran out of bed and quickly turned on the heaters. The power had come back sometime overnight.

At work that day I told people that my power was back, and I asked if they needed any help with anything. That's when it all started. "Can you take care of my lizard?" a co-worker asked me. "Uh, sure, I've never taken care of one before, so you'll have to show me what to do. Bring him after work." She had not had any power for days.

Our new guest arrived and he was pretty big, and in a huge aquarium. It took three of us to get it carefully out of the car without slipping on the ice and bring it into the building. The good news was, he wouldn't be leaving his aquarium and running around. "I wrote down the times he eats and what to feed him," explained the owner. "He's been moved to so many homes the last few days, hopefully it goes well here." She was looking tired. The lizard had to have a heater close to him.

I then received a call from my father. "We have to go to St-Jean – a friend of mine just had a heart attack while shovelling his driveway. Can I bring the cat over?" "Of course," I said, "bring her over." I would just have to make sure the cat didn't bother the lizard or the goldfish.

Things were going well, everyone was minding their own business. Chou-Chou the cat was sitting in the corner of the room staring at the fish, wondering how she could get past the lizard to the fish tank. Then the phone rang. It was my friend Dave.

"James, can you take my mice? One already died and I can't bring them to the arena where I'm staying tonight – my house is freezing!" I always feel bad about the animals in this situation. "Bring them over," I said, "and put a blanket around the cage."

One hour later, I now had goldfish, a lizard, a cat and two little mice in my small apartment. "Janine, do we have any allergy tablets?" I asked. The air was getting stuffy with all kinds of smells and I couldn't open the window, it was another cold night.

"Let's hope tonight goes well," I remember Janine telling me. We went to sleep, the cat with us and the rest of the zoo on the other side of the door. But the sounds that the mice and the lizard made out in the living room drove the cat nuts. Until the other guests calmed down, the cat was meowing and scratching up against the bedroom door. "I hope this isn't going to go on all night," I thought at the time.

Everything was going well until we woke up to the cat scratching on the door. The bedroom was cold. I looked at the alarm clock and couldn't believe it – the power had gone off again. "Oh no!" We went to check on the animals with our flashlight. The lizard's aquarium had no heat at all, and he needs a warm temperature around him twenty-four hours a day. The mice were both in their tunnel but their cage was cold, as was the goldfish water. The cat was fine, with a look of "Who to visit first, the mice or the goldfish?" She was on her own turf now.

It was too late to call anyone, so every hour we tried to place a hot-water bottle under the lizard to keep him warm. The lizard wasn't crazy about it, though, and would give a good fight until he got on top of the bottle. Then he would stay for a while. We had to go through this each time we changed the water. We put a pillowcase around the mouse cage, only to have them bite on it and start to pull it in. Then we decided to put Kleenex in their cage, hoping they would wrap it around themselves.

Suddenly, we heard some water being splashed. "Where's the cat?" I asked Janine. We looked around, and there she was on the bookcase with her paw right into the fish tank and the fish were just going crazy. "Chou-Chou, get down!" we yelled. The cat got her paw out of the water and looked at us to see how serious we were. "Get down now!" The cat finally jumped down and went to the corner of the room, where she proceeded to clean her paw as if nothing had happened. She would later try to get to the mice, but to no avail, as we caught her at that also.

So, all night without power we had to stay up and make sure all the animals, especially the lizard, were kept warm, because if we ran out of hot water, he would be in trouble. The cat, who was trying to con-tribute her help, was knocking on the mice's door again and helping them keep warm with a good exercise of running. Suddenly she opened the cage door and the mice ran out. "Chou-Chou, come here! Chou-Chou, come here!" – like I'm talking to a dog – "Janine, grab the cat! I'll try and find the mice." But Janine was busy trying to get the lizard to stay on his water bottle.

So here I am in the middle of the night, holding a flashlight with batteries that are slowly dying, looking for two mice. We had closed the bedroom and washroom doors to keep the other rooms from making the apartment even colder, so the mice couldn't have been far. Janine caught the cat and held her as she went nuts wanting a shot at finding the mice herself. Finally, after searching everywhere, I found both mice in a corner of the room and was able to put them in their cage. The craziest thing was listening to Chou-Chou purring through all this. We had to head back to the lizard now, as he was all excited watching us run around looking for the mice and we needed to get him on the hot bottle again.

Morning finally came and we still didn't have power. The owner of the lizard came back to pick him up – "I found someone in Beaconsfield with power, I'll bring him there." The lizard will probably have a nervous breakdown before he freezes. Dave picked up the mice and took them to a friend downtown who had power. The fish tank had a blanket wrapped around it, and Chou-Chou was brought to my sister's place in Pointe Claire, where there was power as well as three young kids who would love to play with her. "I just hope Chou-Chou doesn't mind."

What a night: no sleep, no power, and Janine and I still had to go to work. Our electricity came back at the end of that day. Hopefully we never have an ice storm again, but if it does happen, I hope to have a bigger apartment if I have to take care of all those animals for another night.

James Cussen is currently writing about his successful fight against cancer, hoping one day to have it published.

JOAN YORSTON

When my friend Pam moved back to western Canada, she couldn't afford to take everything with her, so she gave me some of her cookbooks, her statue of Buddha and her twelve-year-old pet goldfish in a bowl. The fish was placed on our kitchen counter, in a new fish tank with a filter, and there he swam, day in and day out, for six years.

He never had a name, other than Fish. But we would say good morning to him every day when he was fed, and if I placed my finger on the outside of his tank, he would swim over as if trying to touch me. We kept a small "perpetual" calendar beside his tank and changed the date when he was fed so that we wouldn't lose track and overfeed (or underfeed) him.

On Tuesday, January 6, 1998, we lost our power at 6:57 A.M., just about the time we would normally feed Fish, who was now eighteen years old. I sprinkled some food in his tank and got on with my day.

Only this was not to be an ordinary day, or an ordinary week. Because of the ice storm, we were without power for six days straight, and we, like many others, had to improvise cooking and heating arrangements.

I suppose we were among the lucky ones, because we had a fireplace and enough firewood to keep one room warm. But that room wasn't the kitchen, and as the house cooled off, so did the water in the fish tank. Because Fish was a trust from a special friend, I worried about him, and tried to get professional advice. After numerous phone calls to various veterinarians, I spoke with a "fish expert" who said we shouldn't place Fish near the fireplace, because the extreme changes of tempera-ture would surely do him in. Rather it was suggested that I warm some water in a pot at the fireplace, pour it into a two-litre bottle, place the bottle in the fish tank, and *change it every two hours*.

I could change the water every two hours during the day – after all, we weren't going anywhere. But at night this was a problem; I normally sleep longer than two hours at a stretch. So I changed the water before going to bed, and hoped for the best.

That first cold morning, I woke early and went straight to the kitchen to find Fish floating belly up. I quickly heated some water and replaced the cold bottle with a warm one. After a while, Fish turned over and swam to the edge of his tank for his daily meal.

And so it continued for that week. Every morning Fish was found belly up, but when the warm bottle was placed in his tank, he turned belly down. Up and down, up and down, that was the pattern. But thanks to this regular bottle of warm water, Fish survived the Ice Storm of 1998, a marvellous show of strength and determination at his age.

As for me, I felt that I had fulfilled the trust placed in me by my friend Pam.

Joan Yorston lives in Beaconsfield, Quebec. "I don't have titles or labels," she says, "I am just me."

DOUG TAYLOR

In 1994 we installed an outdoor pond – a figure-eight shape, about thirty feet long and about twelve feet at the widest point; thirty inches deep at one end and six inches deep at the other.

Unknown to me, my sister-in-law had purchased and put three goldfish into the pond. The first winter, I brought the fish into the house and kept them in an aquarium, but found this to be a lot of work, trying to keep the water clean and so on.

Back into the pond the following spring. The fish spawned, and three became thirty-three. Instead of bringing the fish in, I decided to leave them in the pond for the winter. The water in the deep end was kept from freezing by a small pump which had been purchased and installed to keep the water circulating.

The fish survived and – roll forward to the winter of 1998 – now we had about 150 fish living year-round in the pool.

About forty-eight hours after the beginning of the ice storm, we suddenly remembered our fish, but by that time there was little we could do, because the water had completely seized up. In fact we were without electricity for seventeen days.

Roll forward to spring. The water finally unfreezes (this is like ninety to a hundred days with no water circulating in the pond) and I remove the floating dead fish – 150 in all.

A few days later, after the complete thaw, lo and behold, we find three adult fish swimming in the pond. Somehow they had found a spot, probably near a large rock that had been installed in the deep end, which for some reason did not freeze and somehow had sufficient oxygen to keep them alive.

How those fish survived we'll never know. But survive they did, and now we're back up to fifty and counting!

Doug Taylor is a chartered accountant living in Mont St-Hilaire, Quebec. His passion is the animal kingdom.

CHRISTIE CLAYMORE

When we arrived home from vacation, we saw that a lot of changes had occurred over two weeks. As I entered our house, which was covered in mounds of snow, I scanned the area for the bird cage. There it was, but to my horror, a dead cockatiel lay at the bottom of the cage. I gasped and shut my eyes. Next on my mind were my goldfish, Eddie and Freddie. Were they dead too? I sure hoped not.

But the next thing I knew, my brother hollered out, "Christie, are your fish supposed to float upside down like this?"

Well, that answered my question. They were dead too. It was cold in my house, freezing in fact. No wonder my pets died – the heating had been off for three days! One of my mother's friends had been looking after the fish and the bird, but in the past three days she had not come. We were supposed to have been home already, but the ice storm had delayed our getting here. Outside our house, the conditions were terrible: the neighbour's shed had caved in, our wood had rotted and split, and mounds of snow were piled high to the roof.

Christie Claymore lives in Ste-Adèle, Quebec, and attends Laurentian Regional High School in Lachute. She was twelve years old at the time of the storm.

JANET LALONDE

When I had walked my property, I broke down and cried. Fifteen acres of pine trees were moulded into icy cones, with each and every treetop broken. My willows were split into two; the cedars, ash and poplars broken into sticks. The rain coated the trees like shellac on a wooden floor. This was the beginning of the storm, and I had no idea what was to come.

The birds were behaving peculiarly, forever circling the surrounding fields. The air was damp and bitter, and the sky threatening. Power outages were being reported. Driving five miles into Alexandria left me dumbfounded by the damage I saw. A hydro pole with a transformer listed thirty degrees toward the highway. We still had hydro, but that pole signalled a message: we were soon going to lose it.

As I proceeded with errands, there was a terrible sense of panic among the people. I learned where the outages were and how extensive they were, and that we were to receive another storm far worse than the first one. I thought about my veterinary hospital. How was I going to run it for any length of time without power? Food, water and heat . . . my brain began to swirl.

Canadian Tire was the first stop. Residents of Alexandria and surrounding communities were buying water containers, jerry cans, batteries and candles like there was no tomorrow. The shelves were depleted and soon empty.

The grocery store was next. I stocked up on canned food and dry goods and then went on to fill the jerry cans with gas. The final stop was to purchase extra chains and oil for the chainsaw, and order a generator. The dealer had just sold the last one. I should have made him my first stop.

I raced home to fill the water containers, fearing the pole would fall. It did that night, and took ten more with it. We were now in darkness, the hospital without heat. My home, at least, had a fireplace insert for wood, so there was a source of heat for us.

The hospital held animals that had been admitted for surgery or were being treated for illness. They were, in technical terms, "a liability" and I had to provide for them. The local hospital (for humans) was in emergency mode; it had lost power. Family members of elderly patients were asked to come and tend to their care.

As the days went by, homes froze and people moved out to share space in those homes that had generators. The phone started to ring – people had to leave their pets. The real horror was the abandonment of animals. Many of them were left tied outside to doorknobs. The Cornwall branch of the SPCA was filling up quickly; the shelters in Ottawa, Brockville and Vankleek Hill were out of commission.

Four days passed, and I still had no source of heat for the hospital. The temperature in the building had dropped to 12°C. I had twenty-two animals cramped into three small rooms to conserve heat. Finally, at 10 P.M., my generator supplier called; he had one ready for pickup. I loaded my sons into the truck and we had a harrowing drive to Alexandria. The hydro wires that crossed the highway were so heavy with ice, my truck

Janet Lalonde (kneeling), changing the oil in a generator outside her veterinary clinic.
She didn't always find the storm a laughing matter. (Photo: Kathy McGill)

barely passed under them. I wondered if any carried voltage. What would
I do if one fell on the truck? Darkness was everywhere.

When we got home, Mike (nine years old), Paul (eight years old) and
I unloaded the generator. We uncoiled the hookup and threw the switch
on the panel – only to find that the panel operated off a three-prong
220-volt plug, and my generator would accept only a four-prong 220-
volt plug. I started to cry. It was eleven-thirty at night.

I phoned my electrician, but he was still out on calls. I telephoned
again at 6 A.M. and he came right away – ahead of twenty other calls!
My hospital now had lights, heat from a 1500-watt space heater, and
running water (very cold). If we shut everything down, we could run
the washing machine. I felt I could manage the hospital, at least to
provide basic service.

In the meantime, the tree damage had become overwhelming. Limbs
that had trunks of four to eight inches had fallen into and onto the dog

runs of my kennel. One run was operational, but I had three males that would kill each other if allowed the chance. The runs were slick with ice, but the boys and I donned our snowsuits and got busy with the chainsaw. Three hours later, we had opened four runs. We weren't able to move the big branches that lay across the fencing, but at least we could open the gates.

When my parents called from Burlington the following evening, I learned that a state of emergency had been declared. They told me what they had seen on television.

My youngest brother chose one of my lowest moments to phone. Todd and a friend of his – Jules, a recent immigrant from Great Britain – arrived eight hours later with a chainsaw, supplies and smiles on their faces. They cut trees and chipped ice off the roofs for five days. They also entertained Mike and Paul, who were suffering withdrawal from lack of computer games and Nintendo. Meanwhile, I cleaned cages, walked dogs, treated emergencies and pretended to keep a stiff upper lip.

By day five, we still had not realized the full impact of the storm. Supplies were running low, and every woman in eastern Ontario was wearing a baseball cap. The banks were closed, as were the money machines. No one had any cash, and the broken phone lines and loss of power meant Interac or credit cards could not be used. The local merchants, however, were fantastic and opened accounts of credit. On day seven, the banks opened their doors, allowing only two patrons at a time into the darkened buildings. Staff handed out cash from cardboard boxes.

The local grocery store, the Alexandria Loeb, was an even more depressing sight: no frozen or refrigerated food, no meat. The building was dimly lit, thanks to generator power. But the store's operators did everything possible to accommodate the crisis. The staff of the pharmacy whose billing system depended on a scanner would lead you, individually, by flashlight, to the aisle containing the product you needed and then, in many instances, would ask you what you normally paid and charge accordingly. Gasoline was now being rationed; twenty dollars' worth was the limit.

The beer store finally opened on day seven. I was desperate for a beer – absolutely desperate. When I unloaded the case from the truck, I slipped on the ice and sent the beer through the air. It crashed onto the ice and I watched the golden brew froth over the driveway. That was my breaking point . . . I lost it. Jules calmly walked over, opened the case and said, "Well, at least the caps are still on." He proceeded to carry the broken mess away.

We lost track of time and operated by nature's clock. For the most part, I never knew what day or time it was. I lived according to the schedule I established to look after the clinic, my kennel, the children – and, in between, refill the generator and stoke the woodstove day and night.

The abandonment of animals was horrific; so were the deaths of cattle, horses and deer. I have tremendous admiration for two agents of the Cornwall SPCA, Debbie Boulerice and Bonnie Bishop, who worked day and night responding to calls about animals in distress. When the army was called in, soldiers walked door to door checking for signs of humans in trouble; repeatedly they came across animals in need of help, and Debbie and Bonnie reacted. One day we learned of a person in Moose Creek who had abandoned nine dogs for seven days without food or water. Four of them had taken on a porcupine. Debbie and Bonnie drove out and caught all of the dogs, and we spent an evening pulling quills.

Day ten arrived and I, like most, had not showered or bathed in all that time – sponge baths in a cold bathroom were not worth the effort. In fact, it got to the point where I wore the same clothes for four days and nights. Laundry had become a real problem.

We encountered two evenings when the temperature dropped to -31 and -35°C. Despite the woodstove, the basement was only 3°C. I couldn't stand another minute – I had to order another generator for the house. The storm was becoming very expensive, and in more ways than one.

The generator had been working very well until we went down to -35°C. At eleven-thirty that night, the machine began to whine like a baby. I telephoned the distributor, who told me I probably had ice forming in the air hose leading to the carburetor. I removed the hose and thawed the ice, and the machine ran as it always had. At 3:30 A.M., the machine was whining again *and* leaking oil from a hole at the top of the crankcase. The air-filter housing, the hose and part of the carburetor were frozen solid with ice. I took the parts to my truck and thawed them using the heater jets while I listened to a song titled "Spend a Day

With Me." The following morning, we dragged a doghouse from the kennel and built a shelter for the generator so the exhaust would help keep the machine warm.

Thinking all was well, I proceeded to tend to animals in the hospital, when I noticed blue smoke billowing from the doghouse. Where there's smoke, there's fire – and sure enough, the doghouse was on fire. We rescued the generator just in time and put the fire out. The exhaust had been pointed in the wrong direction.

On day eleven, my second generator was ready for pickup. A temporary hookup to the panel allowed me the privilege of heating the hot-water tank. I took a very long shower and savoured the warmth. I just can't tell you how good that shower felt.

My pleasure, however, was short-lived. Later that evening, my domestic long-haired cat decided to investigate shadows flickering on a wall that were created by a large, three-wick candle. Lorus got too close to it and became a screaming feline fireball. We managed to catch him and put the fire out before he got seriously hurt or started a fire elsewhere, but it was another stressful incident that could have been a disaster if we had not been in the room.

The stress the crisis created is beyond anything one could imagine. There was little room for patience, and tempers were extremely short. Yet daily I heard how people were helping each other to remarkable degrees. I think the storm will have created a lot of divorces and a lot of babies.

My power was restored after fourteen days. The sudden change from a comfortable environment to an exhausting "survivalist mode" had made me realize just how dependent I had become on electricity. Following the storm, my home and business underwent major changes. Should we ever have to experience another of Mother Nature's disruptive events, we will be ready.

Janet Lalonde practises veterinary medicine in Alexandria, Ontario. This article has been adapted and slightly abridged from the original version, published in Dogs in Canada *magazine.*

HILDA BENTON

When the power first flickered out, I dutifully refrained from opening the two chest freezers in our basement, hoping that this inconvenience we were experiencing would resolve itself in a day or so. I rescued several casseroles and roasts and left them to chill on the front step. The next morning I discovered the empty containers strewn across the driveway, and our black Newfoundland dog joyfully pursuing lasagna noodles on the icy lawn.

When it became evident that the freezer contents were lost, I began the arduous and depressing task of emptying them out. I would haul the food upstairs and onto a sled, and trudge across the treacherous fields to dump the soggy mess. It was so disheartening to watch our garden harvest floating in that sea of strawberry juice. With frozen fingers I would cut open the half-defrosted bags of chicken and toss them onto the growing heap – again, much to the delight of our dog.

One bag seemed considerably lighter than the others. When I opened it, I'm sure my screams terrorized the wildlife for miles around. An enormous, half-frozen blue jay stared up at me!

My husband, who was enrolled in a bird-carving class, had found this perfect specimen in the fall and had placed him with the chickens in the deep freeze. He had hoped to use it as a model in one of his wildlife projects. Needless to say, the only "wild" life that day was his startled wife!

Hilda Benton lives outside Cornwall, Ontario, where she teaches at St. Anne's School. This piece originally appeared in Ice Storm '98, *published by the* Cornwall Standard Freeholder.

IRIS WINSTON

Live with animals and you will be very clear about the specifics of their personalities. The differences were never better defined for me than through the assortment of annoyance, bewilderment, apprehension and lack of concern my four animals exhibited in the face of the ice storm of the century.

Kona, my small Burmese cat, making it clear that she had been bred for a different climate – *It was never like this in Burma!* – announced her displeasure in no uncertain terms at the first loss of power. Her favourite warm spots – on top of a bathroom heat register or my computer monitor – lost their most desirable property very quickly. Then the house was no longer cozy. A couple of glances at the weather outside and she gave the cat equivalent of a shrug, followed by an irritated mew with a to-hell-with-it tone. Soon she retired to bed. She moved into call-me-when-spring-arrives mode, and buried herself deep under the nearest comforter, emerging only for basic needs or whenever power was restored.

My other cat, Mel, more adventurous but less discerning, just yearned for the great outdoors. In response to each plaintive cry from him, I opened a door to show the full beauty of the storm at its height. He sniffed the air and turned to me reproachfully. *Fix it! I trust you to put things right.* Time and again, he tried a tentative step on to the patio, then decided discretion was the better part of valour and ran back in. A few minutes later, he tried another door in the hope that either the weather was extremely localized or generally improved. He repeated the exercise and the reproach each time he was disappointed, finally braving the elements for a thirty-second sprint around the deck from one door to the next.

Eventually, when he was convinced that all points were as bad as they looked, he gave up and found a comfortable spot in the house. He settled for being an indoor cat during the day, but as soon as darkness fell, he stared out of the nearest window, ever hopeful that the weather was about to improve. He kept the routine up long enough to be certain to get his wish.

The dogs, with no in-house toilet facilities, had no choice but short outdoor sessions and walks each day. The falling branches and cracking trees kept us away from our regular route through the woods. Trips to the open spaces of the local quarry seemed safe enough to me, though the dogs were less certain.

So I fetched the leashes – usually a cause for celebration, happy dog smiles and wagging tails. Not during the ice storm. My border-collie cross, Gilligan, for the first time in the six years since she has been part of the family, said Thanks, but no thanks. She rolled on her back and wagged her tail tentatively. *I surrender and I love you, but you're nuts to even think about going out there!*

This reaction caused Connie, my bouncy standard poodle, to pause in her usual enthusiastic response to the offer of a walk. She generally takes direction from her older and wiser partner. *If Gillie doesn't want to go, then I'm with her.*

Twice daily, I eventually convinced them that we were tough enough to cope, that they really needed to go and that we wouldn't spend very long out there anyway. We headed towards the quarry, where I let them off to run. At least, that was my intention. Not so for Gillie. First she tried to herd Connie and me home as fast as possible. Then, the sound of a cracking tree limb – eerily loud in the silence of the early morning or late afternoon – led her to give up on her charges. She shot back to the house, where she waited anxiously for us to come away from that dangerous winter wonderland.

Connie, obviously torn in her loyalties, cocked her head to one side, pondering whether to follow Gillie's fast-retreating figure or to stay the course of the walk. A moment of indecision and then she remained with me. I am unsure if her intention was to protect or to be protected. She certainly hugged my heels, waiting for instructions on what we were going to do next.

This routine continued for several days. Even after power was restored – just three days in our case – the explosive sounds of branches breaking or limbs collapsing under the weight of snow and ice meant that the woods were a menacing place as far as Gillie was concerned. It was some days after Mel had ventured beyond the patio and Kona had emerged from her comforter nest for more than a few minutes that Gillie finally showed renewed interest in walking. It was her response to the calmer weather, rather than more favourable weather forecasts, that assured me the spectacular storm was completely over. I always listen to my animals.

Iris Winston, a former director of the Canadian Federation of Humane Societies, is a writer who lives in Constance Bay, Ontario, a village on the Ottawa River.

INGRID BIRKER

Day One
No power. No school. Everyone is happy, though Ingrid still has to get dressed and go to work as if it's business as usual. But it is fun for me. The kids and David will be home, and that is fun for a dog! They never tire of giving me belly-rubs, especially when they first get up, and David always gives me great walks. We have a lot of fun because it seems an adventure for them to be home on a school day.

We humans are thinking that only a few Montreal homes are without power and that this storm can't last forever.

Day Two
No power again, mighty strong winds and lots of falling ice. As David takes me for my morning walk, we hear tree branches breaking all around us as they stiffen with ice and crack. There is no warning – one crashes behind the neighbour's car just as he finishes parking, and he gets right back into the driver's seat and backs into our driveway, which is not in the path of any trees, poles or wires. This is my favourite bathroom area. I hope he doesn't block my yellow snow zones for too long.

He will continue to park here for the next seven days. At least the phone is still working. We can call friends and stay with them during the day to get warm.

Day Three
Last night everyone moved into the basement because it was the least drafty spot in the house. Ingrid got out all the camping mats and sleeping bags, and David hauled down all the duvets and pillows. I was especially snug in between Mack and Kendall, the two hot little boys, and they use my warm furry belly to toast their toes before tucking into their sleeping bags.

Sleeping is the warmest and safest activity. We are all together on one big mattress, covered with a mountain of feather duvets, sleeping bags and blankets. I keep my hat and mitts under my pillow.

Ingrid Birker's family setting out for the safety of the Redpath Museum down their ravaged street in Montreal.

Day Four

Ingrid drags all the family except me to the museum even though it is officially closed. It is too cold to stick around the house. They look as though they will be gone a long time. Everyone takes a backpack full of slippers, socks, mitts and colouring books, and David packs tortellini and ground lamb from the almost thawed freezer. They don't take dog food. Maybe they are contemplating camping out at the museum for the weekend. Without me!

We pack up enough supplies to make it through the day (including the Star Wars *trilogy on video), and arrive at the museum to find it occupied by many other like-minded staff. Around 2 P.M., in the middle of* Return of the Jedi, *everything crumbles with an exhausted mechanical moan. We get Kendall and Mack dressed and head outside. After a bit of sliding around on the icy slopes, the kids need a snack. This is not a bad idea and so we head downtown, only to find that everything is closed and people are panicking. The subway has shut down, buildings are being evacuated and traffic is snarled.*

We end up taking a bus through the pitch-black streets. The bus is packed to the ceiling with shell-shocked passengers and we lurch through crowded, chaotic intersections like an overweight parade float. No one speaks. People's eyes are very large and they gaze out the darkened windows in stunned silence. This twenty-five-minute bus ride takes almost two hours.

Day Five

They came home last night after all. I am grateful. I need company and kids more than I need lights and heat. But the water tastes kind of weird.

Spirits are high today. When I scampered out, I found myself frolicking through puddles rather than sliding on those icy ball bearings that were all over the place. The temperature has risen above freezing and melting ice drips on everything. Everyone seems happier and the radio people are talking about the "aftermath" of the storm. Many times the phone rings and there is a lot of relieved laughter as Ingrid and David describe the situation. Ingrid leaves with the boys because she has heard that the Westmount Y is offering free showers and swimming and the shelter at nearby Victoria Hall is offering food and drinks. Even the city buses are free! But they still won't allow us animals to travel on them.

This is the day we can start to laugh. We feel as though the worst is behind us. CBC Radio advises people that they can cook their meals on the exhaust manifolds of any vehicle with four cylinders or more – but don't bring the car into the house!

Day Six

After Ingrid and the boys returned home yesterday, they convinced David that Westmount was the place to go. Free drinks were being given out in the Children's Library and the shelter had provided them with delicious snacks just before they decided to come home. The bad news is that it is getting colder (dropping to -15°C) so I hope they don't leave me alone for too long.

Today is a hard day. When we reach Westmount, it has lost power. Now we are really in a crisis. Where do we go? The army is assembling in front of the shelter. They seem to know what they are doing and look very official. The boys are enthralled. This is the first time they have seen tanks, armoured cars and army personnel in real combat gear (including helmets to protect against falling

STORM SHELTER NOTICE
FOR NDG RESIDENTS

LOYOLA HIGH SCHOOL
2465 WEST BROADWAY
(CORNER SHERBROOKE)
IS AN OFFICIAL CITY OF
MONTREAL SHELTER

X IF YOU NEED A PLACE TO KEEP WARM
OR SLEEP CALL THE CLSC NDG/MTL.O.
@ 485-1670
FOR INFORMATION

X POSTE DU QUARTIER
280-0111

FOR A HOT MEAL, COFFEE DURING THE DAY
CHEZ MES AMIS, 5942 RUE SHERBROOKE, 482-2210

WARM PLACES DURING THE DAY FOR COFFEE, NEWS AND INFORMATION
NDG BLACK COMMUNITY CENTRE, 2121 OLD ORCHARD, 489-3598
NDG FOOD DEPOT, 2121 OXFORD, 483-4680
NDG COMMUNITY COUNCIL, 6525 SOMERLED, 484-1471
HEAD & HANDS, 2304 OLD ORCHARD, 481-0277

One of the many notices posted on trees and lampposts in
Ingrid Birker's neighbourhood.

trees and ice). One of the soldiers says that Montreal reminds him of Sarajevo, but without the bullets.

We wait at the bus stop for a bus that never comes and glance over that day's paper, which has been delivered faithfully to our door every morning even though the mail could not get through. As Quebec sinks ever deeper into crisis, the fashion section heralds spring clothing trends!

Day Seven

We are safe and warm and together. After a very bad day, where the family moved from one blacked-out area to another, they were rescued by Sas at Chad's corner store. Sas told them to go get me so we spent a very relaxed evening in their warm and snug home. When her husband came home, he took one look at me and said, "How could they have dreamed of leaving this cute dog alone?" I am happy that we are together and to see the boys playing again. Even Ingrid's shoulders are back in their normal position. David has taken up smoking. (He is the cover for Sas, who is hiding her habit from her children.)

I spend most of the day playing with the children or helping to feed our two families. In the local grocery store, comfort food items are low; hardly any chips, cheesies, crackers, peanuts, cookies or cakes are left. The good news is that the water is now safe to drink again.

Day Eight

David takes me home and we spend a long time draining the pipes. It is really cold in here. I don't like it when he brings me through the black-ened streets at night. It is a very eerie atmosphere and I really don't like to step on all those black wires on the roads that look like snakes. He has taken my leash off during these moonlit walks and I stick close to his side. Only a few people with generators or fireplaces seem to be left in their houses. At one house David pulls the plug on the ostentatious outdoor Christmas lights.

At Sas's we have a great time. Our families get on really well together and we even celebrated Charlie's sixth birthday. He received the Star Wars *monopoly game, and I spent a few hours teaching kids how to pit Imperial and Rebel forces against each other in order to buy up all the available real estate in the universe.*

Day Nine

David went to work today so Ingrid and the boys take me down to the other side of the tracks to visit A.J. and Emily's house where the power returned on Day Seven. It took us about forty-five minutes to slide over the railway pass and walk the two blocks to their house. Nothing has been cleared or salted or even trodden on in this area. Once we got there, they ate a lot of gorp (good old raisins & peanuts) and read a book about survivors. Mack and A.J. especially enjoyed hearing about the siege of Vienna in 1430 and the attempted invasion of Japan by the Mongols in 1274. I guess it makes our crisis seem minor in comparison.

I carry arnica, the homeopathic remedy for bruising and swelling, in my coat pocket and administer it many times a day. The children are continuously falling on the hard ice and feel sore all over when they come in. I have heard two stories of broken wrists and elbows.

After we return from A.J.'s house, David phones to tell us that he stopped at our house and we have power. He filled the hot-water tank and put the furnace on medium. We decide to have our farewell meal of steak at Sas's house, and then home to bed. We slept together in the basement one last time because it was still too cold in the bedrooms.

Maybe now the dog, Bianca, will begin to act normal again.

Day Ten

I am glad I am not a country dog. We seem to be back to normal here, although the street lights are not on and the family is very cautious about using a lot of power. Ingrid has done the wash but she won't use the dryer and has strung a clothesline in the basement. I was able to bark at the mailman for the first time today and he kind of smiled at me. He brought some overdue Christmas parcels which made everyone excited. Nothing for me – just a bird feeder.

Ingrid Birker is curator of paleontology at the Redpath Museum, McGill University. Bianca is a Bichon Frisé. Ms. Birker would like to credit her mother-in-law, June Singleton, for prompting the writing of this piece.

11

AUTHORITY FIGURES

t was the Sunday after the storm, and I left my mother's apartment early. I had to go into the office and work. But first I headed in the opposite direction, back towards my Pointe Claire home. I wanted to check on the pipes, the roofs, the basement, the general state of the house. As I drove down a hill to the highway, I could see that the intersection ahead was clear. The traffic light was out of action, and at such corners everybody was supposed to come to a complete stop, check in all directions and proceed slowly. This being Montreal, a lot of drivers were doing no such thing. I decided to be a Montreal driver, rather than a safe one.

A hundred metres later, I heard a siren behind me. The first place I could pull over was on the highway itself — an old, shoulderless, two-lane stretch of road, not quite free of ice. The policeman rightly chewed me out, then debated with himself about issuing me a ticket. Finally he decided to let me proceed, less because of my plea for mercy than because our two cars were stopped at a dangerous point. The possibility of an accident was real. There were dark lines under the man's eyes, as though he'd been up for several nights.

His was the most immediate, basic kind of authority: a uniformed man with a weapon. I wondered briefly about the stresses he was under as I continued — strictly within the speed limit, of course — to my deserted home. The officer could give orders to the public, but he had to take orders, too. The emergency conditions meant that while he may have had an unusual degree of power, his own freedom was more than likely reduced. Did he normally have to work so long and so hard? How did he prefer to spend his Sunday mornings?

The stories in this chapter describe the impact of the crisis on seven people who found themselves in a position to give orders. Two are senior, high-ranking officers in the Armed Forces, one a reserve officer, and one a sergeant. But as well as these military personnel, the chapter also includes the voices of a young Quebec policewoman, the mayor of a rural municipality, and the coordinator of emergency services in the Mohawk community of Kahnawake. This is the only chapter where every story is based not on a written submission, but on a personal interview. In each case (and with a varying degree of success), I wanted to find out not just what the individual did, but what he or she felt.

ISABELLE GENDRON

I've been a police officer for the Sûreté du Québec for eight years. During the crisis, I worked in the city of St-Hyacinthe and the surrounding region. I did house-to-house patrols, both day and night; I provided security in the shelters; I did surveillance duty at the firewood depots. I also spent a couple of weeks in a rural municipality, St-Nazaire-d'Acton, working alongside the mayor and councillors in the town hall.

At the start of the storm, police officers were asked to go door to door. If the heating was inadequate, our mission was to evacuate the people to shelters. Some of them were obstinate, and refused to leave. But it was a delicate task – this was their life, their home – and we had to be tactful. In other cases there was enough heat in the home, but if the people were living on their own, and couldn't manage well, we still had to insist on them leaving.

Many people told us they were doing fine at home. But little by little, when they realized that the power would not be coming back for a long time, they became depressed. The longer the crisis lasted, the more depressed people were. It stopped being fun to camp out in the living room. In those cases, our mandate was to visit the people almost every day, and talk to them a little.

At the start, we'd visit them and we'd just say, "Hi, my name is so-and-so, I just wanted to see how you are and check if there's anything you need." And the people would answer, "No, no, we're okay." They didn't know us; they didn't have much to say. But gradually we established a relationship with them. I remember, after a couple of weeks I was visiting one home, and when I asked the couple how they were doing, they began to cry. It was traumatic for them. And it was hard on us, too. There was so little we could do for them, except to give moral support.

The door-to-door work was made even harder because there was ice all over the place. One of my colleagues in the Sûreté fell and broke his leg while on a door-to-door patrol. Some people didn't want to open their doors to us. They were so afraid of being taken away to a shelter that they hid when they saw us coming.

In the rural municipality, I and one of my fellow officers ended up acting as a sort of link between the local council and various other agencies. Communications were difficult. Some work was performed twice over while other jobs remained undone. But it was staggering how hard the council members worked. They were absolutely devoted to the task at hand, even at the expense of their own family life.

Emergency supplies – food, toilet paper, all kinds of things – had arrived for the residents to collect at the town hall; but not everyone came. So the mayor asked me to go to certain families and distribute the supplies. Either because they were out at work or else because they were just too proud, they didn't want to come and pick up a package. Some people refused to accept any help from outside, even when we'd go to their homes with firewood or vegetables. They didn't want to abuse the situation, or profit from it. "No, no," they would say, "give this to someone else who truly needs it." We would say, very gently, "Take it. Please take it."

And we, the police officers, would find our eyes filling with tears. It was difficult to watch people suffering and not to be able to help them more than we could. The public often calls on us because of a problem that needs to be solved: we arrive, and somehow or other the problem gets solved. Even if we can't immediately find a stolen item, for example, the mere fact of our arrival helps to reassure people. But in the ice storm, that wasn't true any longer. We were living through the crisis too.

All this time we were being put up in a hotel in Montreal. Not that we slept much! We'd have to leave the hotel at 5:30 A.M. in order to arrive in the St-Hyacinthe area by 6:30 or 7:00. And it would be 10 or 11 P.M. before we got back to the hotel. On one occasion, we arrived in the evening to find that the hotel had no power. Actually the whole neighbourhood had no power. It was strange, having to use our flashlights in the hotel, taking a shower in the dark, and the men shaving in the dark.

I think the crisis was especially hard on the farmers. Pig farmers and poultry farmers needed to keep their generators functioning twenty-four hours a day, not so much for the heat as for the ventilation. If you don't have ventilation, even for an hour, you have animals that can't breathe and they start to die. The farmers' association, the Association des Producteurs Agricoles, was trying to buy generators wherever it could, all over North America, but it wasn't easy to get them here fast.

I know of farms where the farmers did have a spare generator, but it broke down at the same time as the regular one. And in the space of two hours, they lost half their entire stock. Imagine it: a lifetime of work, disappearing in just a couple of hours! For them it was a terrible catastrophe. And no one could do a thing to stop it happening.

For a time I was on firewood duty. Huge amounts of wood were arriving from all over Quebec, and elsewhere in Canada too, and the army was in charge of distributing it. But pretty soon they realized that some people were coming in to collect wood ten times a day. Instead of just picking up what they needed, they were gathering reserves for the rest of the winter and the next year as well. So the army and the local municipalities asked us to organize a system of control.

It wasn't easy, and I'll tell you why: the firewood was being given out for free. We knew that some people who weren't affected by the crisis were driving to the South Shore to pick up a free supply. We could tell by the licence plates that some were coming from as far away as Laval, where there were no power outages at all. Just by our presence, we deterred some people from making repeated trips for wood, and we also did night-time patrols. But if someone shows up and he says, "Sure, I was here this morning, but that load was for me, now I need a load for my mother-in-law" – what can you do? In the end, we had to rely on the public's goodwill and good faith.

I was also assigned to work at a shelter in St-Hyacinthe. It was located at a big high school, the Polyvalente Hyacinthe Delorme. I'm not sure exactly how many people were staying there – perhaps as many as two thousand. Just before we arrived, they had managed to install a workable system of ventilation and establish an area for smoking. In the previous two weeks, there had been no ventilation and people had smoked all over the place. For older people with breathing problems, or even just for non-smokers, it was awful.

I can tell you, the shelter smelled bad – unbelievably bad. The lineup for the shower was long, maybe as many as two hundred people! People would wait and wait and then finally say, "I'm coming back tomorrow." But the next day, the same thing would happen.

The Red Cross officials were working incredibly hard. The soldiers, too. Everybody was really trying to create a minimum of comfort, a minimum of well-being. But with two thousand people there – the size of an entire village – it wasn't easy.

In a group that size, you find all sorts. The aggressive types, the mentally ill, the chronically sick, the very old, small children, alcoholics, drug addicts: they were all there. I was amazed at the number of children who were left to fend for themselves, because their parents wouldn't look after them. Probably the parents weren't used to it. I spent some of my time just playing with children whose mothers were off in the smoking-room or lying down somewhere.

The alcoholics would hide drinks anywhere they could. They weren't allowed to drink, and they were expelled if they got caught, but they did it anyway. And if they were kicked out of this shelter, they'd just find another one.

I remember one young woman who came into the shelter when she was pregnant. Her belly was already huge. She had to sleep on a camp bed, which must have been really uncomfortable. When she started having contractions, they took her to the hospital. Two or three days later, she was back in the shelter with her newborn baby. The first few weeks of that baby's life were spent on the floor of the shelter. The father wasn't around but the grandmother was there to help, a woman of forty-five or so.

No, it wasn't funny. It wasn't funny. I tried to console one elderly lady who said to me, "The couple next to me are having sex the whole time. I don't want to watch, I don't want to listen, can anything be done?" There was no chance for privacy. You could be surrounded by crying kids or by old people who were coughing, farting, even vomiting.

At eleven o'clock one night I found a little girl wandering alone in a dark corridor. I said to her, "What are you doing?" She was cold, she was worried and she had no idea where her mother was. There could easily have been pedophiles around, who's to know? I was worried for her, so I said, "Come with me." Eventually I found an older sister who could bring the girl to their mother.

I'll never forget the things I saw. There were so many problems of cleanliness, so many people not even bothering to wash, that in one of the other shelters in St-Hyacinthe, the Red Cross organized a "Loto-Douche" – a shower lottery. They'd give you a little coupon that would give you the chance of winning a few small items – a radio, a Walkman – if you took a shower. And it worked!

Not everybody was complaining. Some people said, "I get a hot meal and a place to sleep, that's enough for me." There were people who had jobs during the day, and came back to the shelter just to sleep. The Red Cross managed to organize some special events. Celebrity concerts, movies in the auditorium – I did security when the Montreal Canadiens came to sign autographs. But when you can't go home, life can get very dreary. And as well as all this shared suffering, people had their own private worries. "There's ice on my roof, the plumbing is broken, what's going to happen to my house?" I couldn't answer, any more than I could tell them when the crisis was going to be over.

One of the worst things about the shelter was the amount of thieving. People stole shoes and hats, they stole toothbrushes and clothes – I swear to you, they even stole dirty underwear. Everything you had in the shelter was piled under your bed – but everyone else had access to it. If I hadn't already had a lot of experience as a police officer, it might well have changed my view of human nature. I saw a woman crying and crying, and when I asked why, she told me that she'd gone to a store to buy clean socks – the only socks she had with her were dirty, and she couldn't wash them. She got back to the shelter, went to the toilet for five minutes, and found that somebody had taken the new socks.

But that's not the whole story. There were also the volunteers. A lot of them were displaced from their own homes, but they still wanted to help others. Women worked twelve or fourteen hours in the cafeteria, not just making the regular meals but preparing special treats for the children. Other women would look after children when the parents didn't want to, finding things for them to do all day because otherwise the kids would get so bored. The Red Cross workers showed incredible devotion. And they didn't enjoy extra comforts – they slept on little camp beds, just like everyone else in the shelter.

As for me, I'm the mother of two children. But we live up in the Laurentians, I was working on the South Shore seven days a week, and I was away from my children for almost two months. They were looked after by my husband and their grandmother. I would phone home, but on the phone we'd all start crying. One afternoon I was free, because I'd been working the night shift, and they came into Montreal for a few hours. But in a downtown hotel room, what can a kid do? Watch TV, eat chips, have a soft drink. . . . It wasn't a great visit. I filled the hole inside myself by spending time with other children. For them, it was exciting to play with an officer in uniform.

Yes, it was painful, but it was a great experience. We're an emergency service. When there's an emergency, we have to act. Family life is put on hold.

We have no choice. That's the way it is.

Isabelle Gendron now works at the headquarters of the Sûreté du Québec in Montreal.

ANDREW LESLIE

We were called in on Friday, January 9, at about 2:45 P.M., Alberta time. I received a phone call from my boss, Brigadier-General Dan Ross, and he said, "The province of Quebec has asked Canada for additional soldiers to help in restoring essential services and saving lives. Stand by!" I called my eleven commanding officers, each one in charge of about five hundred to seven hundred soldiers, and told them the news. At about 3:30 P.M. the general called me again and said, "Deploy your brigade to the South Shore of Montreal."

We'd been following the news on television, but we had been told on Wednesday that it looked like the situation was under control. So the Friday call did come as a surprise.

We got the call to go, and by seven o'clock that evening I and my command party were airborne in a Hercules. This means that we had about two hours to get ready for an indefinite deployment. By midnight we had use of an Airbus that had been diverted – it had been flying troops back from Bosnia – and we stuffed aboard the first two hundred soldiers of what would become a total command of about six thousand. The entire brigade left Edmonton within forty-eight hours.

We landed at Mirabel after an all-night flight. Because of the power lines that were down and the massive traffic jams over the bridges, it took us four hours to reach the army's Sector Quebec headquarters, at the Longue Pointe base in the east end of Montreal. We got there at about 9 A.M. and I met with the person who was running the Quebec operation, Major-General Alain Forand. I know General Forand very well; we were in a series of very unpleasant operations in Croatia together. He gave me my orders and told me to get on with it. So my team hopped in a vehicle and drove down to St-Jean – which took another three hours.

The overall situation was, frankly, worse than I expected. There were so many families without heat, without water, without access to the basic necessities of life, that the potential for loss of life was very high.

Once we'd arrived at St-Jean, we started to set up the headquarters at the Megaplex, just down the road from the old military college. Initially it was my brigade alone, but within twenty-four hours we were joined by a battalion of about 650 soldiers from Gagetown, New Brunswick, as well as a locally based reserve battalion of about 800. The first task was to get the soldiers in; the second was to establish contact with the local authorities, be they mayors, reeves, Hydro-Québec, the Quebec provincial police or the Red Cross; and the third was to figure out what had to be done. We used helicopter reconnaissance as well as ground plans.

In all of this, the absolute priority was saving lives. That drove everything we did for the first eight or nine days. After that, we could turn our attention to restoring services – which meant, in this case, helping Hydro-Québec.

So we came up with a plan. In the military, this is what we do! People have this perception of the military as a sort of bureaucratic monster, lumbering from case to case. But when the fecal matter hits the rotary device, we go into crisis mode. We revert to our training. We had been focusing very hard on war management training. And war fighting is essentially management of chaos.

I think none of us slept for the first three days. Every soldier in the brigade has a bug-out kit, and when we left Edmonton, we grabbed our rucksacks and emergency rations and left. On the South Shore we were meeting local officials, of course, and eventually I realized I had to change my clothes. That's when I discovered that everything was in there except for socks. I had been remiss in stocking my bug-out kit with socks, and I had to borrow some from a soldier. This is no big secret. There's no such thing as a secret in the army.

The battalion from Gagetown is a very professional organization. I know the commanding officer, and they just fit in like a glove. The reserve organization were willing to work their hearts out, and they had enough experience to know what Mission Orders was all about. But I did have to beef them up with some personnel from my brigade before they were an equal member of the team.

My headquarters was at the Multiplex, but I only spent maybe four hours a day there. The rest of the day, I was out in the field. On one occasion I was visiting the 2nd Light Battalion of the Princess Patricia's Canadian Light Infantry, and I was at my wits' end getting an idea of what Hydro-Québec's priorities were. I turned to one of my officers and told him to consider himself a "Hydro commando." The area of responsibility covered eight or nine different Hydro regions, and one day one of the Hydro managers said to me, "We can't keep up! Your guys work so hard and so fast, we were planning on them covering two to three kilometres a day, but in fact they're covering twelve or thirteen or fifteen kilometres!"

Another day I was visiting the 1st Regiment of the Royal Canadian Horse Artillery, based in Shilo, Manitoba, and I saw a Hydro-Québec truck being swarmed by soldiers. They were inside the truck, they were up in the cherry-picker, they were all over the place. And no civilians in sight! I wandered over to the soldiers and said, "Hi, guys, how's it going?"

"Great," they said.

"So what are you doing?"

"Well, we're clearing this line."

I said, "Where did you get the truck?"

And they looked at each other and said, "Um . . ."

I said, "Don't tell me you stole the truck!"

Thank goodness, they hadn't. What had happened was this: Hydro-Québec had more wheeled assets than repair teams. One of the soldiers had struck up a fast friendship with a Hydro guy and he had said, "You obviously know what you're doing. Here are the keys to this truck, go ahead and use it!"

By week four, we realized we had done all we could do. Or at least our soldiers were now picking up sticks, clearing tertiary routes and assisting families with debris in their backyards. All good stuff – but not what we were there to do. We had other responsibilities, such as preparing soldiers to go over to Bosnia. The crisis had passed; this was no longer a life-threatening emergency. I was on the last flight out in February.

Looking back at it now, I'd say that out of the one million or so people in the area, there were only one or two idiots who tried to make politics or language an issue. The other 999,999 were very supportive and very grateful we were there. When there's a crisis, people pull together. Many of the soldiers in the brigade are unilingual. But as soldiers, we've been all over the world where people don't speak either French or English. And somehow, we communicate.

Colonel Andrew Leslie is the commanding officer, 1st Canadian Mechanized Brigade Group, based in Edmonton, Alberta.

JOHN SHONE

I'm an officer in the Royal Montreal Regiment, a reserve unit of the Canadian Armed Forces, located in an armoury in Westmount. When I'm not on active duty, I work for an international management consulting company. I joined the reserves in December 1986, while I was a student at McGill University. I'm a transplant from Ontario – I moved from Toronto to Montreal in 1986, fell in love with the city, and never left. Prior to the ice storm, I'd worked at army headquarters for two years and I'd also gone on a tour of duty in the former Yugoslavia.

When the ice storm hit, my apartment in Montreal lost power and my girlfriend moved back in with her dad. The way the deployment of the reserves went, at first they only wanted soldiers, not officers. As a matter of fact, I was called in right after we got power back at the apartment, on January 15. My girlfriend decided to make a chicken pot pie to celebrate, and to have some friends over who were still without power. When we were beginning to eat dinner, I got the phone call. I said, "I'm out of here, enjoy your pie!"

They had started to deploy the 1st Battalion, PPCLI, the Princess Patricia's Canadian Light Infantry, out in Châteauguay. It's an English-speaking battalion, based in Edmonton, and they said, "We need some people who can speak French, who can talk to the population." That's when I was asked to participate.

I was already packed and ready to go. You see, before the regular army was called in, there was a rumour that they would be deployed in Montreal. Then it filtered down that they were going to be housed in the city's various armouries. There was no requirement for reserves at that point, but we knew that if we were going to have a battalion or a company of regular troops show up here, we'd better have some guys on the ground. I started calling in my guys so that we could have people ready to go, just to sort stuff out. Because once the power went out, the telephone system in the armoury went down. Real good, eh? There was no heat, no light, and we needed to set up emergency generators and make sure we had internal communications.

By the time the regular troops started arriving, we had quite a contingent here already. In the first seventy-two hours of the emergency, before the reserves were actually called up, we did a bunch of work for Westmount and other communities. We provided clean-up crews and security for Westmount city hall, we managed to get diesel deliveries to a couple of shelters, and we moved doctors to locations where they were needed. Initially, we seemed to be the only people visiting around different shelters. It was just a matter of time, in my opinion, before headquarters realized they'd need all of these guys with local experience who could speak the language and who knew where stuff was. When the regular troops had shown up and housed themselves here, then they started calling for reserve augmentation. So my guys would come in and get shipped out with the various regiments.

Ultimately they started to put together reserve-formed units to conduct certain tasks. But had they called us up earlier, I think we could have contributed far more than we ultimately did. At headquarters, unfortunately, there seemed to be a fundamental misunderstanding of the reserves – a belief that we couldn't be relied upon to do anything on a large scale, or on short notice. I think the ice storm showed that you can put together reserve units that can actually go out and do stuff. Which I think came as a bit of a surprise to the powers that be.

It's very difficult to give a profile of a typical reservist. We've got university students, college students, people on minimum-wage type jobs, people who are in the computer field and making quite a bit of money – quite a cross-section. We were the first officially bilingual unit in Canada, and there's only a tiny minority of our people who can't work effectively in French. We've got people from many different backgrounds, a decent number of them from South and Central America – it's basically a mosaic. Which is why we always find it amusing when there's talk about racism in the forces. It's just not that kind of place!

When the call finally came, we were deployed very quickly. I was working in Châteauguay, but I was actually housed in a nunnery and retreat centre on Île St-Bernard, in the St. Lawrence River just off from Châteauguay. There's still about a dozen nuns living there, and I thought, "Oh my gosh, they've got a company of infantry guys staying with these nuns, it's going to be, like, mayhem!"

But the nuns loved these guys. They tiptoed around like mice, they cleaned up after themselves, and I've never been around infantry guys whose language was so clean. I'm sure someone had read them the riot act: "There will be *no* swearing!"

I think that to be a nun now, you've got to be a pretty dynamic type of person. There's so few of you and there's so much work to do. So the nuns were extremely open and outgoing. We slept on camp cots in a big dining room – not exactly a lot of privacy, and, of course, not a lot of men's washrooms either. Guys were rushing up and down stairs carrying all their toiletries, just to find one of the rare showers they could use.

We were seconded to a company, which is composed of three platoons. A bunch of guys were clearing stuff up and I was with another group of guys doing foot patrols. We made sure that people were okay, that there was security, no break-ins and so on.

We were working in the really nice part of Châteauguay, down near the river where the big houses are. We helped people bring in supplies of wood and various things. Quite a few people were still in their homes, people who had managed to set up a generator to power their furnaces and coffee makers so they could live. We ran into a couple of houses that appeared to have been broken into, so we called the police – there's not much we could do about that.

One old guy we ran into – he was a Legionnaire, but he'd never served – had his furnace going, and we brought an endless amount of wood down to his basement. He sat us down, fed us and gave us coffee, and when we were leaving, showed us a certificate with a poem on it. One of the soldiers started to write it down on his field message-pad and the old guy said, "Don't worry, I'll make you a copy of it." We never believed it would happen but by the end of the day, the platoon commander had a copy of that poem. The guy had gotten in his car, gone and found a photocopying shop that was open, and made sure it got to us. The gratitude of people was really impressive.

There was another lady whose neighbour had a generator and she was trying to get a power cord in to her furnace. A sergeant and myself showed up, and she was saying, "I don't know how to hook this up." So I'm looking at him, he's looking at me, and we're both infantry guys, we don't know anything about electronics. We go, "Listen, we can try it, we'll do the manual labour, but we can't guarantee anything." She said, "Go ahead," so we stripped the wires and plugged the cord into the box on the furnace. "Okay," we said, "start the generator."

It blacked out the other house, too.

I said, "Well, I guess that doesn't work, you'll have to get someone in who knows what they're doing." What we'd done was leave the wires that come from the external power source attached. So essentially we'd fed the power of the small generator at the house next door into the entire grid, which was dead. Needless to say, it couldn't handle the load.

When the troops had interactions with local people, it was all positive – I didn't hear of any political tensions. Near the end of one day, we'd been doing foot patrols and we were kind of tired, so we waved down a pickup truck and loaded all these army people into the back. At a stop, a car drove by and the two drivers knew each other. The people in the car had just been to Tim Hortons, and they said to our driver,

"Hey, you got some army guys in there?" Then they tossed us this box of doughnuts they'd just bought! It was outstanding.

After a while, the Châteauguay operation shut down because there was no longer a real emergency. The PPCLI were told to go home. My buddy and myself spent a few days with an engineering unit from Edmonton that was out in the Quebec countryside, near St-Constant, I believe, in the "triangle of darkness." The first thing we did was to roll into the town hall. Then they started planning what everybody was going to do that day. I was not very impressed – and I don't think anyone else was, either – at the fact that they had no clue what they were going to do. It was first thing in the morning; they had the Sûreté, the local police, the RCMP, Hydro-Québec; and meanwhile you've got a company's worth of engineers doing nothing, because nobody knows what they're supposed to do.

The civil authorities didn't appear do a lot of forward thinking. They seemed to do their planning when they were supposed to be executing. It was quite frustrating for us, because we're always ready to go! What we found was that they spent a lot of time asking, "Do we do this? Do we do that?" On the first day, what they did was so limited that there was no job for the engineers to do. Nothing to clear, no wood to haul, nothing to cut. Even when the civil authorities had figured out what to do, there was still no reason for these engineers to be there.

This was a combat engineering regiment. So what could these guys do? Well, maybe you have a certain construction capability because you have saws and pneumatic power equipment. But most of the guys in a combat engineering regiment are there to do things like dig up mine-fields. The role of the engineers is mobility and counter-mobility – that's what they're designed to do, not put up power lines. A lot of the stuff they had, like backhoes and bulldozers, was just not required.

You see, my impression is that the army was brought in because of the possibility of huge amounts of civil unrest on the island of Montreal if the last power line went down. It was a security force, more than any-thing else, to make sure that people wouldn't vandalize or just panic. High-rise apartments where the elevators don't work, piles of old people – I mean, the possibility that you'd need hundreds or thousands of extra people was huge.

But once that line had been saved, the soldiers that were stationed in

Montreal went out into the more rural areas. And the thing about the rural areas was that, okay, they didn't have power, but most of them had their woodstoves, their propane- or gas-fired cooking facilities, and their friends. And they had set up some excellent shelters right away in the community halls. They had all-terrain vehicles or pickup trucks. They seemed to have enough security. They could wait it out.

It reached a point where we were running heating-wood distribution centres and cleaning up debris. Only the very specialized military people were involved in helping Hydro-Québec. At one point the Armed Forces didn't have nearly enough people here in the crisis; and then, I think, we had a surfeit of people. It wasn't like the Manitoba flood, where you needed everybody who could fill a sandbag.

John Shone is now a major in the Royal Montreal Regiment. He is not a military spokesperson; the impressions he presents are those of an officer on the ground, and are not necessarily representative of policy or procedure at any level of government. This story was approved for publication in its present form by Major Shone's regiment.

PETER DAGG

I'm a full-time real-estate agent, I drive a school bus, I keep some beef cattle, I rent out land to a neighbour. I have a lot of irons in the fire, but it's the only way to make a living in the country. I'm also the mayor of Elgin, a rural community of about four hundred people in southwestern Quebec, just north of the U.S. border. Elgin is a wedge-shaped municipality in between the Châteauguay and Trout rivers, with about forty kilometres of roads. Half of the people speak French, half English. It's all farms and residences – we have no town centre except our town hall and the old church, which has been unused for a dozen or more years.

During the ice storm we were without power for almost thirty days. We had an Elgin town hall meeting on the first night, the fifth of January, and it was cancelled because we couldn't even get out the driveway. But I don't think many people realized how bad the ice storm was until a few days into it. Our first alarm was, as soon as we could get out, that the roads were basically closed – not so much because of the ice as because of fallen trees. Every single road in Elgin was completely blocked, as if somebody had purposefully cut down trees and just laid them across the road. The damage was incredible. Where the trees weren't down, they formed an umbrella right over the road, so it was absolutely dangerous to drive.

We had no power in my home, but luckily my telephone didn't go out of order. The phone at the town hall was not in operation, so I basically did all my work from home. I went to being a full-time municipal employee. The first thing I did was call to different areas in the municipality, to see what the damage was like and what the feeling was. The phone was so busy, it was unbelievable. People were calling in all the time and their first question was, "When is the power coming back on?" Unfortunately, even as an elected official, I couldn't get a straight answer out of Hydro-Québec.

Once we got out on the roads, we could see it was not going to be a quick fix. It wasn't a case of just a transformer or a breaker – it was massive damage.

Our first priority was to make sure that any emergency vehicles were able to get where they had to go. So the town council and I organized a whole slew of volunteers with chainsaws, trucks, tractors and so on. And we cleared the roads. Road by road – 95 percent by volunteers.

In Elgin, there was less than a handful of people who requested to be taken to a shelter. Almost everybody wanted to stay in their own homes, and probably 80 percent of them had woodstoves. When we got rolling, and we saw how long it was going to take for hydro to be restored, we made arrangements to get three cellular phones, and we set up town hall as a base camp for inquiries and for distribution of firewood. We also had a generator service for people who had no woodstoves, and we rotated these generators through volunteers – three pickup trucks and three crews, who would go around generating electricity for the people who needed it the most.

As for Hydro-Québec, they did not inform us what the problems were. I suppose it was very difficult for them to estimate the scope of the work involved to restore power to this section, let alone to major urban areas. I can sympathize with them. However, we heard more through the media than we heard from them directly. It was impossible to communicate with them – their lines were busy all of the time, and they wouldn't call out. After a few weeks had passed, I managed to make such a lot of noise about the lack of attention to Elgin that Hydro sent one of their lead people here to see what the problems were. But it wasn't until I'd had some interviews with CBC Radio, with the Montreal *Gazette* and with a couple of TV news shows that we had any attention paid to us by the utility. We were one of the last areas to get service.

Seven to ten days after the ice storm hit, we discovered that the provincial government's Civil Protection Agency would be having a meeting in the town of Huntingdon. They didn't call us; we called them. And at that meeting, the story that the army was potentially available to help out came to the table. We thought that might be good for a few of our dairy farmers – we did have three or four farms that were desperate for extra help. The volunteers we had in the municipality were stretched to the limit. So we asked the army to come. They called us one day and said they were coming; they came for a short period of time, we never got to meet them, and they left as fast as they came in. In our municipality, they helped minimally. The suggestion from the army commander at the Civil Protection meeting was that they were willing to help with anything at any time – they were very generous with their offers. However, they didn't produce. I was a little disappointed. Without notice they picked up and left, just like they were on manoeuvres, and they didn't tell anybody they were leaving.

For the most part, Elgin residents helped out Elgin residents. But the Sûreté du Québec – the provincial police force – did a great job. They visited older people at our request, regularly and routinely. It was especially important for the one-third of the municipality that lost its phone service. The SQ did the job that the army was doing in larger places like St-Jean-sur-Richelieu. Later on in the month, we did have representatives from Civil Protection who came to our town hall. Thanks to them, we tapped into the food bank in Valleyfield and we were able to make up food hampers for older people who might not want to travel to town. But this was just in case they were running short. We had no requests for food or clothing – people are more or less prepared in the country.

Civil Protection also put us on to some suppliers of firewood who would deliver wood, basically for free, if we paid the transportation. Unfortunately, it turned out to be a real fiasco. One fifty-foot trailer arrived in the middle of the night from London, Ontario, and the driver wanted to unload. Now everybody was trying to stay warm in a difficult situation, but a team of us went out in the night – only to find that the truckload was absolute scrap garbage. It was green wood, mixed in with snow, that couldn't be burned. It was like it came from a sawmill somewhere, and they just scooped it off the snowy ground and dumped it into the truck. It wasn't even cut up. We started unloading the truck but it was such a bad load that we finally called Civil Protection and said, "This is absolutely unacceptable!" They said, "What can we do?"

It had to be unloaded by hand. The driver didn't know anything about it – he said, "I just work for the company." He called the company to make the complaint, and they said, "It's not our problem – we're just the trucker. We didn't order the wood!" One of our residents has a large family, and we ended up directing the driver there because the family agreed to unload the wood. I think they probably burned it the following winter. That was the worst case, but not the only one. Out of six truckloads of firewood that arrived here, we got four or five loads of crappy wood.

Very discouraging. But once again, Elgin ended up rectifying the situation ourselves. We had seen all kinds of inefficiency, of government intervention with poor results, so we decided to do something properly. We told Civil Protection, "Don't send any more firewood – we'll handle it ourselves." The town council went out and bought firewood from a private person in a neighbouring municipality. We paid the trucker, we paid the supplier, and we brought wood to people. We had volunteers to load and unload it. The distribution was done primarily by two fellows in one pickup – our work crew. This was all possible because Civil Protection gave us a decree saying that anything we deemed important for the security for the population we should buy, and send them the bill later.

We didn't receive any advance training for this kind of emergency, but I've been mayor for twenty years and our council is made up mostly of farmers. Very practical, very common-sense people. They know what people's requirements are. Our municipal inspector, Jim Tallon – he's the guy who deals with potholes, resurfacing, loose dogs, cattle on the road – was the Elgin postman for sixty years, so guess how old he is! I remember seeing this guy, at eighty-odd years, up in the bucket of a front-end loader with a chainsaw, cutting tree branches off hydro lines. And he doesn't even think twice about it!

When the power had come back in most other places, there was a strong feeling here that we were being ignored. I was doing no work as a real-estate agent, of course, but I still had calls in January from people who'd got their power back in Montreal and thought *everybody* had power. One lady who called me couldn't understand why it was impossible to show properties in this area. "We were without power for four days," she told me. "It was awful. Just awful! Why can't we come and look at property?"

Peter Dagg lives on 3rd Concession Road in Elgin, Quebec.

ALAIN FORAND

Two experiences in particular prepared me for my work during the ice storm. The first was commanding five thousand troops in a United Nations sector in southern Croatia in 1995 when hostilities resurfaced. As a peacekeeping force, we were faced with caring for large numbers of displaced persons in a chaotic environment. The second experience was the Saguenay flood, in which we were confronted with an event so sudden that we essentially reacted to what was unfolding on the ground. While the ice storm provided us with a little time to plan, the storm hit quickly, requiring us to react fast.

I was in Montreal when the storm began. My family had remained in Ottawa when I was posted to Montreal, and so I was living in military quarters in the east end of the island. Because my headquarters was in the western part of downtown, I was able to view the extent of the power interruption as I moved back and forth between my quarters and my workplace. My family was more fortunate: they lost electricity only for several hours.

On the first day of the storm, Monday, January 5, my headquarters received an initial request from the Red Cross for five hundred camp cots. They were the first to anticipate problems. When I saw the request,

I said to myself, "Why are they asking for this? We'd better monitor the situation."

The next day, the Red Cross requested an additional five hundred cots. It was on this day that we initiated contact with the Quebec Civil Protection Agency. But they felt that the situation was "business as usual." On the night of the sixth to the seventh of January, it rained constantly, and we began receiving information from our people living in the South Shore and the Montreal area that the weather was creating serious problems. That morning I activated my headquarters.

In the evening of the seventh, I phoned General Christian Couture, the commander of the 5th Brigade located in Valcartier, near Quebec City. The brigade maintains a quick reaction unit of about 450 people on a permanent basis. This group is divided into three parts: a reconnaissance group, an advance party, and the remainder of the unit. By now I was anticipating a request from the civil authorities, so I had the readiness time for the quick-reaction unit reduced. I also asked General Couture to put the rest of the brigade on an eight-hour notice to move. This was no small feat, for the brigade had two of its units in the field conducting winter training and another just back from UN service in Haiti. It was spread pretty thin on the ground.

On the morning of Thursday, January 8, we received a request from Civil Protection to send a hundred troops to St-Hyacinthe. The city was experiencing problems, and when I analyzed the situation, I said, "a hundred is not enough." I told Civil Protection that I would send the whole quick-reaction unit, plus a small contingent of military engineers. The unit was complete in St-Hyacinthe by 2 P.M. and immediately went to work.

Later that morning, I phoned General Couture back and told him to deploy the rest of his brigade to Montreal. I expected additional requests for help from the province of Quebec. The total personnel of the 5th Brigade numbered about thirty-five hundred. At that point I had not had discussions with either the premier of Quebec or the minister of national defence, although I was keeping my superiors at National Defence Headquarters informed. I also instructed that four hundred troops be left behind at Valcartier, in case the base was required to serve as a shelter, or in case troops were needed in the Quebec City area as a result of flooding. I was particularly concerned about the St-François and La Chaudière rivers.

The first elements of 5th Brigade arrived in Montreal at 6:30 P.M., and I immediately got them to begin clearing the streets of obstacles to allow for the passage of ambulances, fire engines, and other emergency vehicles. I also dispatched two hundred troops to the South Shore. The last elements of the brigade arrived in Montreal at 4 A.M. on January 9. Initially my priority was Montreal, because of the very large number of citizens without electricity and also because it is the hub of industrial activities. We learned afterwards from the Montreal police force that the possibility of a complete breakdown of order was in their minds; but this was not made known to us.

I was told that Mr. Bouchard made a verbal request to Prime Minister Chrétien at 4 P.M. on January 8, asking for our help. I contacted Mr. Bouchard's office to explain the actions I had already taken and to describe our priority of work. A written request was not made until the following day. The letter was not very clear as to the support required, but I already had more than four thousand military involved.

On January 9, I contacted headquarters in Ottawa and requested additional troops. I also asked for and received permission to call up the reserves. About two thousand reservists deployed over the next twenty-four hours. Their response was overwhelming and their contribution appreciated.

One thing that needs to be emphasized is the remarkably quick response of the military personnel that deployed from outside Quebec. Colonel Leslie's troops from Edmonton were all in place by January 12. That in and of itself is a major accomplishment. I had also requested the support of the Signals Regiment from Kingston. I needed the expertise of these two hundred troops to ensure communications across the Montreal area and the South Shore. They had to leave their families, who were themselves victims of the ice storm in the Kingston area. The same dedication was displayed by the one thousand troops who were dispatched from CFB Gagetown in New Brunswick. It took them sixteen hours to reach St-Jean due to the treacherous road conditions. In all, I had about twelve thousand people under my command.

Colonel Leslie arrived with his staff and a small advance party on

Saturday, January 10. Later that day, electricity was restored to much of Montreal, except for parts of the west end and the West Island. As a result, I convinced the Civil Protection people that I should shift my emphasis to the South Shore. Not everyone agreed with this proposed shift, including the Montreal Urban Community police force.

As the troops arrived in place, my orders were to decentralize command and control, so as to provide the soldiers with maximum flexibility on the ground. I ensured that they had the resources they required, and I tried to stay off their backs. Briefly, their orders were to assist Hydro-Québec personnel, to coordinate and assist in the running of public shelters, to remove obstacles hindering emergency services, and to respond to other calls for help, including emergency evacuations and the provision of medical services. As an example, we provided some twenty-five field kitchens in the shelters, feeding thousands of ice storm victims every day. We also supported and operated many distribution centres.

On January 12, the government of Quebec asked the minister of national defence to vest the troops with the powers of a peace officer. In fact, this did not give us any more authority than the average citizen already possesses. But in the minds of the population, it created quite a bit of confidence. And that confidence grew. I think that our work created bonds that will last a hell of a long time. The Alberta and New Brunswick troops that deployed in Quebec experienced much the same effect as the eight hundred French-speaking soldiers that deployed from Valcartier to help with the Manitoba floods in 1997. They got the job done. You would be surprised at how far a smile and a helping attitude can carry you.

Much of the success on the ground is attributable to the support that I received from my boss, General Maurice Baril. He was able to isolate me from all of the peripheral stuff that was going on, allowing me to concentrate strictly on the task at hand. Ottawa never asked me to act contrary to the priorities I had established. I must also mention the excellent relations I enjoyed with Premier Bouchard. We received nothing but support from all of the politicians involved.

The biggest problem I encountered revolved around the with-drawal. Around January 21, I decided that the situation was sufficiently stable that I could start sending some of the soldiers back home. You have to remember that we are a force of last resort, in place to carry out essential services that cannot be performed by the civilian authorities. However, people had grown accustomed to our presence and had given us their confidence. When we indicated that we would be leaving, there was a certain reluctance to accept that. I made a commitment that a military presence would remain in the area until twenty-four hours after everybody had regained electrical power. I respected this commitment – the last of my troops, stationed in one of the rural municipalities close to the U.S. border, did not pull out until February 8.

We had excellent relations with most of the agencies we worked with – the governments, the police forces, Hydro-Québec, the Red Cross, and many others. I must point out, however, that it was disconcerting to see how many municipalities did not have emergency plans for a disaster or crisis. The Civil Protection Agency had some extremely good people doing outstanding work, but they did not have a strategic planning capability and they had very few people actually evaluating the situation on the ground. Hopefully, these shortcomings have been considered. I recognize the challenge, as the ministry in question has suffered greatly due to budget reductions.

In retrospect, I look back upon the ice storm effort with a lot of pride. On a personal level, I was proud of the contribution my own family members made in the Farnham area where I am from, an area which found itself deep in the "triangle of darkness." My two brothers were without power for close to three weeks, but they were both involved in organizing shelters. I was especially proud of the way my soldiers performed. They helped restore the situation to normal as quickly as possible. More importantly, they saved countless lives.

Few people know that most of my soldiers worked sixteen- to twenty-hour days, and for this they received a mere twelve dollars extra per day. But even when they were working alongside Hydro-Québec crews who were making close to eight hundred dollars a day, they neither complained nor lost their focus. The troops displayed the courage, dedication, and compassion that has long been their hallmark the world over. I was proud to be associated with such fine women and men.

Major-General Alain Forand commanded all the troops who saw action in "Operation Recuperation" in Quebec during the ice storm.

FRANK MOSES

The storm had been going for about two and a half days heavy. At Petawawa we just missed the tail end of it, but we knew we were going to be called in. Fortunately I had time for a nice dinner with my wife and little boy the night we left.

We ended up going to the Corel Centre in Ottawa to get sorted out. Then we went over to the Quebec side and worked in the Gatineau. We were there for three days, patrolling for Hydro, staying in a small school. Finally we came back to Ontario and down to Martintown, about twenty kilometres north of Cornwall. We were working for the volunteer fire department there, organizing relief, making house-to-house searches, delivering firewood – doing the whole gamut, really.

My platoon and I stayed at the Martintown Community Centre. It fed more than seven hundred people a day, but there were no more than seventy staying there. People would come in for a hot dinner, then go back home. As far as the accommodation was concerned, we put ourselves in their hands – the centre was well-organized that way. I remember a volunteer named Carol Ann. She ran a pub and had no business insurance, so the storm was very serious for her. But she was a rock for the other women. And the deputy fire chief worked really hard. He ran a gravel truck part-time, and he'd have his men stand watch on the generator the town was using. He sorted his town out. Looking at him and his hard work, I was looking at a civilian image of what the army was trying to accomplish.

Our regiment, the Royal Canadian, has been in Somalia, Bosnia, Croatia – it was nice to be working for Canadians for a change. We felt that now we were doing it for the people who pay our salary. When the storm came, we were in the midst of training to go over to Bosnia. But the ice storm really trained *us*. We had to coordinate with the Red Cross. We had to involve ourselves in something other than infantry duties. We became public servants. This was later to prove very useful in Bosnia.

This wasn't the first weather disaster I'd worked in. I was also in Winnipeg during the Red River flood of '97, building the dykes, getting boated out to check on farmhouses that still had functional dykes. It was

In small doses, the ice storm was unforgettably beautiful.
Carolyn Molson took this close-up shot in Ottawa.

a very similar experience in some ways, though we had a lot more volunteers helping us in Winnipeg. Of course the weather was warmer.

A lot of people, because they have electricity, don't really prepare themselves for winter. It's true, we always hear the sensational story. Are nineteen out of twenty people prepared? More than likely. But still, I remember some of the things people phoned me with.

One woman phoned and asked, "Do you have any meat?"

The meat was spoiling in her freezer, while outside it was minus twenty! I said, "Next time, throw it in the snowbank."

"Great idea!" she said. She didn't catch the irony.

There was an old gentleman that lived two blocks away from the centre. I remember Carol Ann saying, "Maybe you could go over and get him to come here." In a case like that, someone in a uniform is a figure of authority. When I went over, I found the gentleman had misplaced his medicine and was trying to heat his house with a gas stove. Pretty soon he was propped up on a bed in the shelter, talking away.

I was in charge of eighteen men. They come from all over the country – in my platoon right now, I have an Inuit soldier. We were away for thirteen days altogether. A lot of us were really proud of what we'd done. But we had to get back, because we were going down to Arkansas to train for Bosnia.

After the ice storm, I was in Bosnia for seven months. Aside from the lack of electricity in certain towns, it wasn't really comparable. There were no shell holes in Ontario. There were no villages half blown apart. The people over there have it a hell of a lot worse than we did even in the storm.

Frank Moses lives in Petawawa, Ontario. He is a sergeant with the 3rd Light Infantry Battalion of the Royal Canadian Regiment.

KELLYANN MELOCHE

I started this job as emergency-planning researcher for Kahnawake in December of 1993, when I was eighteen years old. Now I'm one of three emergency coordinators. I'm the one who mans the office Monday to Friday, eight-thirty to four. The committee I'm on also includes the police chief, fire chief, director of communications, technical services director – they're all directors of something.

On Monday, January 5, I remember sitting here on the couch and thinking, "The winter has been so quiet, I'm getting a lot of planning done!" I was planning a tabletop exercise with my committee for February 3 – a mock disaster. It was about eleven o'clock that night when a police corporal phoned up and said, "I just want to inform you that one section of town has lost power."

The next day, the schools were open and most of us still had power. But with the weather reports I kept getting through the day, and the warnings of heavy ice, heavy rain, I kept thinking, "It doesn't look good." At four o'clock that afternoon, I called the committee and said I wanted to have a meeting within an hour. I gave them an update and told them we should start planning: let's get a couple extra generators in, let's get a building on standby in case we have to put evacuees in there, let's call Red Cross right away and get some blankets and cots.

So we did. And the next day, Wednesday, the whole town was out.

From January 7 to January 15, the power was out. It was the first real emergency I'd had to work with.

The committee would have two meetings every day, at nine and at five. We would brief everyone on what problems we had, and then we would solve them. Our generator in this building did run, so we had heat and light and a couple of sockets – a couple of computers and the fax machine were going. And we got a generator to the radio station right away, so we had community radio.

But the problem was, I thought I had to be here all the time. Sometimes I worked eighteen- or nineteen-hour days. So I wasn't at home. And my six-year-old daughter was there – I'm a single parent. It was difficult, I didn't realize till it was over how I felt I neglected my daughter through that time. Her name is Kaheti:iosta – "she makes the greens beautiful" is what it means – but her English name is Jessie.

She thought it was fun at first, because her grandmother and her aunt and all her cousins were staying at my house. All they had was electric heating in their houses, but I have a propane stove and alternative sources of heat. So everyone went to my house. They took care of my house and my daughter and everything that was in there. In the end there were only two little rooms that they were cooking and living and sleeping in – nine people in all.

I remember one night – actually it was three in the morning – when I walked in. We had been sending out warnings about the kerosene heaters and lamps, because people weren't venting, and when I got home, I'm like, "What's that's smell? It smells like a lamp that's burnt." I'm running around like crazy looking. I check my stove and it's off, there's nothing leaking – and all of a sudden, I see on the counter a kerosene lamp. The glass was smoking and they hadn't shut it off.

I'm shaking everybody, "Wake up!" And my ex-sister-in-law says, "What?" "Did you just light a kerosene lamp?" I say. She says, "Yeah, what's the matter with you?" I say, "Don't do that! I'm telling everyone not to do this, and you're in here in my house doing it!"

That night I felt really nervous and I didn't sleep, because I was thinking, "I could have come into my house and found everyone I love and care for, gone."

My daughter's grandfather did end up getting a woodstove connected. He made modifications to his house during the ice storm – he drilled a hole right through the side of his front door so he could have a venting pipe. It was crazy. But that way, he could get everybody with him, because he was nervous that it was all girls and kids at my place.

The evacuation centre was up and running, in the Knights of Columbus Hall. They got overloaded with food – the cooks were making turkey dinners and ham and all kinds of things. The food was coming from all over the community, from people whose food would go bad if it wasn't stored in a place that had a freezer. So they brought it to the evacuation centre because it was like a public kitchen – you could go there, pick up a plate of food and go back home if you wanted. They were making two hundred, three hundred plates of food a day, and we had maybe fifty people who stayed in the centre.

Half of the hall was tables, the other half was cots. And even that was split up into one area where we had the elders – sort of a quiet, private area – and another where we had parents and kids.

The hospital was one of our biggest worries. It had a generator of its own, but it only kept the in-patient side going – the clinic and the pharmacy weren't powered. One day they came in and said, "We have a problem – we have laundry that can't get washed, because our machines would overfuse." So people on the committee took the laundry, brought it to their homes or across the river where there was power already, got it washed, and brought it back in.

One night I was on duty about eleven o'clock and an eighteen-wheeler with a truckload of wood was coming in. There were only two guys on the shift at the town garage that could help unload it. The assistant fire chief said he was going to get the fire crew to help, and I said, "Well, I'm a volunteer firefighter, it's quiet here, and if you're going, I'm going too." I told the assistant, "If there's anything big, I've got my pager, just call me."

When we arrived, they just had one or two rows of wood out, and the whole truckload to go. So we got up there and we started making a line and getting the wood out. It took maybe two hours to unload the truck, with ten of us grabbing the wood and passing it on, grabbing the wood and passing it on. It was tiring! We would take turns being in the front, picking up the wood. And when it was all done, just as we got back to the office and I was taking off my bunker pants, my fire pager went off. There was a house fire.

I ran with the assistant chief and another guy, a rookie, who responded to this fire. I don't know why the other guys didn't come down – they made it there eventually. One part of the town had got their power back on, and at this particular house they had a kind of radiation-dish heater in their kitchen. There was a pile of clothes in back of it, and the heater caught the clothes. And then the wall, and then the kitchen, started to go.

I'd had the training, but this was my first-ever house fire to go in and put it out. Normally you'd go in behind an experienced officer. But here I'm the one in front, leading the new guy, with David, my assistant chief, watching me and saying, "Are you ready? Are you ready?" I'm looking at the door looking like it's melting, and I said, "Yeah, let's go." When he opened the door, all the smoke and heat just hit you. We had our air-packs on, but you could still feel the heat. He closed the door back again and said, "Are you *sure* you're ready?" We had to crawl in – I didn't have the hose on yet, because I couldn't see any fire.

I'm watching and watching, and all of a sudden I come around a corner and I notice the flame right there. And it went out. I couldn't believe it! That never happens – normally you're fighting there for at least twenty minutes. We keep going, looking and yelling if anyone's in the house, and now I'm turning against another wall and I can see the shadows or faintness of a crib. And I freeze for a minute. I stand there and I'm thinking, "My daughter!" Because when we arrived and were running with the hose, we asked "Is there anyone in the house?" and one of the police officers said, "I don't know." David says, "Kellyann! Kellyann!" and I go and look in, and there's nothing.

Hydro couldn't believe it when we called them. This house had got its power back maybe three hours ago. But when there's a fire, there's a possibility of it extending, and you have to look into the walls to make sure there's nothing. To do that, you have to shut the power off. We called and they're like, "You want us to shut the power *off?*"

After nine days, the stress was hitting. My birthday's on January 15, so it was during the ice storm. I'm a pretty calm person, I'm not a person to yell or snap, and I think straight. But on the fourteenth, it seemed I couldn't do anything. Little petty things, I was having a hard time dealing with them. I was like, "Don't come to me!" And my supervisor, Terry, he's the director of the fire brigade, called me into his office and said,

"I've been talking to the other coordinator, Kevin, and from now on, we're each going on an eight-hour schedule – but first, we're sending you home for twenty-four hours." I go, "What? You can't send me home! I've got to stay here, I've got things to do!" But he said, "Go home."

So those twenty-four hours were wonderful. I loved it. I calmed right down, I spent time with my daughter, I took a whole day to see what they were doing. Doing dishes and having to heat the water, using big pots on the stove. Everybody sharing a little tub to wash their hands and face. Everybody sleeping close together to conserve warmth, and every now and then putting the propane stove on to heat up the house.

I came back to work the next day at five o'clock in the afternoon. I got called in early because there was a big meeting and my supervisor said they wanted me to be there. Just before they were going to finish, the executive director of the Mohawk Council of Kahnawake and some guys from the fire hall walked in with a birthday cake and everybody started singing "Happy Birthday"! I never had such a surprise before. I was shocked! It had really slipped my mind that it was my birthday.

Then after everyone had some cake, it was "Okay, back to work now." But I felt some weight lifted, knowing how everyone cares for one another. Knowing that even though we were there to work and do some serious things, there was still the human side to it.

The power started coming back the next day, the sixteenth. It came in different areas of town, little by little, and then finally here. This section should have been the first, because it has our hospital, our fire department, our police station, our council office, our radio station – everything is in this one section, and it was the last to come up. And even though the power had come on, we still maintained an operating centre through the recovery phase for forty-eight hours after. There was disbelief that the power would stay. Some people in the community were hesitant to go back home.

The co-operation with Hydro-Québec was not all that good. The best information we got was from the guys on the ground, and I can't say enough about the hours that they worked. Our police chief would talk to someone in the Hydro-Québec head office and get told one thing, while the guys on the ground had their work orders and were telling us something different. And the right information was from the work crews.

Something we can be thankful for is all the elders in the community. There are traditional ones who still maintain a woodstove, who still do their shopping little by little, or who still keep these bags of flour and sugar and can make bread without having to go to the store to buy it. A couple of them went on the radio and started telling stories to calm people down within the community. After it was over, they would say, "I'm so glad this happened. I hope it happens again!"

Why? "Because I've never seen my grandchildren for so long. I've never talked to my son and my daughter without them having to look at their watches. Now there was nowhere to go, there was no work, there was no deadline, so they didn't have to hurry." They loved it. It brought everyone together for them, and they started playing all these games – jacks, or a ball-and-stick game, or games that are just made up.

My daughter never complained about my not being there. It hit me really hard *because* she didn't complain. I was thinking, "Is it normal for her not to have her mother around? Or does she understand?" It was during the debriefing afterward when I could start talking and it really hit me. She lost one parent when her father and I split up – then when I was working, she lost another one too. That's how I felt. It was the worst feeling, because everything I do is for her. I built a house at twenty because of her! So did I think I had to prove something, that I had to be here and do things myself?

To try and think of everything, that's what made me forget about what I had at home. Because I was thinking of nine or ten different services. We never declared a state of emergency and we never needed outside assistance, except for one generator for the police station that the Civil Protection Agency took five days to get for us.

Later the committee asked me, "Are we still going to have that big exercise on February third?" I said, "No, I think we'll hold off on that for a while."

Kellyann Meloche is Emergency Preparedness Coordinator for the Mohawk community of Kahnawake, just across the Mercier Bridge from Montreal. After the ice storm, the federal deputy minister of Indian Affairs gave the community an award of excellence.

12

MIGRANTS OF THE STORM

hose of us who endured the ice storm spent nearly a week waiting for the freezing rain to pack up and leave. Instead, its two competing air masses settled above our heads and refused to budge. No wind shoved the heavy clouds away. Virtually immobile, they made us virtually immobile too. Airports and train stations shut down. Highways and bridges were closed. Streets and even sidewalks posed a risk. The sense of entrapment left many thousands of Canadians realizing, possibly for the first time, that their own sense of well-being depends on the capacity to move wherever they like, whenever they like.

We are a migrant people. Only a minority of us live where we were born. The gift of travel, like the gift of light in a winter evening or heat on a winter day, is something we mostly take for granted. Not in the ice storm, though.

In spite of the intrinsic difficulties of travelling, many people did get away. Intent on rescuing loved ones, or simply wanting to return to their homes, others joined the storm. This chapter contains the voices of those people who, thanks to a plane, train, or automobile, experienced the crisis on the move. Their stories are a form of travel writing, though the contributors stick more closely to the facts than do most of the literary travel writers in our time.

Good travel writing conveys a vivid, indeed heightened, sense of place. But often it also conveys a double perspective – for instance, home and elsewhere, ice and thaw – that emerges from the details of the journey. Here is what the storm's nomads saw. Here too is what they thought and felt.

JANE URQUHART

I left my home here in southwestern Ontario at 9 A.M., Saturday, January 10, in the company of several pickup trucks carrying generators. They were driven by farmers engaged in unofficial rescue missions to aid their counterparts in eastern Ontario and Quebec, who had been particularly hard-hit by Ice Storm '98.

My own rescue mission involved the recovery of my twenty-year-old daughter and three of her friends from the university town of Kingston, 240 kilometres away.

My husband and I had spent the past few days discussing whether the kids should come home. The storm missed our part of Ontario, but we had seen the television coverage of the twisted electrical towers, fallen trees and interlaced wires and cables that had covered Kingston's once-bucolic streets since midweek. As far as we could tell, everything was down except for the phones.

Our daughter had been calling us daily. She and four of her friends had moved into one room hoping that their body heat might cause the indoor temperature to rise. She told us they were passing the cat from lap to lap for warmth. It wasn't until Saturday morning, when she said there was no water left and few places to go to get more, that we decided to act.

More than a million people in Quebec and eight hundred thousand in Ontario were without the essentials of life in a cold climate, the worst natural calamity in Canada's history. A state of emergency had been declared; trains had been cancelled. The authorities were asking people to stay off the roads. But I wanted my child out of there.

Highway 401 is one of the busiest in North America. On a normal day, a motorist must fight for space among hundreds of trucks ferrying cargo between Montreal and Toronto. Now it was deserted except for the long convoys of military vehicles heading in to set up shelters and help restore power.

Fifty kilometres outside Kingston I entered a brittle, icy world in which everything had collapsed. Electrical towers had crumpled into oddly human postures. The few trees that had not snapped or split were bent towards the earth as if in despair. Even the outcroppings of limestone were altered, their roughness obliterated by inches of beautiful ice.

Entering the town, I drove through an obstacle course of fallen poles and downed wires, avoiding the streets where the police had put up the most yellow tape. The area around the university was filled with groups of students who wandered through the streets looking for shelter. The phrase "this is a disaster area" kept running through my mind – until I realized this really was a disaster area. It was the kind of scene I and many others in this safe, calm country never expected to see firsthand.

I found my daughter and her friends in the early afternoon, inside their rented house, huddled in sleeping bags. The cat and its owner had already been evacuated. The rest of them retreated, as quickly as possible, to the warmth of my car, leaving behind all those essentials – computers, CD players, curling irons and electric guitars – without a second thought.

As we drove west, leaving the world of ice behind, the evacuees argued about which had been worse, the dark or the cold. We talked about the frail network on which we stake our survival.

We cheered each time we saw a Canadian military convoy heading east, and we cheered again when we saw a fleet of American power company trucks coming up from Detroit to help.

For her novel The Underpainter, *Jane Urquhart won the 1997 Governor General's Award for Fiction. Her daughter's account of the ice storm can be found on p. 22. This article was originally written for the* New York Times.

GREG SILAS

The Typhoon Lounge is a bar on Monkland Avenue in Montreal. I'm the co-owner. Every year we close for a couple of days after Christmas and take the staff up north as a gesture of thanks. Eleven of us went up on Sunday, January 4, and rented a chalet on Lac Supérieur (off the north side of Mont Tremblant). The following day we were on the hill, skiing and having fun. It was dead – everyone else was back at work, the hill was empty and the rain was starting to come down. You couldn't see without your goggles, and you constantly had to wipe your goggles clear of the ice which would immediately form as the rain hit the lens. Eventually you had to use your nails to scrape the ice off.

Even so, we had a good day skiing. In the late afternoon, we all piled back into the van we had rented and headed back to the chalet. It was a big white GMC van, capable of seating fifteen people. Since we had parked on the south side of Tremblant, where all the activity was, we had to first drive around the mountain and then head off to the chalet. It was still raining, and the road was starting to get a little bit slick. We came across a Honda Civic in a ditch. We were all in good spirits and thought to do the good deed of the day, at which point eight guys lifted the car clear out of its problems. Happy with ourselves, we took a picture and finished our way home.

By eight-thirty or nine, our naps and showers taken, we took a vote and decided to eat in the Tremblant village. Although restaurants might close their kitchens early that night, we still decided to go. The problems began right away – the van's tires were spinning in the driveway. We were determined, and finally got the van up to the road, where the rain had put a coating of ice on top of previously fallen snow. The traction was not so bad, as we broke through the ice and created tracks. Once we hit the north side of Tremblant and turned onto the infamous thirteen-kilometre stretch to the south, we realized that the roads were much worse – no salt or sand had been laid. In fact, we had minimal traction. We relied on spinning tires to gain some momentum going up, and gravity to slow us when we approached an incline. Similarly, gravity would give us momentum on the way down, and should we need to slow the pace, we'd steer the van so that we would sideswipe a snowbank. It became quite exciting, sort of a gamble as to how much speed we would need to be able to climb each incline, but without any excess speed sending us too quickly, and out of control, down the other side. The steering had zero control and traction completely disappeared.

After about three kilometres, the road turned right and uphill. The difficulty of course was that if our speed was too great, we would go off the road – but if it was too slow, we would not make the climb. We made it halfway up and then stopped. This huge van started sliding backwards and hit the snowbank. I'm like, "This is trouble." The skating rink on the road acted in our favour, as three or four guys got out and pushed the nose of the van downhill. With very little effort, the van swung 180 degrees and slid back downhill. We tried the hill once again, but arrived at the same problem. Although it was still fun for most of us, we all had a few uneasy thoughts in our head about being stuck in the darkness on the back roads of Tremblant.

Our eating excursion no longer seemed like a good idea, and we decided to head back to the chalet. We began fishtailing everywhere but we managed, using gravity and snowbanks, until we came to one particular hill. It was a hill which turned to the right directly after its peak. As usual, we took the inside of the curve to stay on course and if necessary, slow ourselves with the snowbank. But as we began heading into the decline, we were stunned to see a pair of headlights peering directly at us. A car heading in the opposite direction had run into the snowbank on our side of the road. As I had no steering, we hit the edge of their bumper, snapped off a tire that was sticking out, bounced off the rest of the car, and landed in a snowbank ourselves. It was lucky we did not run right over the other car, as it was a small compact.

Now we were both stuck. We got out and assessed the damage. We had no damage to the van because of its size and strength, but the compact was crumpled. It had four people in it, a girl and three guys, but when we went over and started to talk they were pretty quiet. We couldn't figure it out until they started whispering – they didn't speak English or French.

First we got the van out. We used skis as ice-picks, chiselling away the ice with the bottom of the skis to get down to the gravel. The ice was fairly soft, the temperature must have been about zero. Once we had some traction, I backed up the van from the snowbank and parked it at the crest of the next incline, about three hundred metres away. The other car could not be steered – we just wanted to get it out of the way so the same situation would not repeat itself. After thirty minutes of using facial expressions, hand gestures, and the like, we got the other people to understand what we wanted and they helped us move their damaged car.

One guy was able to say "ski team." Now we knew that the upcoming weekend was going to be the World Cup Freestyle Skiing Championships at Mont Tremblant, so we figured they must be competing.

There was an older gentleman who pointed to himself and said, "coach." He wanted to stay with the car even if the rest of them would have to go with us for help. The coach was afraid someone would steal the radio and heater from their car if he did not stay. We convinced him otherwise and he joined the rest of us in the van, along with their gear. It was already midnight and we had travelled a total of six kilometres (three in each direction).

We still didn't know where they were from, but we could tell they were totally freaked out. Once back at the chalet, we thought that they would loosen up and have a drink with us. The girl and the first two guys were eighteen or nineteen, while the coach was about forty. To our surprise, the whole team, led by the coach, refused to even sit down! We thought, "Okay, we're going to party anyway." After about thirty minutes, one of our staff went over and talked to the coach, he accepted a cigarette from her, and that broke the ice somewhat.

We called Tremblant and somehow, although it was late at night, they put us in touch with the organizers of the ski event. We told them what had happened and they put the Belarus team on the phone, since that team had arrived safely at Tremblant earlier that day. One of them spoke English as well as Russian and did some translating for us. When the organizers came back on the line, they told us that they wanted to come over to our chalet and pick up what we now discovered was the national freestyle ski team of Kazakhstan.

We were excited – we thought this was pretty cool. As it turned out, the Kazakhstan team had come directly from Dorval Airport, rented a car and driven straight up to Tremblant. They were not only tired, hungry, and perplexed – they were also jet-lagged.

It was now 1 A.M., and I tried to convince the organizers not to come until the next morning. They insisted, at which point I gave them directions. At three-thirty, we heard a knock on the door. It was two guys, absolutely drenched. Their car didn't make it, it had got stuck somewhere, and so they joined the group. The number of people in our chalet had now grown to seventeen. By that time, most of the ski team, including the coach, had passed out on their chairs. We got extra pillows for them.

At about 4 A.M., the power went out. The lack of power meant that there was no sump pump, which meant you couldn't use the bathroom. When we got up, we just went to the bathroom in the snow. Most people were up by ten, and the roads were full of sand and gravel, safe enough to drive. The organizers thanked us and went off to get their vehicle. The ski team shook our hands and gave us a bottle of Kazakhstan vodka they had stashed away somewhere.

Upon returning to Montreal that day, we realized that the north was actually a lot better off than the city. We returned to find Montreal in a disaster and our bar out of power. Had we known that the Typhoon had no power, we'd just have stayed on vacation. We tried to operate with candles and battery-operated CD players, but it did not work – Typhoon was closed for nearly two weeks, like so many other businesses.

Tremblant went ahead with the races. But we never found out how the Kazakhstan team did.

Greg Silas is co-owner of the Typhoon Lounge in the N.D.G. area of Montreal.

JONI MAGIL

I am a single parent, and when my eleven-year-old son's school organized a basketball trip to Toronto from January 8 to 11, I was quick to book the time off work and arrange for a lovely weekend for two with my partner.

As the Montreal weather worsened on January 7, I was listening to the news to find the status of train departures. Late in the evening, I confirmed with Kevin's coach that, yes, the trip was on.

Early Thursday morning we were at Windsor Station, once again confirming that all was a go. All the kids from the Selwyn House middle-school basketball team were there, stoking up on a hearty McDonald's breakfast, anxious for their four days of fun and basketball. The train departed. . . .

My partner and I now had our days alone together, but the weather effectively dampened all our outdoor plans and neither of us had electricity. Making some last-minute phone calls, we hopped in the car and drove off to Ottawa. The drive took four hours, but it seemed to be worth it for a quiet dinner out and a stay in a nice warm hotel.

We returned to Montreal late Friday afternoon – still no electricity at my home, so we headed off to my partner's apartment where he had better luck. His pager, set to "vibrate," was jumping across the floor as we entered. Upon retrieving the message, we discovered that Kevin's train never quite made it to Toronto, and the school had been trying to reach me for twenty-four hours!

The train had got stuck in Cornwall and the passengers had spent seventeen hours on the train before returning to Montreal at 2 A.M. My son's coach was thankfully able to secure a car for the boys where they could let off steam away from the rest of the passengers, and he had arranged for all the parents to be contacted so they could meet the children when the train finally returned to Montreal.

At 2 A.M., tired and disappointed, all the boys had disembarked and returned home with their families. Everyone except Kevin, who could not find his mom anywhere.

The basketball coach, Marty Boyle, took my son home with him to his house in LaSalle – he and his wife happily consumed the thank-you gift of candies I had sent along for the host parents in Toronto. The next day, the coach quickly put Kevin to work clearing the fallen trees, digging out the car and collecting wood, and rewarded him with the ever-popular pizza – they also had no electricity, but used a wood-burning stove. They also had a dog, which Kevin seemed happy to play with.

We finally picked him up late on Friday. The street looked like a war zone, with hydro poles down amongst the fallen trees. The house was not accessible by car, so we walked and found my son hard at work. He looked extremely comfortable and at home – a tribute to the coach and his wife, as well as my son's ability to adapt. Happily reunited, after a good laugh over what had happened and the appropriate "thank you's," we were off home to ride out the rest of the storm and put this behind us.

The event was not to be easily forgotten, however! Back at school after a lengthy hiatus, the first assignment for the boys was to write stories recounting their ice storm experiences. Kevin's lovely story contained several references like this: "My mom was off in Ottawa with her boyfriend at a fancy hotel while I was stuck alone at the train station." This sent chills down my spine as I waited for the child-care workers to come and question my parenting skills. To make matters worse, in his immersion program he got to tell his story twice, in English and in French!

To this day, I still get the odd snicker from some parents and staff over what I did during the ice storm. And Kevin does take every opportunity to tease me as he leaves for any school trip – "You're sure you're going to pick me up, right, Mom?"

Joni Magil is a marketing manager who lives in Pointe Claire, Quebec.

GAIL MacLEAN FRASER

After being diagnosed with pneumonia on Wednesday, January 7, I decided to get the heck off the island of Montreal and head by train to my parents in Kingston. Let them take care of me and my energetic pre-schoolers! My two daughters (Susan and Lesley, ages five and four) and I got on the train downtown at 10:10 A.M. Thursday morning. By the time we had left the station, they were fast friends with three graduate students sitting across the aisle, on their way to Kingston from university in New Brunswick for a debate.

All seemed well. The train moved slowly, stopping occasionally, rolling over icy branches that made a neat, sprinkle-breaking sound. We enjoyed the scenery of devastation, ice-laden trees glistening in the morning sun, but didn't notice the time until we finally pulled into Cornwall at about 12:30 P.M. – around the time we should have reached Kingston. We stopped. The line ahead was closed. The train would go no farther.

The lineup started for the train phone. Then an enterprising individual got off the train and found, "Hey, we're in the station!" So another lineup started for the phones inside the station. I took advantage of our three new friends, left the girls under their supervision and got in line. I tried my parents: no answer. The lightbulb in my head went on – if the answering machine wasn't working, the power must be off there too. I called Cliff, my husband, in Montreal, and tried a friend in Belleville – had the blackouts got that far?

VIA announced that buses would be coming from Montreal to take us on to our destinations, some all the way to Toronto. We had to sit and wait. Our train car was a combination of small groupings – there were a few other mothers like myself, heading out with young children. A couple of older ladies helped entertain the children with books and treats, and soon the car was "our home together." I had packed some snacks and didn't have any trouble with food – besides, a generous attendant allowed the mothers to get some sandwiches and drinks before he proceeded to other cars to sell his wares. The train even had ice cubes – my personal loss during the storm. With heat, light and two washrooms, it was an oasis. Why would we want to leave it?

Finally an announcement came. The highway was impassable. No buses would be coming. The train would go a little farther along the tracks to a switchback to turn around, and back to Montreal we would go.

Lineups formed at the phones again. Fortunately, when the train started to pull ahead to turn around, I was *on* the train with my children. But our three friends were down to just one – the other two were in the station. We proceeded down the tracks. It must have taken two hours for the crew to figure out that we couldn't make it to the turn-around spot because of low wires over the tracks. So we backed up to the station. Quite a few people had been in the station and rejoined us on the train. Others took their chances: at least they'd made it to Cornwall, and would try to get transportation west on their own.

We started to back up, slowly, slowly, slowly. By this time my girls were getting more rowdy, rowdy, rowdy. Our car became a self-contained play centre and racecourse. I didn't even realize there was a crowd of boys from Selwyn House School in another car – each car was its own battleground.

I can't remember the time, but soon it became dark. It turned out that one poor VIA employee had a flashlight and a walkie-talkie to communicate with the engineer. He would say "Whoa, whoa!" and jump off the back end of the train (now the front end), pulling branches and debris off the tracks. Then he'd jump back on, say "All clear!" and the train would proceed at, as my father would say, "minus two miles an hour," crawling along, foot by foot. This tediousness, plus the pills for my pneumonia, was very lulling. I was conking out, but the two healthy girls kept me awake. "Watch how fast I can skip to the end of the car, Mommy!"

Finally we reached Coteau Landing. Here we were told we could turn around! It was pitch black – we couldn't see anything outside. Any buildings were in darkness. Was the train moving? What direction were we going? Were there people out there? What was that clunking sound? What was going on? It was getting late – it must have been 10 P.M. by then – and the girls had hit their limit. Overtired and overwired, "I want off this train!" "I want to go home!" Fortunately, the car was not too full. There was lots of space to spread out a child on a couple of seats. I think I managed by 11 P.M. to exhaust them into slumbertime.

But what is this: picking up speed? Oh my goodness, we are actually moving! And, it would seem, "train speed," not "crawl speed." We were on our way. I had kept in touch with Cliff, and knew he would meet us at the Dorval station, on the West Island of Montreal. Our friend Greg had called him with sanctuary: Greg had power at his home in Pointe Claire village, had already sent his own family to Ottawa (by bus, not train – how did he know?) and had offered us his home. It was hard to figure out where we were, lit inside but with no lights along Highway 20 outside, but finally the illuminated Cara food sign went past. We were almost at Dorval!

"Wake up, girls." No response. "Do you want to spend the rest of your life on the train?" One woke up, the other was comatose. Luckily I had already packed up our "keep them amused" articles and was ready when the train stopped. Again with thanks to our helpers from New Brunswick, I managed to toss the luggage, one very sleepy child and one "she's asleep standing on her feet" child out the door to my waiting husband.

It was 12:30 A.M. Friday. We'd spent fourteen hours on the train.

Gail MacLean Fraser lives in Pointe Claire, Quebec.

SABRINA BLANCHETTE

I live on Île-Sainte-Marie, an island outside St-Jean, in the town of Carignan. The whole town is basically rural. My mother's language is English, my father's is French, so I have two first languages.

The ice storm hit at night. At first we thought it was just going to be a one-day thing – losing electricity for a day, no big deal – but then it went to two days and three days, and we started having trouble. We're on a well, and need electricity to get our water. We also have a sump pump in the basement, and the water was rising really high and really fast. It was going to flood the basement. Every two hours, even at night, me and my thirteen-year-old brother and my mother had to empty it with buckets.

School was cancelled right away. People come to St. John's School from all around, a whole bunch of different towns – it's a small school, because there aren't very many English-speaking students in the area. It goes all the way from pre-school up to Grade Eleven. At the time of the storm I was sixteen years old and in my last year.

We lost our phone lines three or four days after the storm started. So then we were really isolated on our tiny island in the Richelieu River, just twenty-six houses. We had no contact with people outside – my mother doesn't drive and since my stepfather was stuck in Montreal, we were relying on my grandfather, who lives up the island, to drive us around. My boyfriend, Jean-François, was out in Nova Scotia at the time – he'd graduated the year before – and I'd been trying to reach him to tell him we needed help. After the first week he got a flight back somehow, and he came over to our house and started helping us. We were exhausted – we'd been emptying out the sump pump for a week. Finally we were able to disconnect the old pump and put in a hand pump instead, which made our job somewhat easier.

The basement and the ground floor were absolutely freezing, because we have our woodstove on an upper level. But upstairs we were roasting. We spent all our time in that little room. We had a lot of work to do, but it was fine, I enjoyed it. It was fun not sitting and watching television every night. I heard people complaining that the ice storm was so traumatizing, but I didn't feel that way at all.

More than two weeks after the start of the storm, my mother went with my aunt to a payphone in Chambly. She called the school, just to leave a message saying that in case they needed to reach us they should call my aunt at work. And by some fluke, the secretary went to the school, where they'd had a flood, and decided to check the messages. They were already preparing a trip to B.C., and were going to leave the next morning. The secretary phoned my art teacher, Louise Dupuis, who is like my best friend, and told her they'd found a way to reach us. So my art teacher called my aunt at work – and my aunt came home that day ranting and raving, saying, "You can go to B.C.! You can go to B.C.! I don't know exactly what it is, but it's free, and you have to leave tomorrow morning!"

We were all like, "Whoa, slow down, what are you talking about? Is this for real?" My mother went to a payphone with a flashlight in the dark, phoned to get the details, and found out that me and my brother Steve would have to be at Dorval Airport at 9 A.M. for a ten-day trip to B.C. The B.C. Department of Forests was paying for the tickets, thanks to a deal with Canadian Airlines, and Air Canada also helped out. The trip was mostly for Grades Ten and Eleven, but younger siblings could come along too. We packed all our things in the dark – we even had to pack dirty clothes and wash them when we got there. Next morning we got up at six o'clock and my grandfather drove us to the airport.

I'd been into St-Jean, but it was still very dangerous, because there were wires and poles all over the place. But I'd been nowhere other than that since the storm began. When I got into the airport, there were lights everywhere and I went, "Wow, I haven't seen this in a long time!"

There were about seventy-five of us altogether, split into two groups. Not all of them were from our school; some came from Richelieu Valley High in McMasterville. We flew from Montreal to Toronto, Toronto to Calgary, and from Calgary on to Kelowna. Everyone was talking about what they'd been going through. All of us were in the same boat, really. All of us were still without power. It was my first time on a plane – I'd never been further west than Perth, Ontario, and I was very, very nervous. I'd promised myself I would never, ever get on a plane. I was sitting beside my little brother – he was so excited and I was chewing my nails. The scariest part was the flight over the Rockies, because it

Sabrina and Steve Blanchette were thrilled to escape
the ice storm en route to Grand Forks, British Columbia.

was just a small propeller plane and it was making a lot of noise. I was
like, "If we crash, we'll never be found!"

We got to Kelowna and there were lots of reporters and photographers around. We had a three-hour drive in a school bus to get to Grand
Forks. We didn't know anything! We didn't know who we'd be staying
with or what we'd be doing there. They took us to a big auditorium in
Grand Forks Secondary School and sent us off with our host families.
Me and my brother hoped that we'd be with the same family, but we
weren't. I was with the Kabatoff family, which had two teenage girls.

The first thing I wanted to do when I got to their house was take a
shower. I'd managed to take a shower a couple of times at the military
base in St-Jean, where they had generators, but still it had been a week
since I had a real shower. They said, "Would you like us to show you
around?" and I said, "No thank you, I want to take a shower first."

They were very nice people. Grand Forks is a small town, and everyone was pretty laid-back and totally friendly. You'd be walking down the road and people would roll down their window and say, "You're from Quebec, aren't you? Hi, nice meeting you!" I was surprised by how warm people were.

We were supposed to go to school, but it was their exam period. So out of the ten days we were gone, we only had a day and a half in school. The rest of the time we visited museums – there's a lot of Russian influence because of the Doukhobors who settled in the town – and an art gallery, and we visited the B.C. Department of Forests, which had paid for a lot of the trip. We went tobogganing and sliding, we went alpine skiing and cross-country skiing – we did all kinds of things! Of course I was homesick a little, but I had a really great time. They even put on a sock hop for us one night. Everyone was dancing, it was a lot of fun.

I couldn't call my mother because the phone line was still down. I'm sure she was worried about us, but we did just fine. The power came back in my home the day that we all got back from B.C., so it was still cold in most of the house and the power supply was still fragile – there was just one light on. We got back just before the weekend, so we had a couple of days at home before we went back to school. By then it was the beginning of February. And at the school, a lot of people were jealous. They were like, "I wish I'd heard about the trip!"

It was sad leaving Grand Forks. I was crying on the bus: I felt like they were my family! A lot of us were crying. One boy got back home and he convinced his father to move to B.C., because he'd fallen in love with a girl there. The father did agree, but then, in the end, they didn't go – I don't know exactly what happened. I called my family in Grand Forks again, but they never called or wrote back – it was kind of sad. But my brother Steve did hear from his family. And in October, nine months later, about twenty students from Grand Forks came here, to visit Quebec. They weren't quite as fortunate, because they had to pay for their trip.

Sabrina Blanchette is now a fine-arts student at Dawson College in Montreal.

DOROTHY LAMB

They were huddled at the station – the old man, his wife and daughter, waiting for what was to be the last train. It was bitterly cold. The surrounding trees were encased in thick ice, and broken limbs were strewn everywhere. The woman had a cane and was clearly in a great deal of pain. They had tried to buy tickets, but the machine was broken, so all they could do was stand and wait for the train. They had been in the cold for three days now, and the daughter was taking her mother into the city to another daughter who was still with power. As the train came into the station, they kissed the old man goodbye, having failed to talk him into coming with them. He refused to leave the home. Struggling, they boarded and sat in the first available seats.

They were in the same clothes they had worn and slept in ever since the power went off. Wearing layers of clothing, coats, scarves and tuques pulled down to their eyes – it was obvious they hadn't recently washed. The daughter took off her tuque and tried to make herself presentable, but the mother just sat there stoically. Presently they arrived at the station, where there were many stairs that had to be navigated with great difficulty.

Up in the station, the daughter led her mother to a seat at a table in a restaurant and went to get her a hot drink. The mother looked around her – it was a different world from the one she had been accustomed to in the past few days. Most important of all, it was warm. Surrounding her were the inner-city people – all the women looking very smart in their short skirts and heels, and the men trim in their fashionable clothes. None of them seemed concerned with what was going on just outside the centre of the city – or with the suffering that people were enduring just trying to keep warm and look after those weaker than themselves.

The woman looked down at the twenty-year-old quilted snowpants showing beneath her coat and realized she was still wearing her husband's old tuque. She quickly pulled it off, and her hair saw the light of day for the first time since the cold set in – it stood up in white spikes all over her head and she knew she looked like a witch. A low point indeed. She was unable to hold back the tears. Her daughter, returning with a hot drink, saw them before she could lower her head, and she put her arms around her mother and kissed her. Then her tears began to flow too. Whereupon they looked at each other, wiped their tears and started to giggle. They were safe and warm – they had much to be thankful for.

Dorothy Lamb, the elderly lady in the above memoir, is seventy-six years old and lives in Roxboro, a west-island suburb of Montreal. She calls this story "The Refugees."

SALA PADLAYAT

I was up north when the storm began, in Salluit and Kuujjuaq. We heard what the weather was like in the south, it was on TV all over. My husband was down here – me and the kids had gone up for the Christmas holidays. He told me to stay up there until the power was on in Dorval, where we live. So we stayed in Kuujjuaq for a couple of days.

I work at the Kativik School Board building in the N.D.G. part of Montreal. The board is in charge of education for all the Inuit communities of Nunavik, or northern Quebec. A lot of N.D.G. had no power. We didn't have work in that time.

When I got to Dorval, there was still ice all over. But the power was on and we also had a Coleman stove, the kind that you pump up. We had two children with us – the others were back up north – and they were off school for a while.

The ice was not strange to them. They had seen a lot of ice up north, only we don't call it an "ice storm." The word in Inuktitut is *irralinijuk*. We do have this kind of weather up north, it happens once in a blue moon. Like when you have to fly, you notice these things happening, once in a long time.

But for Montreal, it was strange to see ice everywhere. I had never seen this much ice hanging off buildings.

And it was a different kind of ice, I noticed. When we chop ice up north, it's easy to chop. But trying to chop ice down here, it sticks – it doesn't crack.

I talked to other people at the Kativik School Board. If they had no power, they would gather in one place, somewhere that had heating or a fireplace. They don't expect this weather to happen down here, they've never heard of it before. It was as strange for us as it was for you.

When I think about all the problems that people had with the storm, to me it shows that they are too advanced. Some of them are not able to go back and think of natural things that they could use around them.

But I was impressed with the people who were working together. When I've been down here, your neighbour doesn't even say hello to you. You're just another face to them. But when something like this happens, you can see that they're human beings, too.

It's too bad it takes an ice storm to make people see that.

It's not just that the weather is changing – it has changed. It's not the same as before. Spring comes earlier now. How do we feel about it? Well, even if you feel anything different about it, you don't have any say. You just accept it.

Some people have no patience. If a plane doesn't come, they get mad, they get frustrated. But what can you do? It's not in your control.

It just happens. Things happen. You can't say you're going to be prepared for the next time – how do you know there's going to be a next time? But it's good to know there would be people willing to help other people.

Sala Padlayat is a pedagogical counsellor for the Kativik School Board.

ANNE and JOHN LUSBY

We missed the ice storm! It was not our fault and we did not plan this, but we just did not know it was going to happen.

On January 2, 1998, we flew from Ottawa on our trip of a lifetime to Australia and New Zealand. There was snow in Vancouver, so we spent the afternoon at the airport. In Hawaii there was a freak storm that knocked out the power at Pearl Harbor and prevented us, and all the Japanese tourists, from visiting the memorial sunken ship, the USS *Arizona*. Our plane did not land as scheduled in Fiji, due to high winds. So we did experience weather problems – but we were unaware of what was happening back home. It wasn't until we were watching CNN in our hotel in Sydney that we learned that eastern Ontario had been declared a disaster area, the troops were being sent in to help, and Prime Minister Chrétien was postponing foreign travel.

We phoned home and were reassured by family that they were coping. There was nothing we could do, and so we enjoyed a wonderful holiday. We received newspaper cuttings with amazing pictures of familiar areas transformed by ice.

When we returned at the end of February, we realized all we had missed. The landscape had changed. No one wanted to hear about our trip or see our pictures; they had too much to tell us about their experiences. We listened, we saw pictures, we watched videos and we heard the sound of the branches breaking and trees falling.

We bought *The Ice Storm*, but we could not really join in with the conversations. We felt we had somehow failed our community by not being a part of this event. It was a time when people really worked together and helped each other. We even admitted, to a friend who had had his basement pumped out by the local fire department and had been without power and drinking water for days, that we were sorry we had been away and had missed the storm. He suggested psychiatric counselling and told us to count our blessings.

During the first anniversary of the ice storm, we kept quiet and just nodded as friends and family reminisced. It was easier that way.

Anne and John Lusby live in Brockville, Ontario. John is retired; Anne works as a case manager with the Access Centre for Community Care.

13

"A BOUQUET OF LIGHT"

BY KAREN MOLSON

Noroît Farm, Lanark Highlands, Ontario,
Tuesday, January 6, 1998

'VE BROUGHT YOU some really romantic coffee," Ralph says, waking me up.

"What do you mean, romantic coffee?"

"I melted snow and ice, and brought it to boil on the woodstove. Power's out."

"Oh." That really is romantic. I prop myself up and slurp gratefully. Unfortunately, other implications are not so sentimental. No water, no shower, no flushing toilets. . . .

"How bad is it outside?"

A rampart of ice separates us from the rest of the world. Trees are falling everywhere. Warily I shift from the chair near the window to the couch near the supporting wall. I visualize headlines in the *Lanark Era*: TREE CRUSHES FARMHOUSE IN LANARK HIGHLANDS. COMPUTER FOUND AMONGST RUBBLE. . . .

Not too many years ago, no one spoke of ice rain. Meteorologists said "freezing rain," "drizzle" or "ice pellets." Ice rain is something new, something in between, something much more deadly.

So far, it seems all the birches and aspens are down. From the back door, we can see farther than ever. The horizon is altered. Thundering cracks and shudders, and great slow-motion smashes ripple through the

Spears of ice outside Karen Molson's home in the
Lanark Highlands of Ontario.

antiseptic air. The branches of the big maple tree at the front door are
bent to the ground, and limbs lean in mute resignation, near surrender. . . .

God threatens wind. His breath teases, topples
whole forests of seized trees.

Ralph says, "One more day of this, and we're moving." He adds,
"Quebec says, 'One more day of this, and we're separating.' " He is poking
at a roast lamb that he has set on top of the woodstove. He says the fire is
so hot he could bend metal in it. "White-hot," he says. "Forge-hot," he
says. Maniac stops licking his paw and yawns.

Wednesday

A big metal bowl on the floor contains ice and snow packed snugly around a carton of milk.

Ralph tried to buy a generator today; found the one he wanted in Perth; said, "I'll be right back after I go to the bank"; but by the time he got back it had sold and there were none left. He took some firewood to people who were running out, filled water containers for us and some of the neighbours, and ploughed their laneways with the tractor.

I feed the fire all day long, plan the day's stew, tomorrow's soup, set pots of water boiling. I know now that the back left corner near the pipe is the hottest place on the woodstove, and that an old cookie rack placed at the front, just above the door, is the best place for toasting bread.

We stand outside and listen to the forest fall. One tree at a time, sharp hollow cracks splintering into the night like gunfire. *I surrender. . . .*

"It's a phone call."

"A phone call?"

"From the outside world." This is said with a hint of something that could either be nostalgia or awe, or both. It's our nearest neighbours, Randy and Christine. For two days our only telephone feedback has been a busy signal. Our radio (with its ebbing batteries) warns about road conditions and says, "Don't drive anywhere unless it's an emergency." So few cars have gone by that when we hear the sound of one approaching, way off on the highway, we both look up.

It's not so bad now that the phone works. Is it ever loud though, jarring, intrusive, like an alarm. . . .

The saddest sound of all is the sound of trees falling. On our hundred acres we've lost thousands.

"A state of emergency has been declared," says the radio.

"Every time we open the freezer it means an hour less time before the meat will be spoiled," Ralph says. We pool our food resources with Randy and Christine. They found an old "carpet-sweeper" in their attic and have started using it. I suddenly remember we have a washboard, a curious antiquity, a decoration on the laundry-room wall – I carry it in triumph to the kitchen, to scrub the soiled linens in soapy water heated by the stove.

I have come to love the way light grows, the way a flame leaps from wick to wick, repeating itself. Light has taken on a whole new significance: how short the days are, how fleeting. The most glorious, ruby sunsets, as though the day displays a gallery of signal flags – *Canada expects everyone to do their duty* – before light is extinguished again, engulfed by dark and silence. Even now, midday, there is hardly enough light in this room to write.

Thursday

Lillith (my notebook computer) is propped open here on the coffee table, humming softly, encircled by her permanent rim of candles. Her breathy whirring and my fingers ordering the muffled clicking of her keys are the only sounds in the room. This is day three of the ice storm, day three of being huddled at home having no electricity or water. I have exactly an hour and forty-five minutes to use Lillith until her battery runs out. I feel like someone stranded who has only life-saving rations of food for a day, holds out for three days and, in spite of no hope of rescue in sight, says, "Oh, what the hell," and gobbles everything at once. But at least they know the pleasure of a bellyful of food before they meet their end. It injects a Damoclean edge into the writing process when one might be forced to stop at any time.

I kneel before Lillith so I can be closer to the candlelight. I observe the staggered heights of wavering flames arranged in an arc around my writing space, and suddenly I realize how beautiful and solemn and reverent it looks, as though the computer is a shrine, and I the devotee.

Yeah, there's paper. And pencils and pens. Already piles of it are billowing around me, spilling over the coffee table, sandwiched between sections of newspaper, stained by coffee cups, splattered by hot wax. The piles of paper keep getting knocked to the floor by cats. (I had to move my work space down here, where it's warm, where there's some light.) But every time I think I might make some headway with work, another log has to be shoved into the fire, or more armloads carried up, or water boiled for washing something. Each day has become directed towards getting ready for the dark. Are there enough candles? How much water have we left? What can we cook on the woodstove tonight?

Except for the chill (thank God for the woodstove), I am becoming enlightened by this experience. First of all, I love the enforced isolation.

Secondly, I love living in the past on the same land as our ancestors the pioneers, when neighbours regularly called upon neighbours for help and the mingling of resources went on unthinkingly, when what was had was always shared by all. A new sense of belonging has evolved; a new sense of being connected to the land, animals and other humans. A new appreciation for the things that were always there.

All night long, waking and dreaming, we listen to the forest fall. Jagged branches are wrenched from trees, crowns broken, maple fragments strewn all over the laneway. Sheathed in ice and silence. Highways are closed, power out for thousands in this area. A clearing has appeared near the pond, which answers the question of where we'll build the new barn. Unconcerned, Elizabeth stands with her wet nose pressed to the window, mesmerized by a red squirrel. (Ralph says that dogs' noseprints are as distinctive as human fingerprints.) Fletcher has draped himself across the floor in front of the fire. I'm sleeping down here from now on. It's too cold anywhere else. Even the plants are trembling.

The blackout has made me more appreciative of my computer Lillith, of music, being able to flush the toilet, microwave popcorn, batteries that work, showers, quilts and blankets.

Saturday

Howard (another neighbour) dropped in. I offered him coffee, a bowl of stew, bread. He has a woodstove at home, so he's not too uncomfortable, but he admits he misses lights. It gets dark too early this time of year. He says he rolled in a snowdrift the other night with a bar of soap!

Howard mused that in the old days men accomplished *less* than what we've become accustomed to. It's only the tools, he says, that have enabled us to accomplish more, but once we're rendered unable to use the tools, we have to accept accomplishing less – set a new standard, to still feel worthwhile.

Sunday night

Ralph came back with the generator this afternoon, but I hadn't seen or heard him drive up the lane. A piercing scream emitted from the parlour and my first, split-second thought was *Oh my God there's a strange woman in the parlour and her hair just caught fire from one of the candles and it's all my fault*, and then I realized that Ralph had come home, hooked the generator up before entering the house, and the TV, which happened to have been left on at high volume, was blaring some crime show. *Help! I'm not ready to come back to 1998 yet.*

Adrian (our brother-in-law) tracked down a generator in Wingham, near where he lives in Teeswater, Ontario. From here, Teeswater is 583 kilometres, a six- to seven-hour drive. Ralph left at 4 A.M. to meet Adrian halfway, in Peterborough, where they loaded it into the back of the van. Once the generator got here it was connected to the freezer and I could run water, flush toilets and clean dishes while Lillith was recharging. The moment I was finished all the above, the generator was gone – lent to the next neighbour and the general store, and then on to Ann's, and after that to our neighbour Mike. Ralph is exhausted but doesn't stop.

Like many of the others staying home to keep the fires going, my actions have become a simple progression of things that make sense – like going to bed earlier, getting up earlier, and sharing food with neighbours. We're coping with this catapult into the past as though we've been doing it all our lives, whether boiling linen in a big black pot on the cookstove, listening to the slowly rising whine of the kettle as the fire pitches and crackles under it, smelling wax and stew, or hanging wrung-out linens to dry near the fire.

Somewhere in Ireland (or so it is said) there is a stew that has been simmering on a fire for five hundred years. The same cast-iron pot, the same stew, every day, sniffed, examined, stirred, some eaten, then some added to it. I like the idea; it's very calming.

The generator, I am surprised to learn, cannot run the furnace, nor the oven, nor the hot-water heater, nor even the washing machine on cold cycle. It can, however, help keep the freezer contents frozen and, better still, run the water pump attached to the well, which means that I can with a simple wrist motion command cold water to tumble like the Pierian Spring from the taps.

So now Lillith is plugged in, and humming happily.

I tried to "bake" a panful of squares today, on top of the cookstove, and burnt them. I feel useless near the hearth these days. I also feel useless to help storm victims. While Ralph is out ploughing neighbours' laneways, lending the generator, helping haul trees off roofs, delivering firewood to those who've run out, what am I doing? Shouldn't I be volunteering, offering our home and hospitality to others? We offered to some, and they said, "No, thank you." Everyone else I know is just staying put. I feel guilty that I'm enjoying *having* to stay home and stoke the fire. I love it that my arms ache from lugging huge cauldrons of water from room to room, hauling wood from the basement. I love it that my hands are red and blistered from scrubbing clothes on a washboard, my hair grimy from rinsing in the bucket of soapy water. I am experiencing discomforts that our ancestors took for granted. . . . Indeed, they'd scoff at us now, having become so inexorably dependent upon something they never had.

Oh hell. The liquor store is closed until Friday, at the order of the municipality.

Convoys of army trucks in the road slow down at laneways; young and eager recruits spring from the back of them like insects.

Suddenly, storm news dominates the media.

Stories are emerging of heroism, of old people discovered huddling in cabins, a young soldier who rescued a woman who'd fainted from carbon monoxide poisoning, dogs licking masters' faces to wake them up to fire, tireless Hydro workers, shelter volunteers, our own brother-in-law Adrian, who has now made three trips here and delivered dozens of generators – *It is a far, far better thing that I do, than I have ever done.* . . .

Monday
Ralph thought he broke his toe. He rammed it into the foot of the armchair and pain exploded. I dashed for the hammer and ran outside, hacked off some chunks of ice on the woodpile, wrapped them in a towel and set it by his foot. After a few minutes he determined it wasn't broken, but it sounds terribly sore nevertheless.

Tuesday
I've become a maven of snack food.

"This has been particularly hard on farmers in the rural areas," says the radio announcer. I sigh and munch the last bag of chips. They say the grocery stores in Lanark and Perth are open again, but their shelves are bare of canned goods, candles, matches, kerosene, cereal, batteries and snacks.

All over the village of Lanark shuffled grimy, unshaven men, their clothes black from their chests to their knees. I crossed the road to go to the grocery store, and sure enough, I found the shelves bare of cereal, cans, snack foods, batteries, and all candles except for one: a beautiful oyster-coloured Mary, Mother of God, with a wick protruding from the top of her pious head. I didn't buy her. Not because she was eighteen dollars, but because I couldn't bear to burn her.

When I glanced at the mirror upon returning home, I saw the female equivalent of those grizzled men: just as dirty, probably as smelly. In fact I look like a madwoman, hair sticking out in tufts all over the place.

CBC Radio has special storm coverage, and every half hour they interrupt the music to give a list of overnight emergency phone numbers for each township. "... If you need help, please call ... If your life is in jeopardy, or you need immediate fire assistance, your first call should be to your local emergency official...."

The moon is so luminous it seems to pulse with light, and the sky is the colour of the skin on a rubbed plum.

The temperature is dropping. I can feel the cold creeping in. So can Elizabeth. She is curled in a ball as tight as she can squeeze.

Thursday night

This is day ten of being without electricity. I slept near the woodstove last night with all the blankets piled up around me, and *still* the chill crept into my bones. Outside it was minus thirty! Elizabeth, crouched at the end of the bed, was trembling so hard that the mattress vibrated. I lifted up a corner of the covers and she slunk in next to me.

There was a message of sympathy to all of us from the Queen in the newspaper today.

When one occupies a very small part of a large disaster, looking out for oneself and one's neighbours, it doesn't seem dramatic at all. It is next to impossible to realize its collective impact. DEATH BY DRIZZLE, said one headline. In the newspaper's city section (city section!), psychologists warn that stress is climbing.

Hopetown got power back last night! There is a big handpainted sign at the M & S General Store: "Showers Here – Don't Be Shye." We bought some more candles and batteries.

I had a lovely bath, with water heated to the perfect temperature on the woodstove, shampoo, soap and a facecloth. First, I lifted the full cauldron with my capable pioneer arms and set it upon a wooden chair pulled nearby, its crossbar slung with towels. I leaned over it and washed my hair. The overlapping of shadows and yellow candlelight . . . the sound, over and over again, of warm soapy water wrung from a cloth, splashing softly into warm soapy water . . . my head immersed in heat, hair swishing in it, lifting, swishing again . . . the easing of steam from my hands, then the peeling of clothes from my shoulders, then elbows, the scrubbing of a dry towel, and my skin becoming pink.

I light candles in all the windows, light the lantern on the front step, and haul the pot of hot water into the kitchen to do the dishes. That's the routine. In the evenings we play Scrabble with the fierce concentration of masters. As long as we can stay tolerably warm, I can actually enjoy this.

Saturday
The soldiers came again this morning. Ralph was up and dressed already. I sprang from the pull-out bed, where I'd been keeping warm and resting from being up, on and off, all night to feed the fire, and unthinkingly answered the door in my long underwear. The soldiers asked if we were all right. (The generator had broken down, but Ralph thought he could fix it.) I wanted to ask them for something because they seemed so earnest, but couldn't think of anything we needed. They told us the township hall in Middleville is offering hot meals three times a day, and volunteers are there with coffee in the afternoons. I decided we'll drop in tomorrow if our power's still out.

Sunday
Ralph went to the general store to have a shower. I swept the rooms, shook the rugs outside, and started soup in our biggest stainless-steel pot over the woodstove, with some bones that had thawed in the freezer. I made dumplings and dropped them in. Voilà, Ice Storm Soup.

We went to Middleville after lunch. We had, we confessed, come for the company as much as the food. The ladies all broke out in smiles. "Nothing wrong with that," one said. "We can all identify with a need to see other humans, when we feel so isolated." Murmurs of assent.

In the township hall's basement are tables, chairs, counters, cupboards, and everywhere plates of cake, carafes of coffee, bowls of fruit, bread, butter, juice, rows of pies, pots of stew. Between mealtimes, there is only a handful of displaced persons mingling for coffee. A row of stalwart volunteers sit on chairs against the wall. They include a modest cook who's obviously not used to spending time with so many women, for he blushes even when asked his name. "Francis," says Marion, the coordinator. "His name is Francis. He's an amazing cook." The other ladies nod in agreement. The ice storm dominates every conversation.

The door opens and a half-dozen men stomp in, their faces reddened by the cold, all in the uniform of the New Heroes: Hydro workers. They nod recognition to the volunteers and sag into the nearest chairs, looking dazed. I start to ask them questions. Eddie, Marc, Dan, Dave and Brian have been working sixteen-hour shifts. I ask them about the limits of human endurance. What their breaking points might be. How long can a body sustain such long hours before fatigue affects the quality and safety of the work? I visualize exhausted men leaning slowly, dazedly, then toppling, from cherry-pickers. . . .

Marc shrugs. He says he could go on for two more weeks, maybe a month like this. But he misses his family in Sudbury something fierce. I ask Dave, who's from North Bay, how long he's been here. He squints, concentrates. He's almost too tired to remember.

Eddie stands up to leave and takes out a map covered with crisscrosses and code numbers. It is a feeder map of the Dewitts Corners station, so well-worn from being folded and unfolded that it makes me think of a reconnaissance map, and these men – who share a uniform and a tired camaraderie – as soldiers in combat against an awesome, wrathful, ultimately unaccountable enemy.

Tuesday, January 20, 1998
Friends, Bill and Lois, who had their power restored a few days ago, arrived with a completely cooked, stuffed and seasoned turkey, cranberry sauce and dessert. I had wrapped potatoes in foil and roasted them in the fire. What a meal. We ate and ate.

The power came back on this afternoon! Day fourteen. Ralph said, "It wasn't that bad – like two weeks of ice fishing, without the fish."

Laurie, who works at the general store, is glad to have power back, but she and her husband have decided to "get rid of" their television. She was beaming when she told me about their decision, and said the kids were in full agreement. "We never had actual conversations before the power went out!"

I, too, find I want to preserve something that evokes our thirteen days of serenity. I hesitate to switch on the (unnatural, blinding) electric bulbs. Candles now illuminate the kitchen; flames, at staggered heights, cluster in the windowsill above the sink. In the next room, more candles bloom next to the Scrabble board in the centre of the coffee table, creating a bouquet of light.

Karen Molson is a writer living in Lanark Highlands, Ontario. She is currently working on a biography of the Molson family.

INDEX OF CONTRIBUTORS